Hitchcock and the Cold War:
New Essays on the Espionage Films, 1956-1969

Edited by Dr. Walter Raubicheck,
Pace University

Copyright ©2018
Pace University Press
41 Park Row
New York, NY 10038

All rights reserved
Printed in the United States of America

ISBN: 978-1-935625-30-8

Library of Congress Cataloging-in-Publication Data

Names: Raubicheck, Walter, 1950- editor.
Title: Hitchcock and the Cold War : new essays on the espionage films, 1956-1969 / edited by Walter Raubicheck.
Description: New York, NY : Pace University, [2019] | Includes bibliographical references and index.
Identifiers: LCCN 2019014433 | ISBN 9781935625308 (paperback)
Subjects: LCSH: Hitchcock, Alfred, 1899-1980--Criticism and interpretation. | Spy films--20th century--History and criticism. | Espionage in motion pictures. | Cold War in motion pictures.
Classification: LCC PN1998.3.H58 H546 2019 | DDC 791.4302/33092--dc23
LC record available at https://lccn.loc.gov/2019014433

Table of Contents

Introduction
by Walter Raubicheck — Page 5

"A Girl Like You" and a Film (Un)Like Another: Sequentiality in *Notorious* and *North by Northwest*
by Rebecca Martin — Page 17

How Deep the Rabbit Hole Goes: *North by Northwest*, *The Matrix*, and the Third Pill
by Craig Arthur — Page 45

What the O Stands for: The Cold War Games of *North by Northwest*
by Jeffery Longacre — Page 73

"Ceci n'est pas une Allemagne": On the Treachery of Images and the Deconstruction of Hitchcock's Thriller in *Torn Curtain*
by Robert Dassanowsky — Page 107

Espionage and Humanity: The Cold War in Hitchcock's *Topaz*
by Walter Srebnick — Page 139

The Unreliable Narrative in *Torn Curtain* and *Topaz*
by Randall Spinks — Page 169

"Even our friends spy on us": Espionage and Emotion in Hitchcock's *Topaz* and *The Short Night*
by Ken Mogg — Page 195

Down and Out in Mysterious Morocco: Ontological Uncertainty in *The Man Who Knew Too Much* (1956)
by Niklas Salmose — Page 243

Index — Page 267

Notes on Contributors — Page 279

Torn Curtain (1966) Paul Newman, Julie Andrews, Lila Kedrova
Courtesy of Universal Studios Licensing LLC and the Hitchcock Estate.

INTRODUCTION

By Walter Raubicheck

Alfred Hitchcock made a dozen espionage films and was preparing a thirteenth when age and illness ended his professional career. No other major director made as many, several of which rank in any critic's list of the greatest Hitchcock films. He should be known as the Master of the Espionage Film. Yet to the general public today he is known for his two shock and horror films of the early 60s, *Psycho* and *The Birds,* while to academic film scholars and theorists he is most highly regarded for his psychological thrillers such as *Rear Window* (1954) and *Vertigo* (1958), because they lend themselves visually and thematically to the most recent psychoanalytical and feminist approaches to film study. The essays collected in this volume make a case for his spy films of the 1950s and 1960s as being among his most important achievements because, more than the other films he made during this rich and productive period, they contain his most salient political views as well as revealing fully the complexity of his moral compass. The Cold War as the historical setting for the second *The Man Who Knew Too Much* (1956), *North by Northwest* (1959), *Torn Curtain* (1966), and *Topaz* (1969) inspired Hitchcock and his screenwriters to create narratives marked by a distinct moral ambiguity that, while present as a subtext in the spy films of the 1930s and 1940s, now became the thematic core of the later works. The dehumanization that was the inevitable by-product of Cold War intelligence activities is now the true enemy, not the vague Eastern Europeans of the '30s films or the Germans of the films of the '40s. The moral curtain separating good from evil has been torn.

Hitchcock's first great success in England—after nine silent features and seven sound ones—was *The Man Who Knew Too Much* (1934), his first movie to concentrate on espionage, the plot being driven by the murder of a British agent in Saint Moritz and the subsequent kidnapping of the daughter of a couple who, friends of the agent, have been given information by him about a political assassination to take place in

London. Hitchcock followed this triumph with a series of espionage films in the next four years: *The 39 Steps* (1935), *Secret Agent* (1936), *Sabotage* (1936), and *The Lady Vanishes* (1938); the only non-spy film he made during this period was *Young and Innocent* (1937). In 1936, he wrote,"It was purely a coincidence that three of my films in succession—*The Man Who Knew Too Much, The 39 Steps*, and *Secret Agent*—should all have a background of spying, though not such a coincidence that they should all be 'comedy thrillers'" (Gottlieb 23). He goes on to explain that in the case of his adaptation of John Buchan's novel (*The 39 Steps*) and his adaptation of several of Somerset Maugham's Ashenden stories (*Secret Agent*), the authors had provided much of the action but that it was he, Hitchcock, who provided the comedy. At this point in his career the director clearly does not want to be associated with the espionage story in particular, but admits that those stories do often provide a suitable action framework on which to build what he thinks is his ideal film: the comedy thriller. In the '40s this would change: the Second World War and its immediate aftermath would be the raison d'etre for two spy films that are among the his best movies in this period, *Saboteur* (1942) and *Notorious* (1946). It would be ten years before the director returned to espionage with the second *The Man Who Knew Too Much*, and now it was the political climate of the mid-1950s that renewed Hitchcock's interest in the spy genre.

When one thinks of spy films of the 1960s, one immediately thinks of the James Bond films starring Sean Connery. Yet it is generally agreed that the Bond film series was directly influenced by the great artistic and commercial success of Hitchcock's 1959 masterpiece, *North by Northwest*, his second espionage film of the 1950s. Fleming wanted Hitchcock to direct the first Bond film, and he wanted Cary Grant to star as Bond. Because of other commitments that had been made by the director and the star, this coming together of Hitchcock, Fleming, and Bond never happened, yet it is easy to see how the tone of the Bond films (as opposed to the novels) reflects the influence of what is probably Hitchcock's greatest comedy/thriller.

Ironically, his last two spy films, *Torn Curtain* and *Topaz*, were at least partially inspired by Hitchcock's desire to make a realistic Bond film in that they eschewed the frivolity of the mid-60s Bond movies and instead portrayed realistically the challenges and costs of modern

Introduction

espionage. Indeed his last project, *The Short Night*, would have had the same artistic goal, as evidenced by the unfinished screenplay by David Freeman. So a Hitchcock comedy/thriller initiated the most successful series of spy films ever, and three of his last five projects were attempts to de-glamorize the spy film genre itself and depict the dehumanization of the very figures who serve as protagonists in these poisonous chess games between the East and West. As the Bond series relied more and more on camp and special effects, Hitchcock's spy films became less like his comedy/ thrillers of the 1930s and more like dramatic psychological studies of the real-life secret agent.

Certainly John le Carré is partially responsible for the change: Martin Ritt's successful 1965 adaptation of *The Spy Who Came in from the Cold* impressed Hitchcock and opened up possibilities for his transformed concept of the spy film. The only spy film from the '30s that features a conflicted spy is *Secret Agent*, in which John Gielgud's Richard Ashenden is repelled by the cold-blooded killing required for his assignments, especially when a man wrongly identified as an enemy agent is killed. In the late '60s, Hitchcock would make two realistic spy films in which the thematic focus is the main character's struggles with the human costs of espionage, and again, the screenplay for the aborted *The Short Night* from the '70s is still much closer in tone to *Torn Curtain* and *Topaz* than it is to any of his earlier spy films.

Several of Hitchcock's espionage films fall into the "wrong man" category: those films in the canon in which a previously innocent, uninvolved protagonist is suddenly plunged into a dangerous, absurdist universe and must struggle to survive, often forced to discover untapped resources within himself in order to do so. *North by Northwest* fits this pattern perfectly, as do *The 39 Steps*, *Saboteur*, and *The Man Who Knew Too Much* (1956). In fact, both *Saboteur* and *North by Northwest* can be regarded as Hitchcock's later adaptations of *The 39 Steps* to the cultural and political realities of the United States in 1942 and 1959 respectively. In these four films the protagonist is not a professional spy as he is in *The Secret Agent*, *Notorious*, *Torn Curtain*, and *Topaz*. In the latter films the protagonist is the "right man," but in pursuing his task he comes to see much that is "wrong" about his profession, and at the same time he is responsible for putting others, usually a woman, in both physical danger and psychological distress.

8 Hitchcock and the Cold War

Robin Wood has written that "the espionage plot [is] typically with Hitchcock, a cover for the film's real concerns with gender relations and sexuality" (275). Of course, this can be said of all his plots, but the spy films in particular are noteworthy for the way they highlight the plight of the main women characters in the male-dominated universe of international intrigue. Think of Iris Henderson (Margaret Lockwood) in *The Lady Vanishes*, being assured by the male authority figure Doctor Rank that her memory of her friend Miss Foy is merely a delusion, and particularly Alicia Huberman (Ingrid Bergman) in *Notorious*, who agrees to sleep with the enemy because the American intelligence agency asks her to do it for her country, only to be rejected and humiliated by the American agent she has fallen in love with. Each of the Cold War films contains at least one female character, and sometimes several, who are controlled or manipulated by a male, whether it be Eve Kendall in *North by Northwest* being used as a pawn by both the American intelligence agency and the "enemy" spy organization, or Jo McKenna being abused by her husband and forced to take sedatives against her will in *The Man Who Knew Too Much* (1956). In *Torn Curtain*, Sarah Sherman (Julie Andrews) is presented as the protagonist in the first half of the film as she is lied to and mistreated by her fiancé Michael Armstrong (Paul Newman), and in *Topaz* Juanita de Cordoba (Karin Dor) is murdered after she tries to help the American cause in Cuba and Nicole Devereaux (Dany Robin) is cheated on and lied to by her husband, the French agent Andre Devereaux (Frederick Stafford). Hitchcock creates tremendous empathy for these female characters both by the use of point-of-view editing and by close-up shots that capture the women's confusion and pain. In all twelve completed spy films, the men perpetrating the espionage come to represent a ruthless patriarchal order that treats women as tools of the trade and dispenses with them at will. In the films we are discussing in this book, only a non-spy character such as Roger Thornhill (Cary Grant) in *North by Northwest* challenges the masculine spy machine: "I don't like the games you people play, Professor," he says to the spymaster (Leo G. Carroll) as he attempts to free Eve Kendall from the soul-crushing world into which she has been conscripted. Of all the male protagonists in the four Cold War films, only Thornhill, the non-spy, instinctively understands the importance of love and trust and the relationships built on these values.

Introduction

Hitchcock is often described as being "non-political" (if such a thing is possible), but certainly the espionage films are always directly concerned with the contemporary realities of international politics. In Hitchcock's 1930s spy films, the enemy is never precisely identified, but then-recent events in Europe and the post-Great War context both implicitly suggest that the opposition spies are German and that the Englishmen who assist them, such as Professor Jordan in *The 39 Steps*, are Fascist sympathizers. By 1940, the year *Foreign Correspondent* was released, the villain, Stephen Fisher, is a traitor who is explicitly working for the Nazis, and war is just about to be declared between England and Germany. In *Saboteur*, released two years later, the main villain, Charles Tobin (Otto Kruger), is a wealthy German sympathizer who presumably finances Fry (Norman Lloyd) and the other saboteurs. Along with *Lifeboat* (1944), *Saboteur* is Hitchcock's most obvious attempt to bring the war and the Fascist threat to democracy into his work in a way that preserves the melodramatic requirements of a thriller without coming across as propaganda. In his post-War spy film, *Notorious*, Hitchcock explores the threat of Nazi exiles who have emigrated to Brazil after the fall of the Reich.

The same pattern is repeated in the spy films of the '50s and '60s. In *The Man Who Knew Too Much* (1956), Hitchcock's first espionage film with a Cold War background, the kidnappers of the McKennas' son, the Draytons, seems to be a normal English couple, but the film's description of the assassination plot reflects the international tensions of the mid-1950s and therefore implies that they are Communists. Likewise, in *North by Northwest*, the late 1950s setting certainly encourages us to believe that Vandamm, Leonard, and their accomplices are Communist agents.

In both *Torn Curtain* and *Topaz* (and *The Short Night* screenplay), the enemy are explicitly Communists, whether of the Russian, East German, or Cuban variety. In these films Hitchcock, the anti-Fascist of the 1940s, has declared his anti-Communism in the 1960s. Yet this is where the pattern falls apart: in the films of the '30s and '40s, the protagonists—whether British or American—are clearly associated with the positive values of freedom and moral courage, as are England and America. This certainty is questioned in *Notorious* because of the way Alicia is manipulated by her American espionage employers, and it is further compromised in the Cold War spy films as the ethical practices of intelligence agencies in England and the United States are continually scrutinized and found wanting. Moral certainty has given way to moral ambiguity, which marks the films discussed in this book with a distinctive tone that separates them from all eight of Hitchcock's earlier espionage films. As Donald Spoto has remarked, "for Hitchcock, a political film is the grand excuse for getting beyond politics to the core of moral and philosophical issues that lie beneath" (430). I would suggest that in the Cold War films the politics generate the ethical issues; the two are inextricable.

This ambiguity gives *North by Northwest*—with an original screenplay by Ernest Lehman and starring Cary Grant, Eva Marie Saint, and James Mason—a layer of meaning that belies its somewhat common reputation as "light entertainment" in comparison to its immediate predecessor, *Vertigo*, and its immediate successor, *Psycho*. Beginning with the setting of the United Nations for the film's first killing, followed by the shot of the Capitol Building outside the window where the American intelligence chief, the Professor, blithely consigns Thornhill to his presumed fate, and continuing to the conclusion on and near Mount Rushmore, the movie deliberately sets acts of violence and death against monuments of national and international prominence. Even the dialogue supports the significance of these images: "Perhaps you ought to start learning how to lose a few cold wars," Thornhill says to the Professor when he learns how the latter has been using Eve Kendall to spy on Vandamm. Here the Professor represents the United States government symbolized by the Capitol and Mount Rushmore, and it is this government, as well as the Communist one, that the film indicts for its dehumanization.

Several essays in this collection discuss the political content of *North by Northwest* from disparate perspectives. Rebecca Martin, in "'A Girl Like You' and A Film (Un)Like Another: Sequentiality in *Notorious* and *North by Northwest*," examines the relationship between the 1959 film and one released thirteen years earlier at a quite different moment in world history, *Notorious*. Martin rejects the truism that Hitchcock was not interested in politics as well as the one, perpetuated by Hitchcock himself, that the MacGuffin in his films is always meaningless. Commenting on the specific historical and cultural contexts of 1946 and 1959, Martin shows how both films are related in complex fashions to the genre of melodrama and to the central issue of gender relations. Responding to

Introduction

Donald Spoto's claim that the latter espionage film is a kind of sequel to the earlier one, Martin demonstrates that despite some similarities in narrative and character, *North by Northwest* is a "cooler," more cynical film, its comedic elements aside, precisely because of the attitudes of Hitchcock and his screenwriter, Ernest Lehman, towards the political atmosphere of its Cold War setting. One of the differences she emphasizes has to do with the acting styles of Ingrid Bergman and Eva Marie Saint, as well as the ways they are dressed, lighted, and photographed: the earlier film presents the character as a woman in a melodrama, the latter as a woman of modernity.

Craig Arthur, in "How Deep the Rabbit Hole Goes: *North by Northwest*, *The Matrix*, and the Third Pill," also touches on gender conflicts in the 1959 film, but does so by expanding on the premise of Claude Chabrol and Eric Rohmer's *Hitchcock: The First Forty-four Films* that a pervasive Platonism characterizes these early and mid-career movies, and everyday reality in Hitchcock's work is like the shadows on the walls of Plato's cave, a play of appearances. Arthur connects this concept to the Wachowskis' *The Matrix* (1999), in which Neo, the protagonist, is offered the choice between a red pill that will show him how the Matrix is the false reality he has mistaken for the Real and the blue pill that will return him to his former life of illusion. Drawing on Jean Baudrillard and Slavoj Žižek, Arthur suggests that Roger Thornhill's descent into the life-threatening world of espionage is equivalent to taking the red pill and being compelled to learn what lies beneath the false security of his Madison Avenue world. But Arthur also points out that the heroines in Hitchcock's films are always compelled to suffer under the blindness and oppression of the "reality" Thornhill is now estranged from, "the artificial territory of the patriarchal map." And Arthur finally posits the existence of a third pill, the one moviegoers take when they buy a ticket and temporarily escape the illusions outside the theater for the ones provided by the filmmakers: if the film is Hitchcock's, we can at least experience the value of empathizing with the subjective perceptions of characters trying to negotiate the Hitchcockian Matrix.

Jeffrey Longacre, in "What the O Stands For: Cold War Games in *North by Northwest*," reads the film as a satire with elements of farce: a satire on the absurdities and the duplicities of Cold War espionage values and tactics. Using Louis Althusser's concept of interpellation,

Longacre shows that the film focuses on the problem of identity in a world in which the state replaces the self with ideology. "George Kaplan" doesn't exist, but Roger Thornhill himself exists only as "a floating signifier signifying nothing" in the metanarrative being spun by the Cold War spymasters in Washington, who are indifferent to his near-certain elimination by Vandamm and his associates. Hitchcock continually uses doubling in the film as a tool of his satire—Thornhill/Kaplan, Townsend/Vandamm, the assassination of the real Townsend versus the mock assassination of Thornhill in the cafeteria at Mount Rushmore, the old world Townsend mansion versus Vandamm's modernistic home in Rapid City. These insistent binaries point to the kind of thinking employed by the Professor, the moral absolutism of Cold War politics. Ultimately the film indicts this absolutism as madness, perfectly encapsulated in the acronym for a Cold War preoccupation: MAD (Mutually Assured Destruction). Hamlet's madness is assumed (existing only when the wind blows in the unreal direction of north-north-west), but in the world depicted ruthlessly by Hitchcock in this film it is pervasive.

Torn Curtain (1966), whose original screenplay about an ostensible American defector by the novelist Brian Moore was inspired by the real-life British defectors Guy Burgess and Donald Maclean, was met with popular and critical indifference or occasional hostility upon its release. It was Hitchcock's first attempt to de-glamorize the spy film at a time when the Bond franchise and its offshoots were the dominant genre in American film, and as such it meant that all the comedic charms and high-intensity pursuit-and-escape motifs of *North by Northwest* would be absent or at least muted, like the film's color scheme. And although the film would feature two of the most popular and glamorous stars of the time, Paul Newman and Julie Andrews, Hitchcock would again insure with his direction and his camera that their performances would be restrained, subdued. Seen today, the film stands with its successor, *Topaz*, as audacious departures from techniques, tones, and narrative strategies that had always worked for Hitchcock in the past but which he declined to use now in order to make serious espionage films that undermined the certainties of the Cold War mentalities of both East and West.

Robert Dassanowsky in "'*Ceci n'est pas une Allemagne*' On the Treachery of Images and the Deconstruction of Hitchcock's Thriller in

Torn Curtain," acknowledges that the film favors neither the East nor the West in its depiction of American and Soviet intelligence activities, but he reads the film primarily as a metanarrative that self-consciously exposes and rejects the basic ingredients of the thriller structure Hitchcock had been building for thirty years. The film combines backlot photography, obvious rear projections and matte shots with occasional on-location shots to call attention to its own artifice. Combined with the recurrence of scenes set in repositories of art—especially the East Berlin art museum and the theater—the cinematography calls explicit attention to the artificiality of the world it depicts as well as of cinema itself. *Torn Curtain*, for Dassanowsky is thus a "performance" of a Hitchcock thriller and not a genuine one; yet as such it can also be read as a commentary on the insubstantiality of Cold War assumptions about nationhood and morality, as well as an indictment of the "theatricality of politics."

In 1969 Hitchcock released his second Cold War spy thriller inspired by actual historical events, *Topaz*, which stars John Forsyth, Karin Dor, and the French actors Frederick Stafford, Michel Piccoli, and Phillippe Noiret. Again Hitchcock wanted to make a film about the human cost of international espionage, with both the East and the West seen as the perpetrators. But the source novel by Leon Uris, based on the political realities surrounding the Cuban Missile Crisis of 1962, was fervently anti-communist, and Uris himself was the original screenwriter, to be replaced ultimately by Samuel Taylor, who had written *Vertigo*. In our volume Walter Srebnick points out that the result ideologically was one of the film's true weaknesses: the even-handed treatment of East and West evident in the dialogue is undercut by the visual content, which favors the American intelligence operation and indicts the Communist ones, particularly in its depiction of the Cuban agents as slovenly and brutal. The film's cool reception, according to Srebnick, was also due to the fact that much of the American public had turned against the Vietnam War by the time of the film's release, and the events of 1962 regarding Cuba now seemed to be a foreshadowing of the misguided military engagement with another Communist government in Hanoi—this time at the cost of much American life. What seemed noble in 1962 now seemed oppressive. So Hitchcock and Taylor's attempt to present a truly human story about the Americans, the Cubans, the Russians, and the French who are all hurt physically or psychologically by the espionage surrounding the Missile Crisis is undercut by the film's persistent anti-communism. Instead of telling the "story" (the text's emotional core) of the human costs of espionage that they truly desired to tell, the film relies too heavily on the "plot," which concerns the attempts of the West to defeat the Soviets and prevent nuclear catastrophe.

In assessing both *Torn Curtain* and *Topaz*, Randall Spinks draws on both Charles Tilly and Noam Chomsky to establish an economic power context for the films' Cold War background. Following Tilly in implicating both Communism and capitalism as examples of a "giant protection racket," Spinks highlights Chomsky's claim that the United States bore primary responsibility for Cold War atrocities, compelling the Soviets to respond aggressively. From this point of view the American ideological system during this period served as an "unreliable narrative." Hitchcock's films are imbedded within that system and make use of that narrative at the same time that the director instinctively subverts them, due to his innate cynicism, apolitical tendencies, and profound awareness of human fallibility. Hitchcock was no dissident, but both films can be read as treating the Western suspicion of Communist expansion as a psychological projection of the West's own imperial designs on the Third World.

Ken Mogg sees *Topaz* as ultimately describing "the toll taken by espionage on human lives." His focus is on the film's "emotional appeal," which gives it a timeless quality. Aware of Hitchcock's cynicism, Mogg demonstrates how it is countered in *Topaz* by a sense of the sublime and by the compassion that is elicited from the audience for the most obvious victims of the Cold War spy games, such as Juanita, murdered by her Communist lover, and the tortured Mendozas—all highlighted by the montage of suffering humanity from the film that are the last images we see. He then turns his attention to the last project of Hitchcock's career, *The Short Night*, of which we have only the unfinished screenplay by David Freeman.

It is fascinating and quite revealing that Hitchcock's final project was one more "realistic" spy film, this one based on the life of George Blake, a double agent who made a daring escape from a British prison and fled to the Soviets. In 1968 Ronald Kirkbride wrote a novel about Blake's experiences, *The Short Night*, which became a primary source for Hitchcock's projected film, along with a book by Sean Bourke, one of

Introduction

Blake's fellow inmates who was involved in the escape, *The Springing of George Blake*. Hitchcock went through several writers, including Ernest Lehman and Norman Lloyd, before settling on Freeman, who, after the director's death, wrote a book about his time working with him, *The Last Days of Alfred* Hitchcock, which contains the unfinished screenplay. Mogg sees the projected film as dealing with the same conflict one finds in *Topaz*: the "life-threatening" world of espionage set against the human need for compassion, which in this last projected film is transmuted almost entirely into libido, the life-affirming passion between the protagonist Joe—who has been hired by the CIA to murder the Blake-character, Brand—and Brand's wife Carla, who becomes Joe's lover. Although Freeman acknowledges that the screenplay needed revision, the draft we do have, according to Mogg, indicates the film would have made "a strong statement about the importance of a loving relationship in an absurd universe." *The Short Night,* based on Freeman's script, would have ended Hitchcock's career with still one more espionage film, this one forming a triptych with *Torn Curtain* and *Topaz*, sharing those films' moral dichotomy—Cold War spying in opposition to love and family.

Hitchcock's first espionage film after 1946's *Notorious* was his remake of 1934's *The Man Who Knew Too Much*, starring James Stewart and Doris Day, with a screenplay by John Michael Hayes, who had written *Rear Window, To Catch a Thief,* and *The Trouble with Harry*, between 1954 and 1956, the year the remake was released. Although *The Man Who Knew Too Much* is even less precise about the national identity of the villains than is *North by Northwest*, the Draytons, whose job it is to kidnap the McKennas' son Hank, seem to be British Communists who are supporting a terrorist/anarchist movement to disrupt the international order of the 1950s by assassinating the prime minister of an unnamed European country. Niklas Salmose in this volume sees the film not only as reflecting the state of international tensions in the mid-'50s, but also as an examination of the beginnings of a postmodern society, one characterized by a fragmented social order that constitutes a rupture with modernity. Globalization and the undermining of colonial dominance are inherent factors in the film, which critiques dominant patriarchal ideologies and grand narratives, while its self-reflexivity is perhaps its clearest postmodern trait—not only in terms of its status as a remake, but also in its use of Technicolor and rear projections, both of which call attention to the constructed quality of the narrative. Also, James Stewart's portrayal of Doctor McKenna, in its combination of aggression and likability, represents "the postmodern condition of a male in distress." Throughout the film, too, runs what Salmose calls "cold war paranoia" that is conveyed through an array of modern modes of transportation as well as modes of communication, especially the telephone. It is fitting that a film that depicts the post-war, fragmented world should end with a fragment, a brief denouement in which the McKennas finally rejoin the guests who have been waiting for them at their hotel, apologizing for their prolonged absence but explaining nothing. The film, for Salmose, is an "important transitional postmodern text."

Hopefully this volume will contribute to the ongoing reappraisal of Hitchcock's continued engagement with espionage fiction, a relationship that should put him among the grand masters of the genre such as John Buchan, Eric Ambler, Ian Fleming, and John Le Carré. As far as espionage cinema is concerned, no other filmmaker has created as many classic films. As far as espionage itself is concerned, the current spy games between the United States and Russia, which are dominating international headlines, make Hitchcock's Cold War films more timely and prescient than they have been since *Topaz* was released in 1969.

NOTE: It should go without saying that when all the authors here discuss these film texts in relation to the script and the dialogue, they are including the respective screenwriters in the term "Hitchcock."

WORKS CITED

Alfred Hitchcock in *Hitchcock on Hitchcock, Volume 1: Selected Writings and Interviews*, ed. Sid Gottlieb. Univ. of Cal, 2015
Spoto, Donald. *The Art of Alfred Hitchcock*. Doubleday, 1976.
Wood, Robin. *Hitchcock's Films Revisited*. Columbia UP, 1989.

"A Girl Like You" and a Film (Un)Like Another: Sequentiality in *Notorious* and *North by Northwest*

By Rebecca Martin

At a moment of dawning distrust in *North by Northwest* (1959), Roger O. Thornhill (Cary Grant) asks Eve Kendall (Eva Marie Saint), "How does a girl like you get to be a girl like you?" While the line may sound as if it belongs in a flirtatious, throwaway dialogue, the fact that it occurs at a turning point in the relationship between Roger and Eve insures that it carries layered meanings. It also echoes a line, and a theme, from *Notorious* (1946) that finds Devlin (Cary Grant), an American agent, accusingly saying to Alicia Huberman (Ingrid Bergman), "You almost had me believing…that a woman like you could change her spots." In both cases, the man's stipulation of what the "woman" or "girl" is "like," while superficially comprehensible, also signals a move into a labyrinth of identities and issues of likeness that carry meaning well beyond the relationships between the characters. There is a mystery at the heart of these two films that is anchored in the historical and psychological contexts of very dissimilar war times, the end of the "hot" war and the heart of the subsequent Cold War. The idea of "likeness" as employed in, and enacted by, these two films will underpin this investigation into Alfred Hitchcock's handling of historical and political specificity, identity and social relations, and genre conventions, in particular certain aspects of the melodramatic mode. The director will retain the mode's drama of peril and rescue, its focus on high emotion—and its suppression—made visible through bodies that speak without words and the use of objects, such as tea cups or matchbooks, that may be more articulate than the characters. Other aspects of traditional melodrama he jettisons or works to complicate, even undermine. Gone are the clear-cut distinctions between evil and innocence and the stereotypes that conveyed those qualities. These distinctions and traditional assumptions become objects of serious play in Hitchcock's hands in both of these films. If *Notorious* is the original in this two-film sequence, then *North by Northwest* is its ghostly double, more colorful, even garish, but moving toward less legibility, greater insubstantiality and greater skepticism.

I borrow the idea of the two-film sequence from Donald Spoto who, in *The Art of Alfred Hitchcock*, notes that *North by Northwest* "is in a way the sequel and conclusion of *Notorious*" and goes on to call attention to certain narrative resemblances (303). I accept Spoto's formulation as a helpful way to conceptualize the connections between the films. It provides a framework for exploring some of what the earlier film seems to leave undone, particularly in its conclusion, and it highlights the characterizations and situations that echo. Drawing attention to the likeness of the two films also invites scrutiny of their differences, though. Spoto says of *Notorious* that it is the film "in which a tippling blonde was nearly sent to her death by a character played by Cary Grant after he blithely turns her over to the enemy." On the other hand, "In *North by Northwest*, Grant seems to get his just deserts: he's the tippling businessman nearly sent to his death by a duplicitous blonde" (italics original). And, finally, "behind it all in both cases is a depraved political order, with government leaders committing mayhem in the name of necessary intelligence activities" (303). This essay will show that the similarities that superficially tie the films together are more complicated than they appear and that the ways in which the films differ are far more significant and mark their mooring in two very different "war-time" environments.

In a passage from François Truffaut's 1962 interview with the director, Hitchcock insists at length that the "story" of *Notorious* "is that the girl is to sleep with a spy in order to get some secret information" and that "*Notorious* was simply the story of a man in love with a girl who, in the course of her official duties, had to go to bed with another man and even to marry him" (168-9). These points are made in the context of a discussion of Hitchcock's well-known use of the MacGuffin, the object or information of seemingly vital importance (a secret, a document, a formula, e.g.) that puts the plot and characters in motion, but is in itself "beside the point," and, in fact, "it doesn't matter what it is" (138). In his conversation with Truffaut, Hitchcock goes into detail about his decision to cast a wine bottle filled with a sample of uranium sand as the MacGuffin in *Notorious*. He notes that the producer balked at using a prop that was specifically linked to the atomic bomb, a prospect that rather than seeming too grim seemed far too fantastic in pre-Hiroshima 1944. Hitchcock offered to change the "gimmick" to industrial diamonds that the German armament retooling project would need, but then the project was moved to another studio and the objection was dropped. To accept this denial of significance (neither Hitchcock's first nor last, and one of many) and indirection on the director's part keeps us from looking squarely at the specificity of this wine bottle MacGuffin. Hitchcock recounts to Truffaut his story of a trip in 1944 with writer Ben Hecht to the California Institute of Technology to gather some information about "how large…an atom bomb" would have to be, and the producer's rejection of the carefully-researched concept (168). One year later in August of 1945 just before filming began, the atomic bombs were dropped on Hiroshima and Nagasaki. The emotional impact and meaning of that wine bottle and its contents to an audience in 1946 is different from the weight that Hitchcock might attach to it in 1962, when the period of 1944-1946 was a memory, and to what anyone seeing the film today might see in it. It's a MacGuffin all right, but one that is displayed in a specific historical context and carries weight as a specific historical referent and one whose meaning changed spectacularly between the producer's hesitation in 1944 and the film's release on September 6, 1946.

The choice of this MacGuffin and the argument I will make about strong conceptual ties of *Notorious* to its place in the World War II timeline and at the dawn of the Cold War are curiously and significantly linked. At the outset, this argument will contradict two truisms about Hitchcock that he took great care to maintain. The first, already noted, is that the MacGuffins that populate his work are invariably "actually nothing at all" (Truffaut 138), and the second is that Hitchcock often resisted attaching any importance to the political content of his films (Corber 200; McElhaney 78). The year 1946 was situated between the coining of "cold war" in 1945 by George Orwell and the use of the phrase in a 1947 speech by American political advisor Bernard Baruch, which placed it into the American vocabulary ("Cold War"). When *Notorious* opened in 1946, one world war was officially over, though trailing damage, damage repair and suspicion into the post-war era. Like director Charles Vidor's *Gilda*, which opened a few months earlier in April, *Notorious* acknowledges what was a very real fear at the time: that pre-war settlements of Germans in Latin America and Nazis who fled to Latin America at the end of the war would make common cause to sustain Nazi ideology and to rebuild the German war machine. Whether this dangerous confluence of sympathies was happening in Brazil, as in *Notorious*, or in Argentina, as in *Gilda*, or in other Latin American nations with significant ethnic German populations, both the US government and much of its population believed that German influence in the southern hemisphere posed political, military and economic threats (Friedman 4-5). *Gilda's* much-derided subplot featuring (apparent) Nazis in Buenos Aires who seek the return by Gilda's husband, Ballin Mundson, of documents verifying their ownership of a tungsten cartel, and the subplot in *Notorious* regarding unrepentant Nazis in Rio de Janeiro and their control of uranium ore, touch upon issues that were far more real to audiences in 1946 than they seem to today's viewers and critics. Newspapers of note, such as the *New York Times*, the *New York Herald-Tribune*, and the *Washington Post*, frequently featured frightening headlines about Nazi Party inroads in Latin American politics and German forces massing in places such as Colombia preparing to attack the Panama Canal, from the late 1930s into the post-war period, as detailed by Max Paul Friedman (55-7). There were reports of sleeper agents, akin to John Huberman, Alicia Huberman's unrepentant Nazi-sympathizer father. Most such reports were misinformed, exaggerated or simply wrong, but a lingering Nazi threat south of the US border would have touched a nerve with American audiences. Hitchcock's choice of uranium-laced sand in a wine bottle as the MacGuffin in *Notorious* was also quite prescient, linking as it does the atomic bombs dropped on Japan in 1945, the supposed resurgent Nazi threat of 1946, and the proliferation of atomic weapons upon which the tense, tenuous, decades-long balance of the Cold War was to be based.

In noting that Hitchcock professed little interest in political content in his films, I only repeat his own denials. I do not mean that his works do not take ideological positions or that they do not convey particular political values or depict events relevant to their times. Of course they do, and many critics, prominent among them Robert J. Corber, have explored the ideological underpinnings of his work. As in the case of the MacGuffin, though, perhaps the director's insistence distracts us or makes us underestimate the weight of historical context in some of his films. *Notorious* is one of them. One biographical factor that is likely to have had a critical though unquantifiable effect on how Hitchcock infused politics into *Notorious*, which began filming in October 1945, is that he had spent a month of that summer in London as an advisor on what was to be a documentary film about the liberation of the concentration camps. His long-time friend Sidney Bernstein, who in peacetime had been a theatre and film producer and who would go on to found the Granada media empire, was chief of the Film Section of the Psychological Warfare Division of the Supreme Headquarters Allied Expeditionary Force (SHAEF). One of the jobs of the section was to coordinate the photographic material being shot by cameramen as the Allied forces entered the camps (Frontline). The British film, given the title of *German Concentration Camps Factual Survey*, was not completed that year due to shifting political balances and shifting propaganda needs. It is impossible to imagine that Hitchcock remained untouched and unaffected as he was viewing during June and July photos and films of the camps, their dead, their survivors, and their German apologists. He was watching films of starving prisoners who were still alive inside the camps, an experience of unimaginable immediacy, as well as viewing films of piles of corpses and the heaps of items taken from them, all within days or weeks of the original filming.[1] The footage is described by Toby Haggith, Senior Curator of the Department of Research at the Imperial War Museum where the unfinished reels of film long resided, as '"much more candid"' and raw than other documentaries from the period, and certainly this was long before such images became more familiar through repetition and more distant through the passage of time (Macnab). In his review of the documentary that was finally released as *Memory of the Camps* in an abbreviated version in 1984 and then in a more complete and restored version in 2014, Richard Brody of the *New Yorker* notes that a significant part of the film's impact comes from viewing the horror and "astonishment" of Allied troops who enter the camps unprepared for what they would find. Though Hitchcock's role in the production is not entirely clear and will probably never be known, some of his contributions are documented. According to Bernstein, Hitchcock instructed that some shots should reveal the surroundings of each camp, including nearby villages and their inhabitants. The geographical context would emphasize the close proximity of a camp to populated areas where "'they must have known about it'" (qtd. in Brody). In addition, Hitchcock encouraged the use of "wide establishing shots which support the documentary feel of the film and showed that the events could not have been staged" (Frontline), and "'long tracking shots, which cannot be tampered with'" (McGilligan 373). While Hitchcock's advice about narrative structure and shot set-ups speaks to his sensitivity to the relationship between technique and viewers' perception, as well as to maintaining an aura of unimpeachable material veracity in the film, his work also may be seen as a way to contain and control images that in all likelihood were far more overwhelming and certainly more real than anything in his films. As Steven Jacobs succinctly notes, "In 1945… the atrocities were facts, not memories" (274).

The original 1946 trailer for *Notorious* blares in print "Notorious woman of affairs! …Adventurous man of the world!" The trailer thus sets up from the outset the meeting of two sophisticated types, where the woman is identified by her questionable past and the man by his active public life in the present. The reference to her notoriety tells us that her disreputable life is public knowledge; as Bosley Crowther of the *New York Times* says in his August 1946 review, Alicia Huberman is a "lady of notably loose morals." In another film, this notorious woman would be destined for the role of *femme fatale*. It is of interest to see that even in Crowther's review, he accepts as conventional the features—"routine ingredients of a South American Nazi-exile gang, an American girl set to spy upon it, and a behind-the-scenes American intelligence man"--that actually tie the film to contemporary accounts and alarms in his own newspaper, as noted earlier. For Crowther, what injects life into the routine "'thriller' elements" of the film is the acting of Bergman and Grant, especially Bergman, of whom Crowther writes in superlatives. He notes that "the crux of the melodramatic action is the peril of the girl" and goes on to say that "there is rich and real emotion expressed by Miss Bergman in her role, and the integrity of her nature as she portrays it is the prop that holds the show." Very little criticism and few contemporary reviews diverge from this perspective: Bergman's performance is amazingly rich, subtle and deeply emotional without recourse to excess, gesture or lengthy dialogue. Alicia's "Mr. Sebastian has asked me to marry him" is delivered with minimal movement (a slow, slight rise of the chin) and a neutral, almost deadpan expression that is given resonance by the eye movements that accompany the plain statement. Her eyes are looking down as she begins to speak, they are raised slightly but are unfocused, then they are raised a bit higher to look at Paul Prescott (Louis Calhern), to whom her statement is addressed. Her facial expression does not change while she speaks this emotionally-charged line. The feeling and the cost of suppressing the emotion is signaled by the slight eye movements and the mild lift of the chin. The tone of voice by its very neutrality conveys both the depth of emotion and the pain of repression. Joe McElhaney, in "The Object and the Face: *Notorious*, Bergman and the Close-up," has provided the most comprehensive and meaningful analysis of Bergman's acting in this film and of Hitchcock's focus on her face in "119 close-ups and 72 extreme close-ups, a combined total of 191 shots in a 101-minute film" (66). McElhaney notes that "Bergman's close-ups are both acts of seduction for the viewer and pieces of evidence definitively establishing this 'new' kind of beauty," that is, "naturalness" (73). Her face, not her body, is the instrument through which her naturalness and her eroticism are expressed. Noting that both Claude Chabrol and Eric Rohmer see in Bergman's films with Hitchcock "'the story of a face,'" McElhaney takes this point further, saying "Bergman's face is not simply functional for Hitchcock, shaped by the dynamics of montage, but is also innately expressive so that his films with her seem to be (whatever their other concerns) *about* the face" (74, italics original). Bergman fills both the screen and the viewers' experience in a way that, as we will see, Eva Marie Saint does not in *North by Northwest*. That absorption is a very significant part of the viewing experience and the film's emotional resonance and impact, but there is another way in which the character of Alicia Huberman is given depth and complexity that is unusual in Hitchcock's films, which he himself preferred to think of in terms of a smoothly-plotted fiction into which his actors fit and provide the necessary emotional effects at times of the director's choosing (Truffaut 111).

    Alicia Huberman exists within a rich, dense web of relationships. The first and most profound of these is her relationship with her traitorous father. She rejects him for his crimes and refusal of American ideals, a point brought home when Devlin plays a recording of her conversation with her father in which she denounces him and insists, "I love this country." It is not a simple love-hate relationship; it has tragic complexity. In the scene on the plane to Rio when Devlin tells her that her father has committed suicide, her reaction is painful to watch and reveals the complicated feelings she has toward him. He is both the "nice" father of her childhood and the parent she felt obligated to react against when she learns he is not the man she thought he was. Her confession of those feelings and that history to Devlin makes it clear that her abandoned, decadent behavior has been her response to her father's treason. Her father's attempts to recruit her shocked her and cut her loose from what she thought she, and he, stood for. Her still intense, though conflicted, emotional attachment to her father is fully expressed as she says of his death, "It's a very curious feeling, as if something had happened to me and not to him." Alicia is given an emotional past and a relationship history that goes back in time beyond her recent notoriety and puts that notoriety in a context that enhances viewers' appreciation of her as a feeling person and explains the behavior that might have made her less sympathetic. When Alex Sebastian is identified as her espionage target, another piece of complex emotional history is added when Devlin identifies Sebastian as someone who had "'quite a crush on'" Alicia. She explains he was a friend of her father's and that she "'wasn't very responsive'" to his overtures. In all of the scenes that build her emotional background and both her strength and vulnerability, her character remains firmly anchored to an emotional life and history (a family, friends, family friends). Devlin's generally unemotive, inscrutable facial expressions and the intensity, even harshness, of his gaze are the perfect foil that gives even greater resonance to her reactions and responses. His body is quiet and makes few dramatic moves. He is often shown with one hand in his pocket, but rarely is he relaxed; his posture is upright. As if to offer another point of contrast with Alicia, he is often shown in close-up or medium close-up, but what is revealed is the immobility of his expression topped by the eyes that convey much with their movement. McElhaney notes, "Throughout the film as a whole, Grant consistently underplays. In close-ups, his face is often rigid, a kind of surface in its own right and marked by its absence of telegraphed thought and feelings in contrast to Bergman" (76). Alicia is a woman plunged into contradiction, but he is a man with no attachments and no past except his job. He is a free-floating, enigmatic cipher whose emotions are signaled only with his eyes while his face gives away very little. Alicia has a deep background while Devlin seems to have none.

An additional point must be made about Alicia. She is a warm character, not only because of the depth and detail of characterization that Hitchcock and Ben Hecht give her and that lend weight and reality to the character, but also because of the way she is filmed and lighted. Part of Bergman's "naturalness" is that her face is not fragile or delicate. Even lighted in near-profile, as in the scene on the balcony in Rio when Devlin reveals her mission, her high forehead and relatively broad cheekbones offer a lighting surface that is richly displayed through black and white photography. She is blonde, but the lighting of her hair emphasizes its darker tones, weight and warmth. Her eyes are large and the eyebrows are soft and curved rather than sharply defined; they are aggressive frames for her eyes. Except for her casual, more revealing attire on the evening she throws the party to which Devlin comes after her father's trial, that is, when she is performing "party girl" and cynic, she is costumed in solid colors and attire of relatively simple cut, even her glamourous gowns. In everything she wears, what viewers are drawn to is her face topping the clothing, not the clothing itself. Bergman's height, 5' 9", and slender, not curvaceous, frame also worked in favor of this emphasis. Joe McElhaney has made the important observation that Bergman's height and the frequency with which she acted with shorter men, Claude Rains included, is yet another factor reinforcing the emphasis on her face. In order to draw attention away from the difference between her height and that of the male actors around her, "there tends to be an avoidance of long and medium-long shots"; thus "her expressive power as an actress...is forced to occur from the waist up." He goes on to note, "In this regard, we may think of her as the purest of Hitchcock's actors in that the movements of her body, by the very limitations imposed upon it, must often be repressed or controlled, resulting in the face becoming the primary expressive tool" (73). Let us consider for a moment what this focus on the body means in terms of the director's long association with melodrama.[2]

Notorious is strongly inflected by melodrama, as with most of Hitchcock's early films, but less so, or with greater complexity, than many critics allow. Bosley Crowther, in the *New York Times* review previously cited, refers to the film, first, as a "romantic melodrama," adding that it has "'thriller' elements" that "are familiar and commonplace, except in so far as Mr. Hitchcock has galvanized them into life," and "melodramatic action" involving the "peril of the girl." *Notorious* has been identified with many genres, sub-genres and modes of filmmaking, which is surely one index of its wide and prolonged appeal. What Crowther's choice of language calls up most vividly are melodrama and seriality. Both are embedded in the trope he invokes with "the peril of the girl," which brings to mind early serials, such as those featuring Helen Holmes, Ruth Roland and Pearl White, with their acts of daring, lives under constant threat, last-minute rescues and cliffhanging endings which promise more to come in the next installment. Linda Williams has analyzed melodrama as a "body genre," which, along with horror and pornography, works by transferring (through the visual and the aural) bodily sensation from the screen to the audience. The tear-stained face, or the eyes-brimming-with-tears face, full of anguish, and shown in close-up, is but one of the melodramatic tropes *Notorious* employs. "The girl in peril," the emphasis on highly emotional states, a central, troubled, romantic relationship, a woman whose innocence must be proven or reclaimed, an emotional rollercoaster alternating between "in the nick of time" and "too late," and a last-minute, daring rescue all attach *Notorious* to melodrama. The psychic conflict played out on Alicia's active face and Devlin's impassive one exteriorizes the problem of (self-)knowing and (self-)recognition that keeps them apart and off balance with one another. They both struggle in different ways between an external expression of their true feelings and the guardedness that comes from repeated pain and fear of betrayal. If they could only speak with clarity to each other, the problems would evaporate, but at key moments this is precisely what does not happen. They cannot or do not speak, and their thoughts and feelings, including the effort of repressing those feelings, the confusion about feelings, and the effort to gather strength and say the thing that does not express real feelings, pass through their faces. Numerous scenes provide a visual spectacle of these efforts and emotions. Devlin's taunting of Alicia for her recent sobriety, the scene on the balcony where he breaks the news to her about the government's plans for her, and the scene at the racetrack that ends with Devlin's brutal remark, "Dry your eyes, baby, it's out of character," each offers a spectacle of emotion that evolves less from an excess of emotion than from the simultaneous attempts to repress it. And, finally, the drawing room scene where Alicia hears a clue about the source of the uranium and only a moment later realizes that she is being poisoned ends with tears of another sort, tears from bodily pain, and a physical collapse. Alicia's body and emotional balance are under attack and the battle is played out across her face throughout the film. Interestingly, something in all of this makes Alicia's struggles, pain and suffering less melodramatic than they might be. Perhaps it is Hitchcock's de-emphasis on action in the narrative, as well as the emphasis on repression rather than uninhibited emotionality. Physical mobility, especially in Grant's role, is underplayed and emotional display that is truly excessive is tamped down. Eyes brim but only rarely overflow; eyes dart with emotion but in a passive face; eyes dull with hurt, disappointment or pain but are cast down or simply closed to conceal it.

Devlin's nasty remark to Alicia at the racetrack, "Dry your eyes, baby, it's out of character," reiterates a prominent theme that begins to develop very early in the film. As this gibe shows, Devlin believes that he has Alicia all figured out; he can say, "It's out of character," because he believes he knows her character, who she is at her core. She's a party girl, a drinker, sexually loose and irresponsible. In the earlier scene when they have been in Rio for a few days waiting for her assignment and are seated at an outdoor café, Devlin scoffs at her sobriety, saying "It's a phase." Alicia responds, "You don't think a woman can change?" She anticipates his skeptical comeback, saying "Once a crook always a crook. Once a tramp always a tramp" and says, crestfallen, "I'm pretending I'm a nice, unspoiled child....Why won't you believe me, Dev. Just a little. Why won't you?" These are two of numerous scenes in *Notorious* where Alicia is described as a "type," or her "character" is dissected, or a certain understanding is telegraphed with the phrase "a woman of that sort" or "a woman like you." Every one of those comments comes from men, whether from Devlin, his boss, Prescott, who says, "She's a perfect type for the job," or one of the agents' colleagues, Beardsley (Moroni Olsen), who refers to Alicia as "a woman of that sort." Devlin's confusion about what he really feels for her is indicated within these scenes by the fact that the most painful insults come from him, but he also, tight with anger, defends her from Beardsley's casual slur. His behavior swings back and forth between insults to her, confrontations in which he throws her past and her present into her face, and remarks that simply repeat tired stereotypes about women's supposed changeability ("It's a phase") and disregard for male advice ("A man doesn't tell a woman what to do; she tells herself"). He also refuses to give her crucial guidance when she requests it: "Do you want me to take the job?" she asks, and Devlin replies flatly, "It's up to you." The emotional brutality that Devlin directs toward Alicia rears its head again in the racetrack scene after she and Sebastian have married and she has begun to report her observations to Devlin. At the time when she is literally risking her life to do the mission she has undertaken, Devlin throws her acquiescence back at her with, "I can't help recalling some of your remarks about being a new woman" and "You almost had me believing in that little hokey-pokey miracle of yours, that a woman like you could change her spots." When he insists that the whole choice was hers and "the answer had to come from you," she responds wearily, "I see. Some kind of love test." Devlin says with emphasis, "That's right." He, of course, will be the one who finally has to change. Alicia will revert to the essentially good, well-intentioned, and loving woman who she was before her father's perfidy and Devlin's act of drawing her into espionage. She will recover who she really is and no longer perform as if she is another; she is no carefree, party girl, notoriously performing cynicism and not caring what man she gives herself to. Near the end of the film, when Alex and his mother decide to protect their own interests by slowly killing Alicia, Mrs. Sebastian takes charge, saying, "Let me arrange this one, listen to me. No one must know what she is." Of course, she means that Alicia is a spy, but her remark reminds viewers that throughout the film Alicia has been a victim of mistaken identity—a victim of all of those men who smugly identify her "type" or who congratulate themselves for knowing what she is "like," while viewers have seen the truth in Bergman's luminous face.

Unlike most conventional melodramas that provide closure along with their endings, *Notorious* seems oddly unfulfilling. Devlin realizes that Alicia is being poisoned and daringly rescues her in a manner that requires Sebastian to appear to assist him in order to prevent his Nazi colleagues from learning that Alicia is a spy. Once the threesome makes it to the car, Devlin closes Sebastian out and gives him no choice but to return to his mansion where his suspicious friends and angry mother await him. There is little doubt he faces death, since they did not hesitate earlier to rid themselves of Emil Hupka (Eberhard Krumschmidt) for a much smaller fault. While Devlin and Alicia are last seen in a car that drives away from the house, the film ends with its focus on Sebastian's back as he turns toward the house and walks toward the lighted doorway that frames his waiting co-conspirators. Sebastian is a villain, but a remarkably appealing one. It is quite easy to believe, in fact, that his feelings for Alicia are deeper and more real than those of Devlin, who has been little but a torment to her. The retreat of Devlin and Alicia at the film's end leaves a very open question about what awaits them. She has been rescued; he has identified himself as a "fat-headed guy full of pain," an all-too-brief and unsatisfying explanation for his insults and hardheartedness toward her, and has confessed his love, but what comes next? This pair has a lot of personal debris to clear before the romance can move forward. This makes it even more strange for Hitchcock to focus viewers' attention on Alex Sebastian in the final shot. His terror and disappointment as he goes toward his fate remind viewers of what a sympathetic character he has been. One feels not that he is an unrepentant Nazi going to his well-deserved death, but that he is a man betrayed by love, a sad and foolish man, less than a villain. This feels like an ending constructed with gestures toward closure but one that, quite daringly, given the historical timing, leaves viewers to consider the differences between the winners and the losers. It could be said of both the US government that is ready to have Alicia prostitute herself and of those who conspire to rebuild the Nazi war machine that "behind it all in both cases is a depraved political order, with government leaders committing mayhem in the name of necessary intelligence activities" (Spoto 303). Donald Spoto's analysis of one theme that brings together *Notorious* and *North by Northwest* also can offer a significant statement about the bifurcated ending of *Notorious*, which directs viewers' emotional energy in two directions. The ending undercuts the conventions of melodrama in seeming to make a point of failing to restore moral values and clearly identify the good.

If *North by Northwest* is the sequel to *Notorious*, will the closure of this story be found in *North by Northwest*? At the end of World War II, American and Western attention drifted away from Nazis-in-waiting and toward the Soviet threat. Nations realigned themselves to face this threat and, by 1955, West Germany joined NATO. This felt threat was not focused on ethnicity (German, Japanese) or race (Asian), but on ideas that posed a covert threat because of their intangibility and their ability to slip unnoticed into the intellectual air. In this way, it was possible for these ideas to infiltrate schools and other institutions, families, and even the sex lives of individuals. The constant risk of small confrontations that could lead to nuclear war, the brutal crackdowns on popular uprisings in several Eastern European countries, the occasional splash of spy scandals in Western newspapers, and the brutal conflict in Korea that took 36,000 American lives and made it clear that the war against Communism was to be fought on both an eastern and a western front, were part of daily life in the 1950s into which *North by Northwest* was launched. This awareness was a significant part of the consciousness that viewers brought to films. Who was the enemy and where would the threat come from? It was everywhere and nowhere. In 1950s America, homeowners were warned to construct fallout shelters, and Civil Defense fallout shelter signs went up across the nation on buildings that were judged to provide adequate protection. The nuclear arms race with the USSR began in 1945 and would continue to garner news coverage and attention for more than four decades. Nuclear weapons tests were in the newspapers and on nightly news; between 1946 and 1958, 67 surface and subsurface thermonuclear experiments were conducted by the US in the Marshall Islands, with 23 on the Bikini Atoll alone ("Bikini Atoll Nuclear Test"). Across America, civil defense warning sirens were upgraded, their signals standardized and publicized in pamphlets and newspapers. Children practiced "duck and cover" routines on a regular basis in schools. Soldiers and sailors wore mysterious-looking black PDs, personnel dosimeters, along with their military dog tags. Even the interstate highway system designed and begun under President Eisenhower was spurred in large part by concern for civil defense and evacuation in case of attack ("Highway History: Civil Defense, 1955"). From a contemporary vantage point it is difficult to re-create the mindset in which these issues were pervasive and of immediate concern. America was a very different nation than it was in 1946. When *North by Northwest* opened on 1 July 1959, the American public was more afraid of infiltration and subversion by ideas and of nuclear annihilation than of German armies massing on the southern border. Hitchcock tells Truffaut in his August 1962 interview that

> the MacGuffin is nothing. I'm convinced of this, but I find it very difficult to prove it to others. My best MacGuffin, and by that I mean the emptiest, the most nonexistent, and the most absurd, is the one we used in *North by Northwest*. The picture is about espionage, and the only question that's raised in the story is to find out what the spies are after....the Central Intelligence man explains the whole situation to Cary Grant, and Grant, referring to the James Mason character, asks, "What does he do?" The counterintelligence man replies, "Let's just say that he's an importer and exporter." "But what does he sell?" "Oh, just government secrets!" is the answer. Here, you see, the MacGuffin has been boiled down to its purest expression: nothing at all! (139)

The MacGuffin in *North by Northwest* is, paradoxically, both full of meaning and thematic resonance and totally weightless and inconsequential. The secret's lack of materiality—the very flimsiness of that film, its fragile, imprinted images and the immateriality and lack of specificity of whatever secrets it holds—is part of the paradox exposed by Hitchcock's film. It is one of many factors in *North by Northwest* that differentiates it from *Notorious* and that shows the director's movement toward a kind of cool, bloodless cynicism in the "sequel."

North by Northwest is a film composed with a background palette of dark blues, browns and many shades of gray. A cool blonde, Eve Kendall, and a suave advertising man, Roger O. Thornhill, inhabit its center. Eve is like Alicia Huberman only in her hair color and her falling for Cary Grant. Her differences are meaningful in nearly every respect, and they reinforce the movement from *Notorious* to *North by Northwest* as a movement away from paranoia based on known, specific adversaries (Germans, Japanese) and material threats (armies) toward a more generalized, free-floating paranoia (Communism, the atomic bomb), threats that are abstract (ideas), and characters who are unmoored from their past and lacking in thickness. Where Alicia existed in a web of relationships that created the tensions and disappointments that tore her life apart, Eve is a woman whose background and beliefs are a blank. Alicia makes her choices for reasons that are clear, both to her and to viewers. First, she sets herself apart from her father and his political principles and, second, she reacts to this disillusionment with self-destructive impulses and, finally, her disappointment in Devlin and despair at her situation lead her to accept the grave and dangerous mission she is offered. In the case of Eve Kendall, the only explanation given for her foray into espionage is that she was bored and directionless when she met the charming and debonair Phillip Vandamm (James Mason) and began an affair with him. Only when federal agents approached her and told her that Vandamm was a traitor and a spy did she make the difficult choice to become a double agent. Her involvement in espionage is based on a situation she drifted into and viewers are not privy, as we are with Alicia, to any struggles she may have had between love and her patriotic duty. Alicia is dropped into espionage through her complex web of relationships, and Hitchcock provides viewers plenty of opportunities to see and share her suffering and the emotional strain of her choices; the close-ups and constant focus on her face and the emotions expressed there absorb viewers in her anguish. He does not grant that opportunity in the case of Eve. Eve is quite unlike Alicia and Eva Marie Saint is a very different actor than Ingrid Bergman.

In a switch from *Notorious*, this is more Roger's film than Eve's. In fact, she does not put in an appearance until 45 minutes into the 136-minute film. In physical appearance, Eve Kendall is more blonde than Alicia and more petite, with a small, delicate face, and a strong, direct gaze that can challenge or discomfit any man. Even apart from her innuendo-filled dialogue, there is a knowingness in this face. Hers is a face for modernity, not melodrama. She is often photographed in the full body shots that Hitchcock avoided with Bergman's Alicia. Viewers see far more of her skin, in dresses with deep "V" backs, worn low on the shoulders. She dresses in warm colors, dark reds and burnt orange, or when she's to be taken more seriously, in a stylish, tailored dark blue suit perfect for a female professional, or in a plain gray dress. The colors of her costumes contrast with and heighten the coolness of her skin

"A Girl Like You"

and hair and make her stand out from any background. Her dresses are usually tightly-cinched at the waist with skirts that hug her hips or fit and flare, as does the beautiful red and black cocktail dress she wears in the scenes at the Ambassador Hotel and the auction house. She is often shown in profile, with her bright page-boy appearing to pull her head back a bit, exposing to better effect her long neck, high, smooth forehead, and delicately-shaped nose. Throughout much of her early conversation with Roger, her gaze can only be described as cool and direct, even bold; she shows little emotion and often raises her brows and gives a slight wrinkle to her forehead adding irony to her words. This is an expression of which Alicia Huberman would seem to be incapable. Eve's large, blue eyes practically twinkle mischievously and her mouth is held closed while its corners rise in an ever-so-slight, knowing smirk. When she half-closes her heavy lids over her deep-set eyes, the suggestiveness of the gaze increases because her eyes signal "relaxed and casual" while her conversation signals something more straightforward. A slight dip of head and eyes does not signify sadness or hesitation, but rather reinforces the irony of her words; she lowers her head as if avoiding a direct gaze at Roger, in the pretense of discomfiture. It feels almost as if she would laugh if she looked him in the face. The conversation is, of course, filled with double entendres and thinly-veiled come-ons to which Roger O. Thornhill quickly responds. Eve comments to Roger, "It's a nice face," to which he responds, "Think so?" "I wouldn't say it if I didn't," she says. Then Roger says, "You're that type," but she responds, "What type?" Roger says, "Honest" and Eve's reply is revealing on several levels: "Not really." She is telling him the truth, but because he has decided she is "that type," he believes it to be a very different truth. The word "honest" works in multiple ways here. In part, she is an "honest" woman because she is blunt, but she is not an "honest" woman, because she does not seem to take sexual liaisons very seriously. And she is not being "honest" with him about the fact that she is part of a plot to trap "George Kaplan," the name under which he is hunted. Later, she cannot be "honest" with him without risking her life and her mission of deception, because she would have to admit she has fallen in love with him and that she is an agent of the federal government while also enmeshed in espionage with Vandamm. The "type" Roger has in mind is a certain kind of woman who picks up men on trains and is open in her desire. She's all that. But she is also telling him a deeper truth that he will not discover until the Twentieth Century Limited reaches Chicago. By that time, the truth of her "type" has grown another layer: she has come to care for him and cannot figure out how to save him while also setting him up and, at the same time, keep government secrets from leaving the country.

Throughout the film, though she does appear in many close-ups, Eve is brightly lighted, and while her frame is slight and seemingly fragile, her posture is always erect as if she has strength—and perhaps emotion—in reserve. Eva Marie Saint is not asked to show the range of emotion that Ingrid Bergman must because, in part, it is 1959 and her character actually is a woman who can be direct in expressing her desires. She is not a woman who will wait for Cary Grant to say the right word so that she does not submit herself to further danger. Late in the film, after Grant's faked death at the park's cafeteria, they meet in the woods and apologize to one another. Grant's Roger is far more understanding than was his Devlin character. Devlin rejects the idea that Alicia's doing her patriotic duty should take precedence over the love she has for him. When Eve explains to Roger that she could not have told him the truth about what she was doing while still maintaining her cover, he responds with "I guess not." His comments lack the venom and anger of Devlin's and his "I guess not" is hardly grudging at all. Rather than "undermining her resolve when [she] need[s] it most," he submits. Where Devlin is a wall of withholding and barely-controlled anger, Roger is a lively, humorous cipher, a man without an identity. He is a far warmer character than Eve, because of his humor and charm, but who is he beneath those qualities? The issue of his identity is raised in many ways and this sets him apart from Devlin, whose identity is attached to a few indisputable concepts (job, duty, brutality, repression, censoriousness). Roger is a slippery one who is tied from the beginning to the question of the fake or the untrue by his profession as an advertising man. As he says, "In the world of advertising, there's no such thing as a lie. There's only expedient exaggeration." Shortly thereafter he is mistaken for "George Kaplan" and while the misidentification puts his life in jeopardy, he later discovers that Kaplan is a fake identity set to lure Vandamm. Kaplan does not exist. But neither does Roger who, at the heart of his name, "Roger O. Thornhill," has "nothing." "R.O.T." is

"A Girl Like You" 35

his trademark, "rot," with, at its center, an "O" that stands for nothing, as he explains to Eve. At several points, Phillip Vandamm notes that without question Roger (a.k.a, "Mr. Kaplan") is playing a role, but of course when Vandamm accuses Roger of "overplay[ing] [his] various roles very severely," Roger is at his most honest, but for all the weight his words carry, it is as if he isn't there. If his identity as Roger is not accepted and George Kaplan does not exist, then Roger has no identity. And when he decides that to defend himself he must follow the Kaplan character across the country, he is both pursuing himself and pursuing nothing. In Chicago, when he wises up to at least part of the plot he is inadvertently involved in—the part where Eve seems to be trying to get him killed—his character is infused with suspicion and anger. Here he turns on Eve in a conversation that harks back to their initial chat on the train, but not in a pleasant way, saying "How does a girl like you get to be a girl like you?" to which she replies, "Lucky, I guess." Roger disagrees strongly, "No, not lucky. Naughty, wicked, up to no good. Ever kill anyone? Because I bet you could tease a man to death without half trying. So stop trying, huh?" And shortly thereafter in the auction scene that veers between the comic and the tragic, even deadly, Roger speaks of Eve to Vandamm in the nastiest of terms, saying, "I'll bet you paid plenty for this little piece of sculpture....She's worth every dollar of it, take it from me. She puts her heart into her work. In fact, her whole body." It's this for which Roger later has to apologize. Roger's assumption that he knows what "a girl like you" is, is predicated on the same sexist stereotypes held by Devlin, but information that Devlin had that should have tempered his hostility but for his "fat-headedness," is not available to Roger. Devlin knows what Alicia is doing and why, but in his own blind stubbornness he throws her motivations back at her. One note of distaste left by *Notorious* is that Devlin's extraordinary cruelty is not adequately answered by his confession of being a "fat-headed guy." As discussed previously, when Roger knows the whole truth he not only accepts that Eve must finish her mission, however dangerous it is, but he also accepts that her motivation for undertaking the mission—"Maybe it was the first time anyone ever asked me to do anything worthwhile"—deserves his understanding. And as Roger denounces the fate that he feels the Professor is forcing on Eve, his use of "a girl like her" has changed significantly. Now, when he angrily says to the Professor that no amount of government interest should force "girls like her to bed down" with "the Vandamms of this world," she is no longer the "treacherous little tramp" he denounced to the Professor earlier. She is rehabilitated in his mind, though she is not essentially changed. The choices she made in getting involved with Vandamm and then betraying him have all been made before the film begins. She has made those commitments and this is who she is when viewers and Roger first meet her. The involvement of Roger complicates her mission enormously but does not keep her from trying to fulfill it. The price she pays for having to absorb Roger's ugly accusations and Vandamm's suspicions is high. At Vandamm's country house, it is clear that she is willing to sacrifice herself even if her mission fails and she cannot prevent the secrets from leaving the country. She delays and makes excuses, but this just makes it clear that she realizes Vandamm knows she has turned and that once she is on the plane, it will be the last ride she takes.

The daring last-minute rescue that Roger performs on the airfield brings us back to the realm of melodrama, but this film, far more than *Notorious*, lies mostly outside of that mode. "The girl in peril" trope is clearly active but the man and woman are both in peril multiple times, alone and together. Devlin, on the other hand, does not share Alicia's physical danger until he removes her from Sebastian's home at the end of the film. There are scenes of high emotion in the narrative but the early ones belong to Roger and are played in a comic-shock manner (Roger with the knife and body at the UN; the drunken ride after his kidnapping) that is not in accord with melodrama. Melodrama requires a drawing out of the emotional response, the playing on the nerves that is felt in the auction scene with its close-up of Vandamm's hand caressing Eve's bare neck and shoulders and encircling her neck. The possessiveness of his gesture and the physical sensation that comes through to viewers in the close-up of his fingers being drawn across her skin are chilling. Vandamm then turns his gaze down toward her back and seems to appraise her with the same attention he gives to the Louis XVI chairs and the Pre-Columbian statue. The scene becomes more purely sensational upon Roger's entry. The camera is in close-up as she hears his voice behind her; she turns her head quickly toward the voice, eyes wide; just as quickly she turns back and the full-

"A Girl Like You"

face close-up continues, but her eyes are now wild and shifting in an otherwise passive face. The revelation that Roger was in Eve's room causes her face to turn fearful, as Vandamm lifts his hand from her shoulder, as if from something unclean. As the camera moves between the podium, Eve, the faces of the individual men, and Eve held in place by a wall of men's suited torsos, her visible suffering in the scene is excruciating. Her sharp intakes of breath become more visible and her discomfort more physically exteriorized. As Eve jumps out of her seat to swing her bag at his head, Roger says, "Who are you kidding? You have no feelings to hurt," though her body, as viewers have seen, signals the opposite. Roger says a harsh goodbye and we are treated to a close-up of Eve with her eyes glistening and her head trembling with emotion. This spectacle of suffering stands out for its sincerity among many others that, while they carry significant emotion, are performed as charades of which the viewer is aware. It is not so much that feelings cannot be spoken, as between Alicia and Devlin in *Notorious*, it is rather that one of the plots within the plot requires of Roger, or more often of Eve, a performance, as when Roger confronts her in the Chicago hotel room and she must continue to play her role, as if she does not notice his change in tone or the innuendo carried by some of his remarks. In that scene, much of her performance is done with her back to Roger, so they are both facing the camera. Even with her back turned to him, she stays in her role, cool and seemingly impervious to the implications of Roger's words. These emotions are legible, but they are calculated lies. In one additional scene, Eve's eyes tear up, and that is the scene in the woods, where Roger makes difficulties about parting with her. He discovers he has been lied to about what happens next: She is leaving and going away with Vandamm. As Roger verbally abuses the Professor (Leo G. Carroll) for lying to him and for placing Eve in even more danger, Eve's face is tense with emotion and her eyes fill with tears. The emotional suffering is sincere and does display the "truth" through a tear-stained visage, but the scene is played under duress with the Professor standing to one side telling Roger that Eve has no choice now. She turns and runs to her car; when seated her hand is over a face covered by tears. As Roger runs to her, she turns her damp face to him with "Please don't spoil everything. Please…". Curiously, her face is not shown in close-up at this emotionally fraught moment, perhaps because in the next instant the emotion is undercut when Roger takes a fist to the face from a patrolman. It's the fist that is shown in close-up; that is visual and physical, but it is not melodrama. It is closer to comedy in the way it underlines Roger's ineffective role when he is confronted with both the power of a government that cares more about winning an abstract, invisible, undeclared war than it does about individual lives, and with the power of Eve's commitment.

I have two final points to make. The first point returns to Donald Spoto's comment about the uncaring government machine that entices Alicia and Eve to commit to a higher cause and to place themselves in danger for it. He says that "behind it all in both cases is a depraved political order, with government leaders committing mayhem in the name of necessary intelligence activities" (303). It is true that Hitchcock makes this point clearly in both films. It is also true that the context in which that point is reinforced in *North by Northwest* is different from *Notorious* in important ways. Let us return to the scene in the forest where an outraged Roger confronts the Professor, asserting, "I don't like the games you play, Professor." The Professor responds, "War is hell, Mr. Thornhill. Even when it's a cold one," which firmly situates the dangers and Eve's commitment in the Cold War context. Roger then makes his detailed accusations: "If you fellows can't lick the Vandamms of this world without asking girls like her to bed down with them and fly away with them and probably never come back, perhaps you ought to start learning how to lose a few cold wars." To this, the Professor replies, deadpan, "I'm afraid we're already doing that." While the Cold War had been going on, undeclared, for more than a decade, it was in October 4, 1957, that the launch of the Russian Sputnik satellite added a desperate "Space Race" to the arms race between the West, especially the United States, and the USSR and convinced many in the West that the Soviets had taken the lead in very dangerous ways ("Sputnik: The Fiftieth Anniversary"). Alicia joined the fight against a visible, specific foe and the specific threat it posed, while Eve joins the struggle against an idea, "Communism" (unnamed in the film), and risks her life for a piece of celluloid whose secret information and threat are an empty set. In *The 39 Steps* (1935), the secret carried by Mr. Memory is finally revealed as the design of a silent aircraft engine; in *Sabotage* (1936), it's a bomb; and in *Notorious* the threat posed by resurgent Nazis armed with

"A Girl Like You"

nuclear weapons is obvious and would have been eminently relevant to audiences in 1946. But what is Eve risking her life for? And at whose behest? It is significant that the "Professor" is never given a name, unlike Mr. Prescott and his colleague Mr. Beardsley in their comfortable office in Rio. When Roger demands the Professor's name, he refuses. He sits among colleagues in Washington, D.C., discussing the situation into which Roger has stumbled. One man expresses surprise that Roger could have identified himself as "George Kaplan," because "Kaplan doesn't even exist." The emotions that are expressed around the table range from chilly irony to cold cynicism, with "*C'est la guerre*" thrown out by one, "It's so sad, why do I feel like laughing?" by another, and in answer to "What are we going to do?" asked by the lone woman in the group, the Professor says "Nothing." "Nothing" is then repeated three times and the Professor continues, explaining that Roger's involvement furthers their goal of distracting from their real agent. His safety? "That's his problem." When Mrs. Finley (Madge Kennedy) suggests this is "A wee bit callous," the Professor condescendingly ("My dear woman…") explains that their mission of protecting the agent "right under Vandamm's very nose" is more important. "Goodbye Mr. Thornhill," says Mrs. Finley, concluding the scene. The scene provides information about the background of what Roger is involved in and accentuates both the danger (the real agent will "face assassination, like the two agents that went before") and the cold pragmatism of the bureaucrats. The building in which they meet has a sign with the partial name "Intelligence Agency" visible, but later when Roger asks the Professor what agency he represents, the Professor identifies them all, "CIA, FBI, UNI" as "alphabet soup," further masking exactly what ultimate concerns, beyond the safety of their agent, motivate the organization. Here we learn that Vandamm traffics in "government secrets, perhaps," which is as close as the film ever comes to identifying that motivation. To them, Roger is a no one, replacing nothing, and chasing something without any materiality or identity to give it thematic weight or value. There is no revelation about what, specifically, has been saved by keeping the microfilm in the country, a move that refuses to add weight to the deadly doings. It could be a copy of the dinner menu from the White House or a list of the locations of American missile silos. In the end, this is, as Hitchcock said, his most insignificant, most unimportant, most weightless and abstract "nothing at all" (Truffaut 139).

My second closing point, as touched upon earlier, is that the melodramatic elements in *Notorious* are somewhat muted or balanced by opposing elements. In *North by Northwest*, they play an even smaller role. The tropes are there but without most of the emotional excess and prolonged physical display of suffering brought by the scores of close-ups. The moral polarization of values that is undermined in *Notorious* by emphasizing Sebastian's sympathetic character as well as Devlin's punitive stoicism is further tempered in the later film by the multiple denunciations of the unfeeling nature of the government's use of individuals for its own mysterious ends and by the portrayal of the nameless bureaucrats who sit around a table in Washington, D.C., putting citizens' lives into play in a great, pointless game. In *North by Northwest*, the West "wins" this small Cold War skirmish, but there is no clue as to what that means, what has been won, and whether it was worth the risk. These concerns are folded into a plot that emphasizes the coolness of the Cold War, the coolness of the heroine, and the cool relationship that both the heroine and reluctant hero have with patriotism. "War is hell….even if it's a cold one," says the Professor, whose words imply the contrast of the heat of "hell" with the coldness of this nearly invisible war. Unlike *Notorious*, which takes place in some of the warmer spots of the world, Miami and Rio, the adventures of Roger and Eve take them from New York, to Chicago and to Rapid City, South Dakota, a tour of the northern parts of America. Even the climate is colder in *North by Northwest*. In the later film, also, the many comic notes serve to lighten the plot and mix the viewers' response to the dangers shown. Here, Cary Grant's physical mobility is used to the utmost as he scrambles through cornfields and hangs off of cliffs. In fact, that cliffhanging part of this story has to be accounted for in discerning the role of melodrama in this film and answering the question we started with about seriality and whether *North by Northwest* does indeed provide a "sequel and conclusion" to *Notorious*, as Donald Spoto suggests. Does it provide the conclusion and closure that *Notorious* only gestured toward?

An unforgettable touch—and a true cliffhanger—at the end of *North by Northwest* is the shot of Roger leaning down from Mount Rushmore desperately gripping the hand of Eve, while Leonard crushes the hand that supports both of them. As Leonard falls, the shot of Roger leaning down transitions almost imperceptibly to Roger, in close-up, leaning down from a sleeping compartment on a train and hoisting Eve, now "Mrs. Thornhill," into bed. Then the train rushes into a tunnel. The comic relief at the transition and the instantly recognizable sexual suggestiveness of the train going into the tunnel make this one of Hitchcock's most memorable endings. Patrick McGilligan, based on research by Bill Krohn, reports that *North by Northwest*'s content and dialogue required ongoing negotiations with Production Code censors in 1959. The director's original version of the sleeping compartment scene did not include the line identifying Eve as Mrs. Thornhill. McGilligan writes, "That line was added in February, long after the scene was filmed," and Krohn adds, "'looped over a close up of Eve from the cafeteria scene…with the background removed'" (574). The censors never saw the final shot of the train going into the tunnel, which was Hitchcock's revenge. Much has been made by scholars such as Robert J. Corber of this legitimizing of Roger's and Eve's relationship. These commentators read that development as Hitchcock's participation in reining in and redirecting the immature sexualities of both characters: Roger who resists his proper role as husband and breadwinner, and Eve, who has to be returned to the "private sphere," the sphere of home and motherhood (201). In effect, the ending does this, but it is critical to note that this was not the director's original intention. The scene as filmed left the pair unmarried and ready for another (implied) night of just-for-fun sexual activity. Hitchcock had to trade this away and then moved to undercut it with the unmistakably sexual tunnel reference. The ending as it appeared on screens does participate in the regulation of sexuality for national security purposes, but even here the seriousness of the regulation of sexuality and gender roles must be undercut both by knowing that Hitchcock was content to leave the sexuality unregulated and by the carnivalesque implication of the train entering the tunnel. In one sense, this joining of husband and wife does conclude the romance plot in a way that is missing from *Notorious*, and there is no fearful Sebastian turning toward his own death to distract viewers and divide their attention and emotional response. Does this offer closure when it comes to the big issues, that is, individuals as agents whose actions and desires must be shaped for the state? Must this be the price of "national security"? All of that remains unclosed and unanswered. Was that piece of celluloid of which viewers get only a glimpse worth all the drama and danger? Neither the viewers nor Roger and Eve are privy to what the microfilm contains, so the question stays open, as does the question of the individual's duty toward the state. Is marriage the reward for subsuming individual goals to those of the state? The answer wobbles under the weight of the belated editing of the ending and the lack of any clear link between the question and the pursuit of duty for duty's sake by Eve, as well as the pursuit of Eve for her own safety by Roger.

North by Northwest may bring an ending to the story begun in *Notorious*, but as a serial or sequel it is an imperfect match. This has been demonstrated in the examination of the MacGuffins and their ties to historical context, in one case by its physicality and in the other by its immateriality. The exploration of the characters of Alicia and Eve, Ingrid Bergman and Eva Marie Saint who portrayed them, and how Hitchcock chose to present them cinematically, shows a profound difference in the performances, particularly in the extent to which melodrama inflects them. Though less closely examined, the performances of two very different roles by Cary Grant have been shown to change the gender dynamics in the films in ways significant to the two very different eras they represent and, indeed, to the director's handling of the sensitive political content of the films. Finally, this discussion has followed the thread of the melodramatic mode in both films, demonstrating that Hitchcock's manipulation of the mode can be a gauge of his changing attitudes about issues raised, but not answered, in this two film sequence.[3] Moving forward 13 years in time from *Notorious* into an era shadowed by a new kind of conflict, *North by Northwest* sheds much of the melodrama, including its usually clear-cut values, and much of the characters' mooring in relatively stable social and political systems. *North by Northwest* shows Hitchcock moving toward greater skepticism and pessimism, some of which is hinted at but not fully-developed in *Notorious*. A "sequel" is a repetition but always with a difference.

Notes

1. In his article "Hitchcock, the Holocaust, and the Long Take," Steven Jacobs makes a powerful argument connecting Hitchcock's preference for focusing in close-up on objects "with symbolic and emotional meaning" and the filmic record of those piles of possessions left behind in the camps. He claims that "Hitchcock…suggested the sequence in the final reel covering the possessions of the dead at Auschwitz, the

harrowing montage of hair, wedding rings, spectacles, and toothbrushes" (269). In *Notorious*, one thinks of Alicia's misplaced hair-piece, the key, the dainty, poisoned coffee cup, and, of course, the wine bottle.

    2. The influence of melodrama in Hitchcock's work has been thoroughly explored. Some notable sources among many possibilities are Ness, Pressler, and Modleski.

    3. Space does not permit addressing whether this methodology might be usefully applied to Hitchcock's two final espionage thrillers, *Torn Curtain* (1966) and *Topaz* (1969). A brief glance, though, suggests that an examination of both films might yield evidence of the director's continued concern with the materiality or immateriality of MacGuffins and motivations. The mathematical equation pursued in *Torn Curtain* is the very definition of immateriality, while the *Topaz* microfilm supposed to provide proof of Soviet missiles in Cuba is both fragile and, even more than the wine bottle in *Notorious*, tied to a deeply felt historical moment, the Cuban Missile Crisis of 1962. As for the web of social relationships that form one aspect of the argument in the current study, by the time Hitchcock completed *Topaz*, these relationships—marriages, friendships, family relationships, political alliances—are undermined by infidelity, lies, political expediency, and betrayal of principle until they become nearly indistinguishable from espionage itself. Many fruitful avenues of exploration seem to be present.

Works Cited

Anker, Elisabeth. "The Melodramatic Style of American Politics." *Melodrama After the Tears*, edited by Jörg Metelmann and Scott Loren, Amsterdam UP, 2016, pp. 219-245.

"Bikini Atoll Nuclear Test: 60 Years Later and Islands Still Unliveable." *The Guardian*, 1 Mar. 2014, www.theguardian.com. Acessed 8 Jan. 2018.

Brody, Richard. "Hitchcock and the Holocaust." *New Yorker*, 9 Jan. 2014, www.newyorker.com. Accessed 7 Jan. 2018.

"Cold War." *Encyclopædia Britannica*, 18 Sept. 2017, www.britannica.com. Accessed 5 Jan. 2018.

Corber, Robert J. *In the Name of National Security: Hitchcock, Homophobia, and the Political Construction of Gender in Postwar America*. Duke UP, 1993.

Crowther, Bosley. "Notorious." *New York Times*, 16 Aug. 1946, www.nytimes.com. Accessed 7 Jan. 2018.

Friedman, Max Paul. *Nazis & Good Neighbors: The United States*

Campaign Against the Germans of Latin America in World War II. Cambridge University Press, 2003.

Frontline. *Memory of the Camps. Frequently Asked Questions.* Public Broadcasting Service. WGBH Boston. www.pbs.org/wgbh/pages/frontline/camp/faqs.html. Accessed 8 Jan. 2018.

"Highway History: Civil Defense, 1955." *US Department of Transportation/Federal Highway Administration*, 27 June 2017, www.fhwa.dot.gov/infrastructure/civildef.cfm. Accessed 19 Jan. 2018.

Jacobs, Steven. "Hitchcock, the Holocaust, and the Long Take: *Memory of the Camps.*" *Arcadia*, vol. 45, no. 2, 2010, pp. 65-76.

Macnab, Geoffrey. "Alfred Hitchcock's Unseen Holocaust Documentary To Be Screened." *The Independent*, 8 Jan. 2014, www.independent.co.uk. 8 Jan. 2018.

McElhaney, Joe. "The Object and the Face: *Notorious*, Bergman and the Close-up." *Hitchcock: Past and Future*, edited by Richard Allen and Sam Ishii-Gonzalez, Routledge, 2003, pp. 64-84.

McGilligan, Patrick. *Alfred Hitchcock: A Life in Darkness and Light.* Harper Collins, 2003.

Modleski, Tania. *The Women Who Knew Too Much: Hitchcock and Feminist Theory.* 3rd ed., Routledge, 2016.

Ness, Richard R. "Family Plots: Hitchcock and Melodrama." *A Companion to Alfred Hitchcock*, edited by Thomas Leitch and Leland Pogue, Wiley Blackwell, 2014, pp. 109-125.

North by Northwest. Directed by Alfred Hitchcock, Turner Entertainment and Warner Home Video, 2000.

Notorious. Directed by Alfred Hitchcock, Criterion Collection, 2001.

Pressler, Michael. "Hitchcock and the Melodramatic Pattern." *Chicago Review*, vol. 35, no. 3, Spring 1986, pp. 4-16. JSTOR, doi: 10.2307/25305355.

Spoto, Donald. *The Art of Alfred Hitchcock: Fifty Years of His Motion Pictures.* 2nd rev. ed., Random House, 1992.

"Sputnik: The Fiftieth Anniversary." *National Aeronautics and Space Administration*, NASA History Web, 10 Oct. 2007, www.history.nasa.gov/sputnik/. Accessed 9 Jan. 2018.

Truffaut, François. *Hitchcock.* Rev. ed., Simon and Schuster, 1985.

Williams, Linda. "Film Bodies: Gender, Genre and Excess." *Film Quarterly*, vol. 44, no. 4, Summer 1991, pp. 2-13.

How Deep the Rabbit Hole Goes: *North by Northwest, The Matrix,* and the Third Pill

By Craig Arthur

"Sometimes reality is the strangest fantasy of all."
—Voiceover in the trailer for Michelangelo Antonioni's *Blow-Up*

"You're here because you know something," Morpheus (Laurence Fishburne) tells Neo (Keanu Reeves) in *The Matrix* (the Wachowski siblings, 1999). "What you know you can't explain. But you feel it. You've felt it your entire life. There's something wrong with the world. You don't know what it is but it's there like a splinter in your mind, driving you mad."

Morpheus offers Neo a straightforward binary choice. He can choose to take the blue pill and the story ends. He wakes up in his bed and believes whatever he wants to believe. Alternatively he can take the red pill and find out "how deep the rabbit hole goes." With its focus on activities taking place out of sight of the overt world, the spy genre too, whether on the printed page or onscreen, offers us a metaphorical red pill. Spy novels and movies foster our fascination with the idea that there is a more real bedrock reality than the artifice of what is immediately visible to us. The genre creates the illusion we are glimpsing a more dangerous and complex nether region, reminding us that our safe, comfortable existence amounts to a dream world, an illusion of safety and invulnerability. And as Ian Fleming observes in *Casino Royale* (paraphrasing Novalis), "You are about to awake when you dream that you are dreaming."

Alfred Hitchcock's various forays into espionage are no exception. *North by Northwest* (1959) is part of a long tradition of Hitchcock spy films stretching back to the first version of *The Man Who Knew Too Much* (1934), highlighting an unseen reality outside the world we know, depicting male protagonists thrust—most often against their will—into a more complicated and dangerous existence than they are accustomed to. At the same time, Hitchcock spy films such as *The 39 Steps* (1935), *Notorious* (1946), the remake of *The Man Who Knew Too Much* (1956), *North by Northwest*, *Torn Curtain* (1966), and *Topaz* (1969), also emphasize the compromises imposed upon women, required to suppress their true capabilities and desires to conform to the artifice of a patriarchal order.

That unseen reality reflects what Eric Rohmer and Claude Chabrol identify as the "ever-present Platonism" in the director's work as a whole, not solely his espionage films. Discussing *Rear Window* in *Hitchcock: the First Forty-Four Films*, they point out, "As in Edgar Allan Poe's stories, this work is constructed on the implicit base of a philosophy of Ideas. Here, the idea—even if it be only the pure idea of Space, Time, or Desire—precedes existence and substance" (26). They compare *Rear Window*'s wheelchair-bound Jefferies (James Stewart) spying on his neighbors to Plato's chained troglodytes watching the flickering shadows on the cave walls: "Everything happens as though they were projections of the voyeur's thoughts—or desires; he will never be able to find in them more than he had put there, more than he hopes for or is waiting for. On the facing wall, separated from him by the space of the courtyard, the strange silhouettes are like so many shadows in a new version of Plato's cave. Turning his back to the true sun, the photographer loses the ability to look Being in the face" (26).

The Allegory of the Cave is most explicit in a science fiction film like *The Matrix*, where the distinction between the world of illusion and reality is a clear cut split between the mental prison of a simulated dream world and bedrock reality. The simulated dream world, the matrix, is everywhere, Morpheus explains: "It is all around us, even now in this very room. You can see it when you look out your window or when you turn on your television. You can feel it when you go to work, when you go to church, when you pay your taxes. It is the world that has been pulled over your eyes to blind you from the truth.... Like everyone else you were born into bondage, born into a prison that you cannot smell or taste or touch. A prison for your mind." When Neo swallows the red pill, he learns that AI machines harvest humans as an energy source, keeping them imprisoned in pods, hooked up

How Deep the Rabbit Hole Goes 47

to a shared simulation of reality, a virtual construct, oblivious to their true situation. Actual bedrock reality is a post-apocalyptic wasteland. ("Welcome," Morpheus says, exposing its desolation to Neo for the first time, "to the desert of the real.")

In *North by Northwest*, the parallel with the allegory may not be as obvious—certainly there is no literal brain-in-a-vat sci-fi epiphany. The parallels are not even as immediately apparent as the ones Rohmer and Chabrol point out in *Rear Window*. All the same, *North by Northwest's* protagonist, Roger Thornhill (Cary Grant), is another chained troglodyte and his journey out of the cave to enlightenment echoes that of Neo.

North by Northwest and *The Matrix* open the same way. *The Matrix* starts with the graphic of streaming green digital rain of half-width kana symbols, letters and numerals representing the coding for the virtual reality world of the matrix. The digital rain then switches to the green numerals of the trace program to find the phone number from which Trinity (Carrie Anne Moss) is calling. The agents—the guardians of the matrix—are trying to locate Morpheus and his associates because they threaten to expose the artificiality of the virtual simulation. *North by Northwest* opens with Saul Bass's similar use of graphics to metaphorically depict what is happening in the narrative. Intersecting lines on an unnatural, sinister green background mirror Vandamm's henchmen attempting to close in on the American agent, George Kaplan, who threatens to expose Vandamm (James Mason) as a foreign spy. They are seeking to protect the subterfuge of Vandamm's espionage activity just as the agents are protecting the artifice of the matrix.

Saul Bass's intersecting arrows of fate knit into a lattice—a literal matrix grid that serves as a figurative symbol of the construct of our reality. The green background changes to the steel and glass grid of 430 Park Avenue, as an archetype of a Manhattan skyscraper.[1] The modernist exterior reveals nothing of the building's interior. Instead it provides *North by Northwest's* twentieth-century urban cave wall onto which the shadows are projected. Reflected in the glass, are images of the New York traffic. We see their reflections but not the actual traffic itself, just as we only know the inner world of our own perceptions, not our external reality.

The discrepancy between perception and reality—the inability to separate the shadows on the cave walls from actual forms—is what leads Vandamm's henchmen to mistake the hapless Roger Thornhill for the non-existent George Kaplan. And in this instance the American intelligence officials are playing the puppeteers, manipulating the projected shadows, using the non-existent Kaplan as a decoy.

Mistaken for Kaplan and abducted at gunpoint from the Oak Bar in New York's Plaza Hotel, Thornhill takes a plunge down the rabbit hole into a nightmarish reality he previously did not know existed, which contrasts with Neo's in *The Matrix*. Neo's decision to take the red pill is voluntary. Thornhill's is involuntary. No one offers him a blue pill that will allow him to wake up in his bed, his nightmare over, his charmed but morally shallow existence back to what it was beforehand. The metaphorical red pill is forced down his throat much like the bourbon his abductors force him to drink before bundling him behind the wheel of a stolen car to make it look as if he were the victim of an accident, driving while intoxicated.

Thornhill would prefer to take the blue pill. He is content with his cave dwelling existence, surrounded by pedestrians in the urban Manhattan treadmill unaware they are chained prisoners in a cave. He is on that same treadmill, perpetually on the move from the moment we first see him emerge from the elevator, dictating to his secretary while walking. That said, his blue pill is redder than that of those around him. He is simultaneously both prisoner and puppeteer, consciously manipulating perceptions in both his professional life as an advertising executive and his everyday public interactions. Just as Hitchcock doesn't necessarily have a conscious neo-Platonic intent yet is able to make films Rohmer and Chabrol cite as possessing an ever-present Platonism,[2] so Thornhill is able to appeal to the troglodytes' susceptibility to imaginary ideals, even if neither he nor they are conscious that anything lies beyond the shadows on the cave walls. He is able to because the archetypes are ingrained in our imagination.

According to Plato, the archetypes were imprinted on our souls before birth. But Plato's concept of imagination reflects what Samuel Taylor Coleridge also believed was "a repetition in the finite mind of the eternal act of all creation in the infinite I AM" (*Biographia Literaria* 263). The Cave Allegory and theories of imagination are an attempt to explain what we cannot explain, inventing a theory that embellishes the puppet show of flickering shadows on the cave walls of the mind into an external absolute reality; Plato and Coleridge are just as much chained prisoners as everybody else. Coleridge's theory differentiates between imagination and fancy when really the Platonic concept of an external absolute reality amounts to fancy also. As puppeteer, Thornhill exploits this susceptibility to fancy, embellishing humdrum reality to make it appear closer to the sublime. For instance, he instructs his secretary to send a woman, presumably one of his ex-wives, a gift of candy, "The kind…you know…each piece wrapped in gold paper? She'll like that. She'll think she's eating money."

Thornhill's very identity is built around such embellishments. He has added a superfluous middle initial to give his name more flair, becoming Roger O. Thornhill instead of plain Roger Thornhill. When Eve Kendall (Eva Marie Saint) asks him what the "O" stands for, he replies, "Nothing."

The empty initial, as others have pointed out, sums up his nothingness as a person. He is a hollow man, a sugar-coated blue pill, a human placebo in an immaculate suit. He is obsessed with his personal image ("Do I look a little heavyish to you? I feel heavyish. Put a note on my desk in the morning, 'Think Thin'"). Image gives him the power, in Eve Kendall's words, to "sell people things they don't need…make women who don't know you fall in love with you."

He refuses to acknowledge any fault in his manipulation of reality. When his secretary chastises him for lying in order to jump the queue for a taxi, he responds, "in the world of advertising, there is no such thing as a lie, Maggie, only the expedient exaggeration." He is tempting providence, as he will discover when trying disprove the fiction he is George Kaplan. Vandamm dismisses Thornhill's insistence he is Roger Thornhill, labelling it "expert play acting" that makes "this very room a theatre," and later in the film accuses him of "overplaying his various roles." This is an expedient exaggeration rather than a lie given that, for Thornhill, his identity is a performance, an exercise in perception management. Kaplan's identity is nothing more than an image attached to a name and a wardrobe full of suits moved from one location to another; Thornhill too is an "empty suit" always on the move. Kaplan's non-existence is an expedient exaggeration of his own hollowness.

Thornhill's ordeal, then, equates to indirect retribution for his hubris. He is paying for the choices he has made up until now. He does not want to see beyond the shadows on the cave walls and only leaves the comfort of the Oak Bar because he is forced out at gunpoint, reinforcing Plato's argument that any cave-bound prisoner is reluctant to confront the outside world and must be dragged out by force and made to confront the true light of the sun. (How else would we expect them to react? As Plato points out, are they not likely to be pained and irritated?) This is even true for Neo in *The Matrix*. In spite of his voluntary decision to swallow the red pill, his initial reaction to the truth is one of horror and dismay.

North by Northwest is more sophisticated than *The Matrix*, however. Whereas Neo leaves the confines of the matrix and enters the supposed "desert of the real," Thornhill's plunge down the rabbit hole leads him to a place where bedrock reality still remains elusive. The Wachowskis borrowed the "desert of the real" term from Jean Baudrillard. But Baudrillard was uncomfortable with their appropriation of the concept, claiming they had misunderstood or distorted its meaning: "The most embarrassing part of the film is that the new problem posed by simulation is confused with its classical, Platonic treatment... *The Matrix* is surely the kind of film about the matrix that the matrix would have been able to produce," as quoted by Steve Poole in *The Guardian*. In other words, the film's concept of reality as the product of a higher intelligence manipulating our perceptions—in the case of the matrix a hostile AI harvesting our bodies—amounts to another blue pill rather than a red one. (The same is true of Plato's theory that imagination is the product of the light of true Being.) For Baudrillard the actual desert of the real is a state of hyperreality where simulations of reality are no more or less real than the reality they simulate, where there is no longer such a thing as a lie, as Thornhill would say, only expedient exaggerations.

North by Northwest's New York setting exemplifies this twentieth-century disconnection from reality. A dumbfounded Salvador Dalí, on his first visit to America in the 1930s, witnessed workmen spraying soot onto a brand new New York skyscraper, "ageing" the edifice to resemble centuries-old, smoke-blackened European buildings. "New York: why, why did you erect my statue long ago, long before I was born, higher than another, more desperate than another?" he later wrote. The city is a blue pill environment. According to Rem Koolhaus's *Delirious New York: A Retroactive Manifesto of Manhattan*, "Not only are large parts of its surface occupied by architectural mutations (Central Park, the skyscraper), utopian fragments (Rockefeller Centre, the U.N. Building) and irrational phenomena (Radio City Music Hall), but in addition each block is covered with several layers of phantom architecture in the form of past occupancies, aborted projects and popular fantasies that provide alternative images to the New York that exists" (9).

An example of Koolhaus's phantom architecture is evident in the soundstage reproduction of the mural glimpsed in *North by Northwest's* Oak Bar scene. The Everett Shinn mural depicts old New York, showing the demolished Vanderbilt mansion formerly adjacent to the Plaza, horse-drawn cabs and pedestrians battling the elements, with the newly built hotel on the edge of the composition. Thornhill, with his phantom middle initial, is at home in this phantom environment where nonexistent entities like George Kaplan are indistinguishable from actual people.

The Martini—Thornhill's drink of choice at the Oak Bar—is itself a symbolic blue pill (in contrast to the red pill of the bourbon Vandamm's men force him to drink and which he later asks the Professor to buy when plotting a distraction that will allow him to escape from the locked hospital room and rescue Eve Kendall). In Somerset Maugham's short story "His Excellency," the World War I secret agent Ashenden says he moves with the times: "To drink a glass of sherry when you can get a dry Martini is like taking a stage coach when you can travel by the Orient Express" (155-6). As Peter Conrad remarks in *The Hitchcock Murders*, the Martini "pays tribute to modern mobility, since liquor is fuel" (170), providing the ideal drink for somebody continually on the move like Thornhill, but even more fittingly a hallmark of someone reluctant to pause and question the hollowness of his existence.

The ability to travel by train rather than stage coach allows us to forget the tyranny of distance and travel in more comfort. Yet it also requires placing our trust in fallible mechanical contraptions, in taking the blue pill and ignoring the complexity and danger of the engineering technology concealed within. Modernity is anchored to this blue pill, this illusion of invulnerability and infallibility—the safe coziness of drinking Martinis in the Oak Bar or on the Twentieth Century Limited and forgetting the more complex and dangerous world beyond the shadows on our mental cave walls.

We like to pretend nothing can go wrong. Mistakes do not occur; everything works smoothly. Hitchcock disabuses us of this notion. He reminds us of the precariousness of mechanical contraptions and how even the most minor malfunction can derail characters' lives. In *Young and Innocent* (1937), Erica (Nova Pilbeam) becomes embroiled in the plot because the policeman won't accept that the starter on her father's car is broken and needs to be operated by a piece of string, causing her to intervene and drive it herself. In the 1956 version of *The Man Who Knew Too Much*, the bus driver's unexpected sudden braking causes Hank (Christopher Olsen) to accidentally tear off a Muslim woman's veil, providing the catalyst for the McKennas' introduction to the world of espionage by triggering their interaction with the spy Louis Bernard (Daniel Gelin).

Elsewhere in Hitchcock's films, contraptions devised to produce safe thrills go awry. In *Strangers on a Train* (1951), the merry-go-round is sent spiraling out of control when the operator gets hit in the crossfire. And even watching a movie becomes deadly for one audience member in *Saboteur* (1942), when an actual gunfight breaks out in the theatre while a gunfight plays out onscreen in the movie within the movie, erasing the safe vicarious distance we enjoy as cinema goers.

The *Saboteur* theatre scene is an example of how our modern immunity to the consequences of reality results in a hyperreality where the boundaries between illusion and reality become blurred. In "The Precession of Simulacra," Baudrillard likens this to the map in Jorge Luis Borges's parable "On Exactitude in Science," where cartographers perfect their skills to such a degree they create a map so exact it is the same size as the territory it represents, covering the entire empire at 1:1 scale, corresponding to it point for point. Subsequent generations ignore the map, abandoning it to the "Inclemencies of Sun and of Winters. In the Deserts of the West, still today, there are Tattered Ruins of that Map, inhabited by Animals and Beggars; in all the Land there is no other Relic of the Disciplines of Geography" (Borges 325). But for Baudrillard the territory no longer "precedes the map; nor does it survive it. It is nevertheless the map that precedes the territory…whose shreds slowly rot across the extent of the map. It is the real, and not the map, whose vestiges persist here and there in the deserts that are no longer those of the Empire, but ours. *The desert of the real itself*" (*Selected Writings*

166). We exist in the map, not the terrain, forgetting how complex and dangerous the real is because we've been conditioned to believe the illusion that we are immune from reality. Yet its chaos—the persistent vestiges of reality—is ever present, impinging on our lives from the space outside our everyday perceptions, as Roger Thornhill finds out and Hitchcock films so often remind us. (The audience member getting shot in *Saboteur* is an example of a vestige of the terrain penetrating the map.)

Thornhill never gets an opportunity to sit and enjoy his blue pill Martinis in peace. At the Oak Bar he is dogged by the earlier oversight of asking his secretary to call his mother, realizing too late that his mother is at "one of those brand new apartments—all wet paint and no telephone yet." His associates seem to have difficulty grasping the problem. One of them, Nelson, hard of hearing, cups a hand to his ear. Thornhill's mother, Clara (Jessie Royce Landis), is an example of what Slavoj Žižek identifies in Hitchcock as the dominance of the maternal superego (*Everything* 5). Her unseen presence inhibits his ability to relax and enjoy the situation. Her disapproval of his drinking haunts him even before he arrives at the bar. ("I'll have had two Martinis at the Oak Bar, so she needn't bother to sniff my breath," he tells Maggie *en route* to the Plaza.) Later, too, on the Twentieth Century Limited, the train makes an unscheduled stop and the police board the train before Thornhill gets a chance to finish his Gibson. In both instances the chaos of the terrain outside the map is impinging on artificial order.

Thornhill's decision to send a telegram to his mother from the Plaza at the same moment Vandamm's men page the non-existent George Kaplan is what plunges him down the rabbit hole. He signals the bellboy and the two watching henchmen mistake him for Kaplan and abduct him at gunpoint. Suddenly Thornhill, like any number of Hitchcock protagonists before him (from *The 39 Steps, Young And Innocent, The Lady Vanishes, Saboteur, Strangers On A Train, Rear Window*, the two versions of *The Man Who Knew Too Much*, to *The Wrong Man*), is thrust into the disorder that, in Robin Wood's words, "Hitchcock sees as underlying—or as surrounding—all human existence: the chaos of our unknown, unrecognized 'Under-nature'" (105-6).

That under-nature is another name for the terrain outside the map, the invisible nether regions we do not ordinarily see beyond the flickering shadows on the cave walls. (In terms of *North by Northwest* and the spy genre in general, it is the world of espionage.) The difficulty for Thornhill is that his exposure to this nether region, his involuntary consumption of the red pill, does not automatically bring with it the clarity to see things as they truly are. The truth does not reveal itself to him in a way he can decipher.

At first glance he is entering a more solid reality than the one to which he is accustomed. The sign at the entrance to the grounds of the Long Island mansion where his assailants take him reads, "Townsend." The connotations suggest town's end, signifying that Thornhill is crossing a frontier from the glitz and superficiality of his Manhattan existence to the enormous lawn and brick and stone of the Townsend mansion, radiating Old Money and respectability. Except its apparent solidity is a masquerade. The Townsend mansion is not the bedrock reality outside the cave. Philip Vandamm is not Lester Townsend.

Neither Vandamm nor Thornhill realizes that the other party is not who they think. ("Games, must we?" Vandamm asks, confused when the man he thinks is Kaplan insists on addressing him as Townsend rather than as Vandamm and playing innocent, demanding to know why he was brought to the mansion.) Nor is the audience aware yet that a deception is taking place. We accept Vandmamm's Townsend at face value. We, like Thornhill, accept the apparent solidity of the illusion, unaware that the rock of the world, as F. Scott Fitzgerald puts it, was founded securely on a fairy's wing.

Similarly, when Thornhill goes to Kaplan's hotel room at the Plaza, the puppeteers' shadows on the cave walls continue to deceive him. It is impossible for him to see past the falsehoods—the wardrobe of suits, the dandruff on the hairbrush—to realize that Kaplan is material without being real, to borrow another Fitzgerald phrase. Thornhill is still mistaking the unseen puppeteers' shadow dance for reality. He is caught in limbo between the other troglodytes—the police, his mother—refusing to believe in the world beyond the visible shadows on the cave walls ("You gentlemen aren't really trying to kill my son, are you?"), and his own inability to know anything beyond his perceived reality.

It is an inability we all share. Our perceptions, our measurement of reality via shadows on the cave walls, will always be an exaggeration of reality. Our internal compass will always point to a non-existent heading, mad north-northwest, as Hamlet would say, pointing to an approximation of north, never actual north, just like the non-existent direction of the movie's title. Such a direction is an expedient exaggeration of north. Bedrock reality will always elude us. Our perceptions will always feed us a distorted version of the truth. It is a bias we cannot escape. Beyond its exaggerations lies absolute nothing, a desolate mental equivalent of the prairie in *North by Northwest's* iconic crop dusting sequence.

The nothingness of the prairie mirrors the psychological territory which circumstances have thrust Thornhill into. Yet the sequence also reminds us how out of place he is surrounded by the bedrock reality of the plain. Still wearing the same medium grey Glen check suit he was wearing when he began his ordeal, he makes an incongruous presence. And as Plato points out, any prisoner freed from the cave, accustomed to the darkness of the shadows, will be dazzled, unable to see things as they are. Specifically, Thornhill does not know what we, the audience, already know. We know George Kaplan does not exist whereas Thornhill, unaware of the danger he is in, still expects Kaplan to turn up for the rendezvous.

Even though there is nowhere visible onscreen for danger to hide, we know the situation is a trap. Thornhill, meantime, remains oblivious. The man Thornhill encounters waiting for the bus on the prairie (Malcolm Atterbury) does not know either. He has no more insight into Thornhill's situation than the occupants of the film's public urban spaces, who see only the shadows on the cave walls. Nevertheless ,the man is less dazzled by the brightness of the light outside the cave. He is better able, like Wallace Stevens's snow man, to behold "nothing that is not there and the nothing that is." He is more accustomed to the heat, for instance. (Thornhill complains about the hot day; the man has seen worse.) The man realizes something is awry, the crop-dusting plane is "dusting crops where there ain't no crops," whereas even after having had this pointed out, Thornhill is still clueless about the imminent attack, still waiting for Kaplan to arrive.

Kaplan will never arrive because Kaplan only exists as an impossible archetype, a James Bond figure—the Platonic Ideal of the secret agent hero rather than an actual entity; in other words, a symbolic fiction. And as Žižek explains in his documentary, *The Pervert's Guide to Ideology*, "If you take away from our reality the symbolic fictions that regulate it, you lose reality itself." That is what happens to Thornhill on the prairie: stripped of the symbolic fictions of the cave walls, staring the nothingness of the real in the face, he is blind, as are we. We can no more comprehend the real than guess the contents of the stolen microfilm later in the plot. (We know something is wrong, we know the situation is a trap, but because we cannot see anywhere for the danger to be hiding, we don't know what it is. What we know we cannot explain, as Morpheus would say.)

Žižek's comment is a response to the binary choice between the blue and red pills in *The Matrix*, and he sees the choice as "not really a choice between illusion and reality." He explains, "Of course the matrix is a machine for fictions but these are fictions that already structure our reality." Hence Žižek craves a third pill, a pill that would enable him to perceive "not the reality behind the illusion but the reality in illusion itself." To do that we need to fictionalize. We need to fictionalize in order to make sense of the reality we cannot otherwise decipher.

This is what Scottie (James Stewart) effectively does in *Vertigo*. He needs to embellish reality to paradoxically find the truth. Judy (Kim Novak) reminds him of the dead Madeleine. But what he knows he cannot explain either. Only through his misguided attempts to achieve a Daliesque conquest of the irrational and create the illusion that Judy is Madeleine does the reality reveal itself—when she puts on the necklace and he finally realizes she is the same woman.

That Scottie is looking at the reflection of the necklace in the mirror when the moment of revelation comes is significant. It is what Lacanian psychoanalysis refers to as an "ah-ha experience," a shock to his ego, akin to Lacan's mirror stage for an infant where the external image reflected in the mirror produces a psychological response. As with Scottie realizing Gavin Elster and Judy have set him up, Thornhill's equivalent "ah-ha experience" is the immediate aftermath of the crop-dusting sequence, when he realizes that Eve deliberately sent him into a trap, but then also again later in a second such moment, when the Professor reveals that Eve is an American agent and his actions have endangered her.

In both instances, Thornhill's only trajectory forward is in a "fictional direction," as Lacan would say, like the fictitious compass heading of the film's title. The subsequent scenes in Eve's hotel room and at the auction represent Thornhill's return to the cave from the outside world of the prairie. In the aftermath of the crop-dusting sequence, he learns to embrace and manipulate the discrepancies between perception and reality to his advantage, rather than trying to disprove the illusion he is Kaplan, much like Neo learning to manipulate the false reality of the matrix to defeat Agent Smith.

The spectators at the auction sit like Plato's cave-bound prisoners, transfixed by the puppet show of the auction, oblivious to the nothingness beyond their perceptions. They watch as a succession of items from the collection of an enigmatic, unseen "Dr. Orlando Mendoza" are paraded before them. The furniture, bric-a-brac, and paintings all amount to imitations of an imaginary archetype, imitations of an imitation, as *Republic* Book X explains. Except here the troglodytes are hostile to any suggestion of imitation. ("How do we know it's not a fake? It looks like a fake," Thornhill demands, intentionally seeking to upset the apple cart. "Well, one thing we know: you're no fake," the woman in front of him responds, "You're a genuine idiot.")

The scene echoes the society party in *Saboteur* where the party goers are ignorant of the jeopardy Barry Kane (Robert Cummings) and Patricia (Priscilla Lane) are in, in their very midst. The guests dismiss Kane's claims their hosts are "a hotbed of spies and saboteurs." ("What's the matter with you, sir? You're drunk. You're not even dressed."), because—as Plato predicted and the *North by Northwest* auction scene also demonstrates—the cave dwellers would react with hostility to anybody returning from outside the cave trying to expose the falsehood of the shadows.

Earlier, Thornhill had similar difficulty convincing either the police or his mother of the truth in the aftermath of his experiences at the Townsend estate. At the auction he no longer attempts to expose what is happening to him, however. Instead he deliberately resorts to theatricality, manipulating the audience's ignorance of the danger in their midst and the emptiness outside their cave walls to create a disruption that will allow him to escape. In his later efforts to assist Eve, after the Professor has revealed that she is an American agent and Kaplan does not exist, he will exploit the illusion that he is Kaplan rather than trying to expose the reality behind it.

The paradox is that rather than the short man with dandruff whose unworn suits grace unoccupied hotel rooms, Thornhill—especially with Cary Grant playing him—gives George Kaplan an identity closer to a mythical James Bond-like archetype. Grant's glamour colors our perceptions of Thornhill. Eve Kendall's comment about Thornhill selling people things they don't need, making women who don't know him fall in love with him, applies just as much to Grant's screen persona as to Thornhill. (There is, of course, a meta element to Vandamm's jibes about him making this very room a theatre or over-playing his various roles. Thornhill offers a surrogate for Cary Grant the film star. He plays himself playing the role as Sean Connery and Roger Moore's personalities would dominate their contrasting interpretations of Bond.)

In the same way, Judy colors our sense of Madeleine in *Vertigo*. We never meet the actual Mrs. Elster but she was likely older and less beautiful than the invented Madeleine, just as Thornhill is more debonair than the imaginary Kaplan, or that Vandamm is younger and better looking than the actual Lester Townsend. As Vandamm remarks on his first encounter with Thornhill, mistaking him for Kaplan, "Not what I expected—a little taller, a little more polished than the others." Ditto Leonard (Martin Landau): "He's a well-tailored one, isn't he?" The discrepancy does not cause them to question whether they have the right man; instead George Kaplan becomes a closer approximation of their Platonic archetype. The illusion is greater than reality.

Thornhill's resourcefulness, his miraculous escapes from the various attempts on his life, and especially his willingness to disobey the Professor and risk his life to rescue Eve from Vandamm's Mount Rushmore hideout, further reinforce the illusion of substance to the Kaplan myth. It is how we would prefer our heroes to act, closer to our imaginary archetype. But that ideal can only be achieved through artificial means, through illusion.

Thornhill's giving a crutch of reality to the mythical Kaplan is no different from what all movies strive to achieve. They create an illusion closer to our imaginary ideal but also allows us as viewers to see more deeply into the human condition, allowing us to find the reality in illusion and see the unknown, unrecognized "Under-nature" Robin Wood refers to. Wood's *Hitchcock's Films Revisited* cites Jean Douchet's interpretation of *Rear Window*, roughly equating Jefferies with the spectator in the cinema and the flats across the court with the screen:

> what Jefferies sees is a projection of his own desires…Each apartment offers a variation on the man-woman relationship or the intolerable loneliness resulting from its absence, and only the one contented couple is passed over and forgotten…all can be taken as representing possibilities before Jefferies and Lisa.…All this offers clear parallels with the spectator watching the screen. We tend to select from a film and stress, quite unconsciously, those aspects that are most relevant to us, to our own problems and our own attitude to life, and ignore or minimize the rest; and we tend to use such identification—again, usually unconsciously—as a means of working out our problems in fantasy forms: often, as it proves with Jefferies, a dangerous tendency but sometimes—again, as with Jefferies—a valuable one. (101-103)

Jefferies's growing obsession with whether Thorwald has murdered his wife reflects his own situation. It offers him a means of exploring the under-nature of his relationship with Lisa. Spying on the Thorwald marriage allows him to explore his own anxieties about how cloying he imagines married life with Lisa might prove and his subconscious desire to be rid of her. At the same time, Lisa's eagerness to break into the Thorwald apartment to look for Mrs. Thorwald's wedding ring and prove the woman is dead mirrors her own determination to disprove Jefferies's conjecture that she is too unadventurous. She wants to find the dead woman's wedding ring as evidence the murder has taken place in order to land a wedding ring from Jefferies on her own finger. Both Jefferies and Lisa desire to see their paranoia—the conjecture a murder occurred—become critical, as Dalí would say. They want external physical reality to conform to their inner psychological reality.

Cinema delivers a similar conquest of the irrational. We like to see our paranoia given a crutch of reality via the events onscreen. Thornhill exploiting the illusion he is Kaplan mirrors Cary Grant manipulating the perception he is the character he is playing, and indeed Hitchcock uses cinema to fulfil our yearning for the Bond-like archetype of George

Kaplan to save the day. James Bond, after all, was dreamt up as a counter to midcentury anxieties, an invention to deflect from collective fears in the same way Kaplan was invented to deflect attention away from Eve Kendall. Ian Fleming created Bond to distract himself from his own anxieties about the prospect of marriage: "the prospect was so horrifying that I was in urgent need of some activity to take my mind off it…So I decided to write a book" (9). But also Bond was a response to Britain's reduced role as a world power amid postwar threats, ranging from the spread of Communism to atomic annihilation.[3]

As Borges explains in another parable, "Ragnorak," 'The images in dreams, wrote Coleridge, figure forth the impressions that our intellect would call causes; we do not feel horror because we are haunted by a sphinx; we dream a sphinx in order to explain the horror that we feel" (321). The idea precedes existence and substance, as Rohmer and Chabrol would say. Whether it is Ian Fleming sitting at his typewriter in Jamaica, dreaming up supranational villains' threats, or Jefferies fixated on Thorwald's marriage in *Rear Window*, both are looking for a sphinx that will explain the horror they feel.

North by Northwest, too, is another sphinx. According to Ken Mogg in *The Alfred Hitchcock Story*, its subject "(insofar as it can be pinned down) might be described as 'surviving' in the twentieth century" (154), or more specifically surviving the twentieth century's disconnection from reality. *North by Northwest* exposes the pitfalls of feeling safer in the world of illusions, exposing the hollowness of the various patriarchal sphinxes that are our false gods in the flickering shadows of the cave walls.

This hollowness is explicit in the graven images of the American Presidents hindering Thornhill and Eve's escape from Leonard and Valerian atop Mount Rushmore in the film's climax. Throughout the film its patriarchal role models are grey-haired (Thornhill's drinking companions at the Oak Bar, the real Lester Townsend, the Professor) and deaf, literally or figuratively, or missing in action (Thornhill's absent father). The patriarchal Old Money of the Townsend estate has been infiltrated by foreign spies. Townsend is killed before he can assist Thornhill. The Professor and his fellow government officials are willing to sacrifice Thornhill and later Eve if it helps them achieve their Cold War ideological objectives. Even the film's MacGuffin, the Mexican Tarascan warrior statuette, is also another masculine false god with a "bellyful" of stolen microfilm. Plus, of course, the Kaplan archetype of masculine perfection is a man who is not only absent, but he also does not exist.

Like the Mount Rushmore statues, Kaplan is another false god, and *North by Northwest* explores the artifice of masculine archetypes—the world pulled over our eyes as Morpheus says in *The Matrix*. Such archetypes are another prison we cannot smell or taste or touch, another prison of the mind, because once again they demonstrate our susceptibility to imagination, to mistaking our internal mental constructs for eternal absolutes imprinted on the soul.

In recent years, *The Matrix* has itself become a touchstone for men's rights activism. The red pill has become synonymous with the metaphor for opening one's eyes to the disproportionate number of men dominating the statistics for work place deaths, suicide, homelessness, victims of violence, as well as poor outcomes in health, education, life expectancy, child custody access, and so on. But with its emphasis on the shortcomings of patriarchy and masculine archetypes, *North by Northwest* offers a greater insight into the construct of masculinity and gender roles than does *The Matrix*.

Much of Roger Thornhill's apparent shallowness stems from his trying to live up to the archetype of a "suit," a provider, "with a secretary, a mother, two ex-wives and several bartenders depending" upon him. Even his inclusion of the empty, superfluous "O" in his initials is a symbol of his trying to live up to the nothingness of such an archetype. His overbearing, skeptical mother reminds him of his failure to live up to her expectations. His personal growth comes when he emerges from her matriarchal influence, but also when he rejects patriarchy, telling the Professor that if "you fellows can't lick the Vandamms of this world" without asking women like Eve "to bed down with them and fly away with them and probably never come back alive, maybe you better start learning to lose a few Cold Wars." But Thornhill has himself placed Eve in danger through his earlier ignorance, mistakenly believing she is in league with Vandmam. The expedient exaggeration of his perceptions, his internal compass pointing again to a non-existent direction, blinds him to seeing the terrain beyond the map. He does not know that Eve is the actual undercover spy in Vandamm's household whereas Kaplan was just a non-existent decoy.

When she explains to Thornhill that going undercover was the only time anyone ever asked her to do "anything worthwhile," Eve blames men like him for her predicament. "What's wrong with men like me?" he asks. "They don't believe in marriage," she replies. "I've been married twice." "See what I mean?" Dysfunctional men have plagued her existence, just as Jefferies's dysfunction in *Rear Window*, his dismissive attitude toward Lisa and his reluctance to marry, are what provoke Lisa to put herself in harm's way to prove herself. Jefferies's attitudes towards her and marriage approximate those of the present day Men Going Their Own Way community. Watching his neighbors and witnessing examples of broken-down relationships between men and women is his 1950s equivalent of turning to the online manosphere as a refuge.

Both Eve and Lisa are victims of the male protagonists' inability to engage with them on an equal, mature footing. As Thornhill confesses to Eve at their first encounter on the Twentieth Century Limited, "Honest women frighten me...I feel at a disadvantage with them." "Because you're not honest with them?" she responds. "Exactly." And later in her Chicago hotel room, he remarks on how when he was a little boy he never even let his mother undress him. To which she responds, "Well, you're a big boy now." As a result, both women end up doing what Lisa terms "a woman's hardest job: juggling wolves."

Hitchcock's heroines occupy the terrain outside the artificial territory of the patriarchal map, existing in a lonely wilderness the male protagonists are oblivious to. They don't see it, much like the eyes behind the sunglasses of the police officer not really seeing Marion's situation in *Psycho* (1960). Devlin initially assumes Alicia has reverted to her old party-girl habits in *Notorious*, drinking heavily, when actually she is being poisoned; Thornhill does not realize that Eve is an American agent but she cannot confide in him, just as Judy cannot tell Scottie that she was posing as Madeleine in *Vertigo*. All Judy can do is become frustrated as he blunders on in his ignorant dominance over her, trying to turn her into the dead Madeleine. And the viewer, having heard the confession letter Judy writes then destroys, can only watch on with a mixture of pity and fear as Scottie plunges deeper into his obsession. Eve's predicament, dealing with Thornhill's ignorance, is a less extreme version of Judy submitting to Scottie's whims. It puts Eve in danger all the same.

How Deep the Rabbit Hole Goes

Even when masculine ignorance of feminine reality is not directly hazardous to the women involved, Hitchcock's heroines are still subjugated to it. In *The Man Who Knew Too Much*, for instance, Jo (Doris Day) had a successful international career as a singer before her marriage to Ben (James Stewart). She has given up her public singing voice to live in Ben's world as a doctor's wife in much the same way Hans Christian Anderson's Little Mermaid gives up her tongue and tail in exchange for two human legs in order to live on land and marry the prince. Yet it is only by recovering her voice—her scream during the Albert Hall concert and reviving her singing career to sing "*Que Será Será*" at the embassy—that Jo is able to prevent the assassination and then later help rescue the kidnapped Hank.

Jo's suppressed voice in marriage goes beyond being forced to quit her singing career. She is subordinated to Ben's rationalism, even though her intuition is more acute than his reasoning. She is the one who intuits that "Ambrose Chappell" is not a person but a place (Ambrose Chapel), whereas Ben chases the red-herring. Ben, the titular man who knew too much, is a man who reasoned too much, who likes to think his internal compass points north.

Often Hitchcock's heroines can be just as ignorant and lacking in intuition as their male counterparts, however. In *The 39 Steps* and *Saboteur*, they are initially convinced of the protagonist's guilt. In *To Catch a Thief*, Francie (Grace Kelly) spends much of the film convinced that John Robie (Cary Grant) has resumed his former life as the cat burglar known as The Cat and is responsible for the recent spate of jewel robberies in the South of France. Even so, Francie's obsession with Robie as a thief, like Jefferies's obsession with Thorwald as a potential murderer, reflects her dissatisfaction with being a chained cave dweller, constrained by the shallow materialism of the social milieu she inhabits. Jewelry does not interest her; she dislikes having cold things touching her skin. Instead, the idea of The Cat breaking into women's bedrooms at night and stealing their diamonds excites her. As Donald Spoto says in *The Art of Alfred Hitchcock*, "Her sexual desire is in fact indistinguishable from her fascination for his criminal record" (228). ("I've never caught a real thief before. This is quite stimulating!") Spoto also points out "that the real thief is in fact a woman is crucial, however, since there is a link by association with Francie" (229).

Her craving for excitement, for the idea of John Robie as a cat burglar, leads her astray. Robie fascinates her for the same reason the Thorwald fascinates Jefferies. To her he represents a manifestation of her latent desires. She, like Jefferies, is another surrogate for us, the spectator, wanting more excitement and glamour than our everyday life has to offer; we like her, are "tourists." The difference between Jefferies and Lisa, however, is that Jefferies's conjecture about Thorwald being guilty of murder are proven correct, whereas Francie is wrong about Robie. She expects Robie to be something more than he is in reality—Batman instead of Bruce Wayne—just as Thornhill's mother is disappointed with him as he is.

Men are expected to live up to unachievable archetypes, measured against non-existent George Kaplan figures. They must don a costume that embellishes who they are, whether it is as simple as Roger Thornhill adding a superfluous "O" to his name, or taking on the mantle of the non-existent Kaplan. They are Bruce Wayne/Peter Parker figures. Their Batman/Spider-man-type alter egos are expedient exaggerations of the people they are without the costumes. Women, on the other hand, particularly in Hitchcock films, reflect the expectation for them to camouflage themselves behind an alter ego less than their capabilities and surrender their mermaid tales and their voice. Their alter egos are, in contrast, equivalent to Superman masking himself as Clark Kent or Wonder Woman living under Diana Prince's various civilian guises. (A possible Hitchcock exception would be Judy turned into the unattainable alter ego of the more glamorous and mysterious Madeleine, except even then she is expected to suppress her real self, abandoning her voice.)

The theatricality in *North by Northwest* reflects these social expectations for men to be more than themselves, whether it is Thornhill becoming Roger O. Thornhill, or Vandamm hiding behind the wealthy, respectable facade of Lester Townsend's Long Island mansion or posing as an art collector to obtain stolen microfilm at the auction. *North by Northwest* is a reworking of *The 39 Steps* and *Saboteur* in which the protagonists, Richard Hannay and Barry Kane, are also average men mistaken for more than they are and the villains similarly hide behind the mask of wealth and respectability greater than their true selves.

In John Buchan's original novel, *The Thirty-Nine Steps*, Hannay refers to this method of disguise as "atmosphere." "If a man could get into

How Deep the Rabbit Hole Goes

perfectly different surroundings from those in which he had been first observed, and—this is the important part—really play up to these surroundings and behave as if he had never been out of them, he would puzzle the cleverest detectives on earth," Hannay observes. " A fool tries to look different: a clever man looks the same and is different" (137). The power of this tactic of playing up to one's surroundings is evident in how we take things at initial face value in *North by Northwest*, too. Thornhill's own approach depends upon that same concept of "atmosphere" (his "Think thin" philosophy, for example).

We assume Vandamm is Townsend because of his surroundings, and even he is bemused ("Games, must we?") at Thornhill seemingly acting as if there is no masquerade, just as Thornhill is later frustrated at the ease with which everybody at the Plaza automatically assumes he is Kaplan. And Thornhill is susceptible to the fallacy that Kaplan exists, based on the visual "evidence" in Kaplan's hotel room. Similarly, all who see Thornhill with the knife in his hand at the UN, either with their own eyes or in the newspaper photo splashed across the headlines, assume he murdered Townsend. Nobody question his or her eyes, mistaking the shadows on the cave walls for reality.

The truth is hidden in plain sight yet nobody sees it, much like in Poe's "The Purloined Letter" where the king is blind to the unconcealed, incriminating letter lying in plain sight and later the policeman trying to recover that same letter from the minister cannot find it in the letter-rack. As Kingsley Amis points out in *The James Bond Dossier*, "Like all Poe's "psychological" ideas, this is shallow perversity: in real life, someone would pick up the letter in the first five seconds. Fictional villains have always tended to go in for the purloined-letter fallacy, pushing their most heinous designs as far into the open as possible as if motivated by an all-but-conscious desire for detection" (128). Amis gives examples of this fallacy in Ian Fleming, such as the prominence of the villains' hideouts and cover identities, the belief that "advertisement is not only the ideal form of concealment but, so to speak, desirable in itself" (129). Vandamm posing as Townsend in *North by Northwest* or choosing to live atop Mount Rushmore reflects a similar exhibitionism, as does his use of a public auction to receive the stolen microfilm instead of via cutouts and a dead drop.

Yet despite the shallow perversity of advertisement as concealment, the initial theft of the incriminating letter in "The Purloined Letter" highlights the extent to which the rules of etiquette involve what Žižek refers to as the third gaze of one "who, at any price must be kept in ignorance as to the true nature of the affair," citing Racine's *Phaedre* as an example: "The configuration here is homologous to that in Poe's 'The Purloined Letter,' where we also witness the duel of two gazes (the queen's and the minister's) against the background of the third (king's) gaze, which must be kept ignorant of the affair" (215). Referring to the society party scene in *Saboteur* as another example, Žižek explains how "both sides have to observe the rules of etiquette—that is to say, the actions each of them undertakes against the adversary have to accord with the rules of the social game; the Other (epitomized by the crowd) has to be kept ignorant as to the true stakes" (215).

North by Northwest's scene in the elevator of the Plaza Hotel or at the auction provide additional examples of both sides having to observe the rules of etiquette under a public gaze that must remain ignorant. In the elevator scene, the laughter erupts when Clara Thornhill's jibe about whether the two men aren't really trying to kill her son threatens to expose that ignorance. Her mockery amounts to a breach of etiquette as are Kane's attempts to alert guests that Mrs. Sutton's house is a den of spies in *Saboteur*. In *North by Northwest*, Roger Thornhill is able to escape the elevator by applying etiquette, insisting the killers allow the ladies to exit first. At the auction he extricates himself by deliberately breaching etiquette to get himself arrested and removed from the auction house. Etiquette is the blue pill that maintains the illusion of order. Manipulating that illusion provides the means of escape.

In the cases of both the elevator and the auction, gender assumptions about men measuring up to female expectations underlie the illusion, with Thornhill's mother poking fun at her son's claims the men are trying to kill him, and the equally matriarchal woman at the auction calling Thornhill a "genuine idiot." These matriarchal figures enforce the etiquette, denying the evidence of a reality outside their insular troglodyte perceptions. They believe in an imaginary archetype of masculine identity and behavior they expect men to live up to. But the irony about these two matriarchs is that, like the queen in Poe's "The Purloined Letter," they think their gaze is the absolute truth when actually it is as blind and fallible as that of the patriarchal gaze of the king or the policeman.

The blind patriarchal gaze is a recurring motif in Hitchcock's oeuvre. As Žižek explains in regard to *Phaedre* and by extension "The Purloined Letter," "It is not by accident that this role is attributed to the king—who but the king, the ultimate guarantor of the social texture, is more apt to epitomize the blind mechanism of the symbolic order as such?" (214-5.) Žižek relates this to Hitchcock's use of gigantic stone statues: the Egyptian Goddess in the British Museum in *Blackmail*, the Statue of Liberty in *Saboteur*, and Mount Rushmore in *North by Northwest*. Vandamm hiding out atop Mount Rushmore, then, is a metaphor for his espionage activities under the unseeing gaze of the king, with the presidents' statues as a metonym for American Democracy itself—as is his earlier occupation of the Townsend mansion without its owner being aware. (Lester Townsend insists the house is completely closed up, with only the gardener and his wife in residence.)

Despite Vandamm's ability to operate in plain sight without the king noticing, he in turn possesses an unseeing gaze. He cannot see the queen's duplicity, failing to realize Eve is a spy. It takes Leonard, analyzing the situation from a gay perspective, applying what he terms his "woman's intuition," to deduce the truth about Eve. This echoes "The Purloined Letter," where seeing what the king cannot is a matter of identifying with the viewpoint of either a woman or a man who does not think like other men. The unconcealed, incriminating letter proves so difficult for the policeman to find because he operates under the erroneous assumption all men proceed—with obvious Freudian overtones—to conceal a letter "in some out of the way hole or corner suggested by the same tenor of thought which would urge a man to secrete a letter in a gimlet-hole bored in a chair's leg" (Poe 292).

Uncovering the deception is a matter of thinking subjectively, placing oneself in an opponent's shoes. Specifically, it is an ability to see things from the intuitive feminine point of view of a woman or a poet. We see this emphasis on intuition versus an unseeing masculine gaze throughout Hitchcock, whether it is Jo's superior intuition to her husband's in *The Man Who Knew Too Much* or Jefferies' suspicions about Thorwald in *Rear Window* while meantime his detective buddy, Doyle (Wendell Corey), insists "Lars Thorwald is no more a murderer than I am." He cannot see anything from a perspective other than his own, falling into the same trap as the policeman in "The Purloined Letter," assuming all men think as he does, and deriding female intuition. ("That feminine intuition stuff sells magazines. But in real life, it's still a fairy tale. I don't know how many wasted years I've spent tracking down leads based on female intuition.") At first we cannot be certain whether Jefferies is applying the same erroneous logic that all men think as he does—assuming that Thorwald has killed his wife on the basis of his own subconscious desire to rid himself of Lisa. However, the revelation that Thorwald did in fact murder his wife means Jefferies possessed the subjective ability to put himself in the man's shoes. Yet he is not intuitive enough to see Lisa clearly and the danger her desire to prove herself will put her in, just as neither the queen nor minister in "The Purloined Letter" are intuitive enough to see they will be outsmarted. It takes the agony of watching helplessly as Lisa is cornered in the Thorwald apartment for him to see subjectively from her point of view.

Roger Thornhill occupies the equivalent middle ground as the minister or the queen. He is intuitive enough to know he can manipulate his fellow blue pill-swallowing, chained prisoners staring at the flickering shadows of the cave walls but not smart enough to question Kaplan's existence or Eve's treachery, for instance. The same applies to someone like Francie in *To Catch a Thief*. She has enough insight to see through the subterfuge of John Robie claiming he is Conrad Burns from Oregon. Yet she lacks the intuition to realize that Robie is no longer the Cat and somebody is framing him for the jewel thefts.

As with Jefferies, Thornhill's character growth comes via learning subjectivity and empathy. He progresses from being patronizing to his secretary at the start of the film ("Use your blood sugar, come on"), and dictating recycled platitudes to accompany the candy he is sending as gift, to genuinely empathizing with Eve and standing up to the Professor, rebuking him for asking women like Eve to bed down with the Vandamms of this world and fly away with them and probably never come back alive. In addition, he proves himself willing to risk his life to save her from Vandamm's clutches.

The king and policeman in "The Purloined Letter" have effectively taken the blue pill and are oblivious to the illusion of their assumptions. The queen has taken the equivalent of the red pill. She thinks she has a better objective understanding of the underlying reality the king cannot see, an awareness of the reality behind illusion. But she herself lacks the minister's even broader perspective, as the minister himself will later be oblivious to Dupin's own third pill perspective. Watching *North by Northwest*, we ourselves move through the three positions. In its first act, the New York and Long Island sequences, we are under the influence of the blue pill. We know the same amount Thornhill knows and watch with the same surprise as the narrative unfolds. That changes in the second act. We become privy to the intelligence headquarters meeting and discover that Kaplan is a non-existent decoy. We have now taken the red pill and are conscious of the subterfuge and the nothingness of George Kaplan. We now know much more than Thornhill does but fail to realize the limits of our knowledge until the Professor's revelation that Eve is an undercover agent demonstrates otherwise, while in the final act of the film's three-act structure, we are aware of the limitation of our previous positions.

The third act places us in a more subjective position. Twice—once when Thornhill stands up to the Professor and attempts to stop Eve going off with Vandamm, then again when Leonard shoots Vandamm with Eve's gun to reveal it contained blanks—we are shown characters being punched in the face from their subjective point of view. We become the ones on the receiving end of the punch, reminding us of our inescapable subjectivity in general. The third act also reverses the situation in the second act where we had a greater insight than Thornhill. When Eve shoots him in the cafeteria, it catches us unaware. Even though we know he has agreed to perform the role of Kaplan, and Hitchcock has concealed what was going to happen in plain sight in the ironic exchange between Thornhill and Vandamm at the auction ("Apparently the only performance that's going to satisfy you is when I play dead." "Your very next role. You will be quite convincing, I assure you."), seeing him play this next role still takes us by surprise. The scene reinforces that we do not know everything. But knowing everything is not crucial. Identifying with the subjective reality of others is. On the one hand we, like Jefferies in *Rear Window*, are turning our back to the true sun when we watch movies, indulging in pure illusion. Cinema is as much a masquerade as Eve Kendall shooting Roger Thornhill in the cafeteria in *North by Northwest*. Eve and Thornhill staging the shooting under the Professor's guidance are once again surrogates for Eva Marie Saint and Cary Grant acting out the scene under Hitchcock's direction. Yet we submit to the illusion, allowing Hitchcock to manipulate us via its artifice because we identify with his intent.

Just as Eve and Thornhill carry out the subterfuge of Kaplan's death to quell Vandamm's suspicions about Eve (to prevent the king discovering the queen's treachery), so we indulge in the illusion of cinema for the sake of the reality we find within that illusion. Thornhill rescuing Eve from Vandamm under the unseeing gaze of the stone faces of the Presidents is a variation on Dupin stealing back the purloined letter from the minister. And cinema, through the implicit base of the philosophy of Ideas Rohmer and Chabrol identify as central to both Poe and Hitchcock, allows us to steal back a semblance of reality from illusion, under the blank and pitiless gaze of the world pulled over our eyes.

We can never escape the hyperreality of our existence. The falsehoods of the reality we take for granted will always loom over us. They will always be there, like Mount Rushmore's stone faces still visible, peering over the otherwise peaceful tranquility of the wooded glade when Thornhill meets up with Eve after his fake death at the cafeteria. No red pill is going to liberate us. Not fully. But the third pill—the pill our movie ticket buys us—will at least give us a subjective insight into a mermaid existence that the etiquette of rational reality outside the darkness of the theatre might not otherwise allow us to explore.

We find our north in a fictional direction. North by northwest.

Notes

1. A building so nondescript and interchangeable that it doubles for 650 Madison Avenue and Hitchcock scholars often incorrectly cite it as that building, amongst other potential New York addresses.

2. Hitchcock himself insisted that he "made *North by Northwest* with tongue in cheek; to me it was one big joke." (Truffaut and Scott 102). But as Wood remarks regarding his interpretation of *The Birds* (1963), "If Hitchcock himself told me tomorrow that the whole sequence was shot purely to give the audience 'kicks,' that the only reason why Melanie doesn't escape is that if she did the 'kicks' would stop, I would merely quote him my favorite aphorism of D.H Lawrence: 'Never trust the artist—trust the tale'" (*Hitchcock's Films Revisited*, 171). The tale can manifest complexities the artist

is not consciously aware of. The same applies to Thornhill's ability to be a puppeteer while unaware of his own unconscious submission to the puppet-show reality.

3. The Bond novels compensate for Britain's diminished international importance in the same way Baudrillard cites movies like *Apocalypse Now* as compensating for the disaster of the Vietnam War: "The Vietnam War and the film are cut from the same cloth, nothing separates them: this film is part of the war. If the Americans (apparently) lost the other, they have certainly won this one. *Apocalypse Now* is a global victory. It has a cinematographic power equal and superior to that of the military and industrial complexes, of the Pentagon and governments" ("The Evil Demon of Images" 17-18). Bond represents a similar "global victory" for Britain, a hyperreal archetype superseding reality.

Works Cited

Amis, Kingsley. *The James Bond Dossier*. Jonathan Cape, 1965.
Baudrillard, Jean. "The Evil Demon of Images." Mari Kuttna Memorial Lecture. University of Sydney, 1984, Power Institute of Fine Arts, 1987, www.monoskop.org/images/4/47/Baudrillard_Jean_The_evil_demon_of_images_1987.pdf.
---. *Selected Writings*. Edited by Mark Poster, Stanford University Press, 1988.
Borges, Jorge Luis. *Collected Fictions*. Translated by Andrew Hurley, Allen Lane, 1999.
Buchan, John. *The Thirty-Nine Steps*. Penguin Classics, 2004.
Coleridge, Samuel Taylor. *Selected Poetry and Prose*. Random House, 1951.
Conrad, Peter. *The Hitchcock Murders*. Faber, 2000.
Fitzgerald, F Scott. *The Great Gatsby*. Penguin Classics, 2010.
Fleming, Ian. *Casino Royale*. Jonathan Cape, 1953, reprinted 1965.
Koolhaus, Rem. *Delirious New York: A Retroactive Manifesto of Manhattan*. 010 Publishers, 1994.
Krohn, Bill. *Hitchcock At Work*. Phaidon Press, 2000.
Maugham, Somerset. *Ashenden*. Pan Books, 1953.
Mogg, Ken. *The Alfred Hitchcock Story*. Titan Books, 2008.
The Pervert's Guide to Cinema. Directed by Sophie Fiennes, presentation by Slavoj Žižek. Mischief Films/Amoeba Film, 2006.
Plato. *The Republic*. Translated by Desmond Lee. Penguin Classics, 2008.

Poe, Edgar Allan. *The Fall of the House of Usher and Other Writings.* Penguin Classics, 2003.

Poole, Steve Poole. "Obituary, 'Jean Baudrillard.'" *The Guardian,* 7 Mar. 2007, theguardian.com/news/2007/mar/07/guardianobituaries.france.

Rohmer, Eric and Chabrol, Claude. *Hitchcock: the First Forty-Four Films.* Translated by Stanley Hocham. Frederick Ungar Publishing, 1979.

Spoto, Donald. *The Art of Alfred Hitchcock: Fifty Years of His Motion Pictures.* Anchor Books, 1992.

Truffaut, Francois and Helen G. Scott. *Hitchcock,* Revised Edition. Simon and Schuster, 1983.

Wood, Robin. *Hitchcock's Films Revisited.* Faber, 1991.

Žižek, Slavoj. *Everything You Always Wanted To Know About Lacan But Were Afraid To Ask Hitchcock.* Verso, 2010.

---. writer and performer. *The Pervert's Guide to Ideology.* Directed by Sophie Fiennes, Zeitgeist Films, 2012..

What the O Stands For: The Cold War Games of *North by Northwest*

By Jeffrey Longacre

Just before the climactic chase on top of Mount Rushmore in Alfred Hitchcock's *North by Northwest* (1959), a scene is staged in the cafeteria adjacent to Rushmore's observation deck in which an American spy named Kaplan has arranged to meet an enemy spy named Vandamm, his lieutenant, Leonard, and his girlfriend, Eve, in order to make a deal. "And now, what little drama are we here for today?" asks Vandamm. In exchange for Eve—who, working as a double agent, has betrayed and attempted to have him killed—Kaplan will do "nothing to stop [Vandamm]" from leaving the country with a statuette full of secrets in the form of microfilm: "I want the girl to get what's coming to her," he states, coldly. "I'm curious, Mr. Kaplan," Vandamm says after listening to the proposal, "What made you arrive at the deduction that my feelings for Miss Kendall might have deteriorated to the point where I would trade her in for a little piece of mind?" "I don't deduce," Kaplan responds, "I observe." Eve, who has been browsing in the souvenir shop throughout these negotiations of which she is the object, returns and says that she is "going back to the house now" and starts to leave. Vandamm rushes after her and, after a brief discussion, he summons Leonard and they head for the exit. Kaplan rushes to physically stop Eve, the object of his contempt, from leaving, who screams: "Stay away from me! You let go! Let go of me!" "Save the phony tears," Kaplan replies. Leonard stops Vandamm from intervening in what is becoming a public scene; spies cannot afford to draw too much attention to themselves. Eve struggles against Kaplan, who pulls her across the room, then takes a gun from her purse and shoots him. He falls to the floor and she shoots him again and flees amidst horrified gasps and screams.

This scene is quintessential Hitchcock: it has intrigue, violence, Cary Grant playing a "wrong man," a duplicitous blond, and above all, suspense. Except that nothing here is what it seems. Kaplan is actually a man named Roger Thornhill (Grant), an ordinary advertising executive who has gotten swept up in these Cold War games via mistaken identity. Eve Kendall (Eva Marie Saint) is actually an American agent posing as Vandamm's (James Mason) girlfriend and confidant, a double agent working for the CIA. She did not actually betray Thornhill, although it appears that way at first to both Thornhill and the audience, but she was merely trying to find a way to save her cover while putting him in the least amount of danger. Kaplan never existed; he was a red herring created to keep Vandamm and his men off of Eve's scent. Most importantly, Eve did not really shoot Thornhill any more than Eva Marie Saint really shot Cary Grant. Manipulating audience expectations, Hitchcock puts a twist on the concept of Chekhov's gun (we first see the gun a few scenes earlier in Eve's purse around the time we find out she has double-crossed Thornhill), which establishes the rule that if a gun appears in Act I of a play, it had better go off by Act III, but Chekhov never stipulated that the gun fire real bullets, and real bullets would be a little too hot for a cold war. This "little drama," this film-within-a-film, is a microcosm of Hitchcock's themes in *North by Northwest*. Hidden beneath the slick surface of a thrilling adventure and romance there is a sophisticated satire of doubling, duplicity, and the binary logic of Cold War strategies, where nothing is indeed what it seems.[1]

Thornhill and Eve finally have their reconciliation just after this scene. All cards now seemingly on the table, Hitchcock allows the chemistry and tension between Grant and Saint to pay off, giving the audience what they want. After apologizing for the way she has treated him, and revealing how she got involved with this business in the first place, she says that she has to get back to the house where Vandamm and Leonard (Martin Landau) are waiting. When he continues to try to detain her to prolong their romantic embraces, she asks him: "Well, whose side are you on?" Revealing his uncommitted status as a free agent in a binary world order entirely dependent upon the either/or logic of picking sides, he responds, "Yours, always, darling," preferring to choose love over war, revealing that he is a sentimental man at heart. "Please, don't undermine my resolve just when I need it most," she pleads. He concedes, but with the caveat, "After your malevolent friend Vandamm takes off tonight, you and I are going to get together and do a lot of apologizing to each other, in private." Confused, she tells him, "You know that can't be." In a game that is never straight, all cards are, in fact, not on the table. The Professor (Leo G. Carroll), the author and director of the mission of which Eve is a part, has determined that Eve is more valuable to the agency, and therefore to the mission and to the national interest, if she leaves the country with Vandamm and continues to play the role of his mistress. Thornhill reacts with outrage and attempts to stop this development, but sentimentality is read as a flaw by the Professor and has no place in his calculated plans. For him, Eve is little more than a pawn on the chessboard of the Cold War: "I needn't tell you how valuable she can be to us over there." Thornhill protests, stating that he will not allow it, but the Professor simply says, "She has to." "Nobody has to do anything!" Thornhill responds, taking the position of free individual, agency over subservience to the fatalistic machinations of institutional or collective agency: "I don't like the games you play, Professor." "War is hell," he tells Thornhill, "even when it's a cold one."

According to James Naremore, Hitchcock was, in general, "a disengaged artist," apolitical. He concedes, however, that *North by Northwest* might best be viewed as an exception to this rule, writing that "Hitchcock's relatively anxious or cynical attitude toward the state is apparent in *North by Northwest*, where he and Lehman satirize the cold war" ("Spies" 10).[2] Developing this general assertion, Alan Nadel more recently argues that Hitchcock's film demonstrates qualities reminiscent of classic farce and that, in fact, "more generally farce could be viewed as the quintessential Hitchcock genre, especially in the way that (in Eric Bentley's words) 'farce brings together the direct and wild fantasies and the everyday and drab realities'" (163). Furthermore, he demonstrates how Hitchcock uses farce to comment on aspects of the Cold War, "suggest[ing] that Thornhill's adventure also undermines the fundamental meaning of allegiance that the concept of the double—be it the double agent, the Communist cell member, or the closeted homosexual—constantly worries with the cultural scheme of Cold War binaries" (Nadel 163). Whether read as farce or satire, however, it is clear that Hitchcock's tone in *North by Northwest* is comic and that these Cold War binaries are the object of his attack. While I generally agree with Nadel and am greatly indebted to his essay, I tend to side with Naremore's identification of the film more broadly with satire, in which the elements of farce that Nadel describes can still function as tonal elements, but within a larger tradition of social commentary.

Northrop Frye, in identifying what he called the four "*mythoi* or generic plots" of narrative literature, labels irony and satire as "The Mythos of Winter," certainly an appropriate mythos for a cold war (162).[3] Frye writes that "satire is irony which is structurally close to the comic: the comic struggle of two societies, one normal and the other absurd, is reflected in its double focus of morality and fantasy" (224). The "two societies" of *North by Northwest* are the ordinary world of surface reality—like the one reflected in the glass and steel of the opening credit sequence, discussed below—and the shadow reality of Cold War espionage. The difficulty of identifying which society is "normal" and which is "absurd" during the Cold War is the point of Hitchcock's satire: in a world governed by the high-stakes logic of Mutually Assured Destruction (with the most appropriate acronym ever: MAD), what does sane even look like anymore?[4] "[Hitchcock's] transformation of madness into a comic nightmare in *North by Northwest*," writes Thomas Leitch, "whose title, an echo of Hamlet's reference to his own whimsical or assumed madness, announces its subject—*the problematic relation between madness and sanity in a world which is itself mad*" (206, italics added).[5]

If satire is dependent upon the ironic contrast of "normal" and "absurd" societies, which are mirror images of each other despite the stark contrast of the surfaces, then Hitchcock ingenuously sets up this juxtaposition immediately in the film's opening credit sequence, designed by Hitchcock's frequent collaborator in the 1950s and '60s: Saul Bass. This sequence establishes the "normal" society that the famous crop duster sequence, which occurs almost exactly at the film's midpoint, is the visual and thematic counterpoint to, which in turn is part of a larger contrapuntal pattern in Hitchcock's film.[6] The film begins in green (even the MGM logo is done in green), suggesting greed, money, envy, and life. It also establishes a palate of cool colors that will dominate the look of the film: a cold look for a world embroiled in a cold war.[7] The green screen is quickly divided up by diagonal and vertical blue lines that form a grid. Subsequently, this grid dissolves into the façade of the Manhattan skyscraper in which Roger Thornhill works. Cars and cabs, yellows and reds, are reflected in the glass, creating an effect not unlike one of Piet Mondrian's late, abstract canvases, their paths seemingly demarcated by the lines in the building, lines that emerged from Bass's earlier animation. Do these lines determine the fate, the direction of these vehicles, or do they simply plot and trace their movement?[8]

Further cuts take us down to street level and into the hustle and bustle of the busy Manhattan streets, all accentuated and given a frenetic energy by Bernard Herrmann's masterful score.[9] Non-diegetic sound dominates this sequence as opposed to the diegetic sound that dominates the crop duster scene, further emphasizing the complementary yet contrasting relationship between these scenes with the city's bustling cool artifice in striking juxtaposition with the fearful and barren naturalism of the open fields of the crop duster sequence, colored in faded browns and yellows. This contrast signifies the two Americas of the Eisenhower era: a slick façade of consumer capitalism masking a desolate, empty interior. One can feel safe in the confines of the city, becoming just one out of many, a face in the crowd, as opposed to the feelings of isolation and exposure revealed in the later scene. The other side of this, however, is that one also becomes dehumanized, a piece of information, a data point, a commodity as *E Pluribus Unum* (out of many one) on American currency guarantees. In the 1950s, in the age of McCarthy, U2 spy planes, Sputnik, and hydrogen bombs, the enemy is anonymous and could be anyone,[10] surveillance is pervasive, and the blue sky seems like the most likely source for death and destruction. These are the poles of signification between which Hitchcock builds his satire of Cold War ideology and discourse.

As the counterpoint to the opening sequence, the crop duster sequence establishes the contrary pole of signification establishing a binary—city/country—that signifies "America." Like the credit sequence, it begins with an extreme high-angle, long shot—or bird's-eye view shot—that shows a bus deposit Roger Thornhill at a desolate crossroads in the middle of nowhere (perhaps the same bus that Hitchcock misses in his cameo appearance at the end of the credit sequence).[11] He is a tiny speck, insignificant, in the middle of parallel and intersecting lines of roads and ploughed furrows (the flat analogues to the vertical grid-lines of the skyscrapers): in both sequences, he is a point on a graph, data to be measured and recorded. "It is on this ground," writes Stanley Cavell, "that the man undergoes his Shakespearean encounter of nothings—the nothing of Thornhill meeting the nothing of Kaplan—the attack on his identity, as it were, but itself" (256). In the next shot, from a different perspective, a ground-level long shot, he is like an absurd, well-dressed scarecrow, one of T. S. Eliot's hollow men perhaps, in the middle of a brown and yellow waste land, under a cloudless pale blue sky.[12] He is a cinematic correlative for a straw man: a nothing, a fiction-within-a-fiction, an incongruity who distracts and disrupts, drawing focus and attention from more serious matters, like an escapist entertainment. The scene immediately conjures familiar modernist iconography from the mid-twentieth century: alienated, helpless, man-alone, confronted with the void and silence of the abyss.[13] Christopher Morris argues, in fact, that "[t]rue 'grounds' of identity in *North by Northwest* are nonexistent, in their place is an empty abyss" (50). Thornhill's helplessness and insignificance are, in particular, what draw the audience into identification—it's Cary Grant!—of him, with him and, at least emotionally, his predicament.

Our identification with Thornhill is underscored through the next series of edits that alternate between Thornhill framed in a medium shot looking, and POV shots of what he is looking at, a favorite method of Hitchcock's for aligning the viewer's perspective with his protagonist. These shots underscore his isolation, in contrast to the crowds of the city, revealing the only signs of life anywhere to be a far-off town and a distant crop duster on the horizon. The soundtrack emphasizes this isolation through the sparse use of diegetic sound—light wind, passing vehicles in the distance, Thornhill's steps on the ground—and the wise decision not to use Herrmann's masterful score until it punctuates this sequence with an exclamation point (which is also in contrast to the forceful use of diegetic sound in the opening sequence). Ostensibly, Thornhill is here to meet a contact who, he hopes, will reveal the secret of George Kaplan, for whom he has been mistaken, and to clear up the international intrigue this ironically ordinary man has been swept up into (ironically ordinary because he is Cary Grant). A car goes by and does not stop. Another car goes by from the opposite direction and does not stop. Thornhill waits. A truck goes by from the opposite direction and kicks up a dust storm, engulfing Thornhill. A car appears almost out of nowhere from behind the lone cornfield and deposits another man in a brown suit and fedora across the highway. Hitchcock frames them both in a ground-level long shot, each on opposite sides of the screen, a road between them, vaguely reminiscent of Vladimir and Estragon waiting for Godot,[14] waiting for the arrival of someone or something that will give meaning to and provide context for their being here in this desolate place. Thornhill crosses the highway to inquire if this is the man he is supposed to meet in the scene's only dialogue. "Then your name isn't Kaplan?" says Thornhill after the man tells him he is only waiting for the bus. "Can't say it is, because it ain't," he replies. Unlike Thornhill, however, he is not a stranger to this land and he is therefore capable of reading the scene and noting significant incongruities: "That's funny," he says, "that plane's dustin' crops where there ain't no crops." Again, nothing is what it seems in this Cold War satire: a crop duster is not just a crop duster. The uses of technology and tools have been repurposed as weapons while maintaining the disguise of tools. Hitchcock suggests that it will take a new perspective to read the signs in this new American landscape. "Throughout," Naremore reminds us, "[Hitchcock] made satiric use of American landscape, turning every colorful tourist stop and national icon into a slightly paranoid vision" ("Spies" 18).

    Left alone again after the man boards the bus (the bus Hitchcock missed in the opening sequence?), Thornhill resumes waiting, but the crop duster begins to circle around and come towards him and also—by way of Hitchcock's carefully paced shot/reverse shot construction—the viewer, closer and louder with each cut. It flies very low, forcing Thornhill to the ground. Circling back, it comes at him again, forcing him to take cover in a ditch as machine gun fire rains down on him. Thornhill tries in vain to stop a passing car for help, but to no avail; he is on his own, exposed. The plane circles back again, leading to the iconic shot of Thornhill running towards the camera, towards the audience, with the plane flying at him over his right shoulder. It is a tracking shot, the first time Hitchcock has moved the camera during this sequence, which accentuates the fearful effect of the shot. Thornhill—Eliot's scarecrow, a modern straw man—takes cover in the dead cornfield, the only cover available. The plane returns and dusts the cornfield, making it clear that nowhere is safe from this airborne death. Running back out into the open, on to the road, Thornhill succeeds in stopping an oil truck—barely—by standing in front of it and risking his life. The plane, relentlessly coming back for another pass at Thornhill, crashes into the side of it in a spectacular explosion and Herrmann's score explodes back onto the soundtrack, signifying the end of the danger and the return to the safe excitement of Hitchcock's thriller; the reality of the fiction (the reminder, signified by extra-diegetic sound, that it is only a movie) replaces the frightening fiction of the reality that, although exaggerated and dream-like, the threat to Thornhill is analogous to the threat of death that hovers anonymously, inescapably in the skies of our ordinary days.

One reductive way of defining "Cold War" is through the absurd idea of a war in which nothing happens and, in turn, becomes a war about nothing. Philosophically, the 1950s were a decade dominated by Existentialism and the Absurd. Long before *Seinfeld*, but only six years after the premiere of Samuel Beckett's *Waiting for Godot* (1953), *North by Northwest* is a film about nothing.[15] Like Beckett's Theater of the Absurd, though, and in line with much modernist art in general, it is about the paradox that nothing is an aspect of the Real: the nothing that is. Hitchcock explores this idea specifically through the relationship between representation and identity, through "the paradoxes of representation, the devious conflations of appearance with reality, and the crisscrossing of identities" (Wilson 1161). Cary Grant, playing Roger Thornhill, who is in turn mistaken for the nonexistent George Kaplan, is an avatar for the cool aloofness of masculine subjectivity in the 1950s, more image than man. He is a cipher, an empty signifier of a masculine ideal, who can be anything and therefore is nothing. As Thomas Leitch puts it: "In his dedication to the 'expedient exaggeration' and superficial charm of the good advertising executive, Thornhill is the organization man par excellence, the faceless son of an absent father, the man defined so completely by parental authority that he has no identity of his own" (209). In modernist iconography, if he is Eliot's hollow man and one of Beckett's tramps, he is also the heir to Wallace Stevens's Snow Man.

Although originally published in 1921, Stevens's modern meditation on John Keats's concept of negative capability, "The Snow-Man," is the perfect articulation of a characteristically Cold War, existential, perspective on being and identity: "One must have a mind of winter," Stevens's poem begins, "[a]nd have been cold a long time" in order to reach a state of negative capability and transcend the limitations of selfhood (becoming an empty field, figuratively speaking, ready for new growth). This means becoming a part of one's environment to the point of transcending emotional or subjective responses to a wintry landscape, responses that might result in the sentiment of a pathetic fallacy, resulting in a catharsis of cold reason (i.e. one must not "think / Of any misery in the sound of the wind").[16] If such a negative state is achieved through the subordination of the pathetic response in favor of pure logos, then one might become a snow man and master of an utterly objective, indifferent perspective, becoming "nothing" and "behold[ing] / Nothing that is not there and the nothing that is." The Snow Man, paradoxically, sees everything because he sees nothing; he is capable of being anything because he is nothing.[17] He is an emptied container capable of filling himself with whatever significance suits his particular situation and environment. When applied to war instead of art, he is an archetype for the quintessential cold warrior: the spy.

Roger Thornhill is no spy, of course. He is an advertising executive, a profession that marries art and commerce, a prototype for Don Draper and Roger Sterling of more recent *Mad Men* fame, a man who trades in manufactured desires and comforting fictions in the service of consumer capitalism.[18] He is the quintessential mid-twentieth-century American hero in contrast to John Wayne, who was himself a nostalgic throwback to a mythical hero of nineteenth-century America, symbolizing the American ideal as opposed to its communist Other. "In the world of advertising," Thornhill says to his secretary at the beginning of the film, after he has lied to a man to steal his taxi, "there is no such thing as a lie, there is only expedient exaggeration."[19] His profession, Hitchcock suggests, is what makes Thornhill perfectly suited for the world of espionage, even if he is an unwitting and unwilling participant in the spy games he gets swept up in, as one could simply replace "advertising" with "espionage" and still have a valid claim. Each profession requires the creation of "expedient exaggerations," of words and narratives that will influence or even determine reality.[20] In the context of the Cold War, whichever side creates the best fiction controls the master narrative and becomes the author of history. In a war that mostly avoided the direct confrontation of a traditional "hot" war, this was the battlefield, which had become abstracted from a real battlefield like the grid that is abstracted from the lines in skyscrapers over the opening titles. The objective for both sides was to win the hearts and minds of the masses, to control the master narrative of history in order to determine its outcome. A strategy to protect oneself against such ideological warfare perpetuated by an invisible enemy who could be anyone, anywhere, was to cultivate a dispassionate and impersonal "mind of winter,"[21] a rejection of emotion and passion—the "red" hot fervor of war and revolution—in favor of the cold logic of consumer capitalism: the nothing that is. If one avoided all ideologies in favor of pure reason, then one could not be singled out and accused of anything.

In addition to all of this, Thornhill is the classic Hitchcockian wrong man to the point of self-parody; he is at the wrong place at the wrong time and raises his hand at precisely the wrong moment to get a waiter's attention to send a message to his mother. Unbeknownst to Thornhill, the same waiter has been paging a "Mr. Kaplan," and a couple of men are waiting and watching for whomever will answer this call. Slavoj Žižek reads this inciting incident as the moment that Thornhill, as empty signifier, begins to be filled with significance, through a psychological interpretation of the hero's call to action. He writes, "we are on the symbolic level: we are dealing with an empty name, the name of a non-existent person ('Kaplan'), a signifier without a bearer, which becomes attached to the hero out of sheer chance" (Žižek 131). While this case of mistaken identity can certainly be attributed to chance—and chance definitely plays a role in it—I tend to lean towards Naremore's intriguing Althusserian reading of this event as an "interpellation." He writes: "Seen in Althusserian terms, *North by Northwest* could be understood as a comic allegory about interpellation, in which the name 'George Kaplan' is revealed as nothing more than an empty signifier" ("Spies" 8, n13). Naremore's reading neatly coincides with my own interpretation of the film as a Cold War satire, commenting as it does on the relationship between individual subjects and the intersecting lines of *Ideological State Apparatuses* (ISAs).[22]

In addition to serving the function of setting the plot in motion, this inciting incident also establishes the primary theme of Hitchcock's film: the problem of identity, particularly the problem of identity as defined and determined by the state as the function of reductive, either/or choices.[23] Thornhill, mistaken as Kaplan, is abducted by the two men, "mere errand boys carrying concealed weapons," and he is taken by car to a mansion outside of the city: Townsend. He asks his kidnappers,

"Who's Townsend?" a question that also implies, "Where's Town's end?" and "Who is at Town's end?" Who is outside the pale of the city, living at the margins? Questions of identity are consistently related to questions of location and geography in *North by Northwest*. Who one is cannot be determined without the corresponding context of where one is, one's location on the grid. As an empty signifier, Thornhill has, perhaps, lived under the illusion that he is a free agent. Again, according to Althusser, subjects fool themselves into thinking that they are free agents when in fact they are not. "There are no subjects except by and for their subjection," he writes" (182).

Thornhill gets no response to his question. Inside the house, he is ushered into the study where he meets the person whom he thinks is Townsend (James Mason), who both is and is not Townsend; he is an imposter posing as Townsend, but he is indeed the man haunting the margins at "Town's end." "Townsend" immediately closes the curtain and turns on lamps; like a director setting the scene for a drama, he is the auteur who controls the scene. "Not what I expected," he says, "A little more polished, a little taller than the others, but I'm afraid just as obvious." When Thornhill demands to know why he was abducted, "Townsend" remarks, "Games, must we?" Constant references to games, theater, and play disguise the severity of the stakes. Thornhill informs him that he has plans to go to the theater, to which Townsend parries: "With such expert playacting, you make this very room a theater." The dialogue here is dripping with meta-dramatic commentary. "He's a well-tailored one, isn't he?" says Leonard (Martin Landau), Townsend's right-hand man, commenting on what they perceive to be a disguise, a kind of theatrical costume, because there's no possible way Cary Grant exists in reality. This comment foreshadows Thornhill's later discovery of a suit allegedly owned by the real Mr. Kaplan that is "for a much shorter man." The disguise for the nonexistent fiction is more realistic than the reality. "My secretary's a great admirer of your methods, Mr. Kaplan," says "Townsend," perhaps a backhanded compliment on Thornhill's method acting.[24] When Thornhill stops him and asks, "Did you call me Kaplan?" Townsend replies, "I know you're a man of many names, but I'm perfectly willing to accept your current choice," implying that Kaplan is just a role among many that Thornhill has adopted, like an actor playing different parts in different productions. Thornhill, of course, insists he's not Kaplan: "my name is Thornhill, Roger Thornhill. It's never been anything else," a perspective that reinforces some essential aspect of identity that is predetermined, not a matter of choice, more than just a name, not a mask one puts on and takes off at will. "I told you, I'm not Kaplan, whoever he is." Cary Grant, as Roger Thornhill, insists.[25] As Stanley Cavell puts it, "in part what or who is 'nothing' is the film character (here, Roger Thornhill) in comparison to the film actor playing him. Cary Grant would be more or less who he is if Roger Thornhill had never existed, whereas Roger Thornhill would be nothing apart from Cary Grant" (252).

The joke that Hitchcock plays underneath all of this is inherent in the very act of casting Grant for this role, another kind of interpellation insofar as the Hollywood studio system might be seen as a communications ISA. By 1959, Grant's notoriety was such that there was no way one could forget they were watching Cary Grant and believe they were watching a Roger Thornhill or a George Kaplan or any other character than "Cary Grant." The idea that Grant would be misidentified as anybody else is a key component of Hitchcock's theme and a major conceit in a satirical reading of this film: image is identity, surface is reality in Eisenhower's America; control the image and you control the identity, control the identity, then you control the agency and subsequently the master narrative of history. A further layer is added to this conceit when one remembers that Cary Grant himself is also a fiction, "a peerless creation" as Pauline Kael once put it,[26] an alias created by Archie Leach, who was, like Hitchcock, an English expatriate in Hollywood.[27]

The construction of character and identity is foregrounded in the expository scene in the United States Intelligence Agency that occurs about a third of the way into the film and serves to provide the audience with some answers about Thornhill, the non-existent Kaplan, and why the former is mistaken for the latter and why he has been pursued, almost killed, and, most recently, framed for the murder of the real Townsend at the UN.[28] The scene of Townsend's murder ends with a striking, and much analyzed,[29] extreme long shot from very high up looking down the façade of the UN building as Thornhill—who is no more than a tiny speck from this distance—runs out of the building and gets into one of the taxicabs waiting outside. The high angle of this bird's-eye-view shot is a near rhyme with the establishing shot of the crop-duster sequence, and the grid of steel and glass on the UN building, which dominates the right half of the screen, rhymes with the title sequence of the film, illustrating that Thornhill is no more than a character or plot point from this perspective, caught in the intersecting lines of much larger forces, which ultimately determine his fate. Therefore, it is no accident that this shot dissolves into the establishing shot of the following scene, which is a close up of a sign that reads United States Intelligence Agency, with the United States Capitol building reflected in it to signify the change in location from New York to Washington, DC.[30] Through this transition, Hitchcock is telling us that here is the authorial presence—the narrative voice—managing the grand narrative. These bland bureaucrats are the modern, ironic equivalent of the Olympian gods that controlled the destiny of classic heroes like Odysseus and Oedipus, of whom Thornhill is a postmodern variation.[31] They write and control the secret metanarrative, the mythos that underwrites history—a fiction that determines reality operating outside of the awareness of most people—in which Thornhill has found himself swept up. Instead of Olympian gods, however, these are bureaucratic Cold Warriors, waging war from a distance at a conference table (with Capitol Hill just across the street serving as an American analogue for Olympus) through the fabrication of fictions.

If Thornhill, as an advertising executive, creates desire through "expedient exaggeration" to sell products, then the Intelligence Agency is the absurd analog to his profession in the shadow world of espionage, creating "expedient exaggerations" to sell the way of life and the political reality that underwrite the existence of advertising executives in the first place: one creates an artificial cultural narrative that is impossible to live up to, yet creates the desire in consumers to aspire to this better, although unattainable, life; while the other creates an artificial historical narrative that is impossible to live up to, which creates the desire in citizens to identify the outliers and destroy the enemies of the way of life authenticated by the advertisers' images of a consumerist utopia.[32] This absurd cycle of image-determined reality is the essence of the American way of life at the end of the 1950s, and this is the subject of Hitchcock's Cold War satire.

The scene inside the Intelligence Agency begins with a close up of the newspaper, the collage of words and images that tell the story of what happened to the general public, with the headline summarizing—by way of cinematic transition—what had happened in the previous scene: "DIPLOMAT SLAIN AT UN" and a picture of Thornhill, looking comically confused, holding the dagger in his hand.[33] This group of Cold Warriors, architects of the metanarrative, is led by a character referred to only as "The Professor" (Carroll), marking him as a kind of personification of the superego or purely analytical function. They meet around a table like a group of writers at a story conference during production to discuss what the appearance of this Thornhill character, a free radical loose in their plot, means to their narrative: "Does anyone know this Thornhill?" The answer, of course, is no; he is no creation of theirs, but he is instead a variable that has infiltrated their narrative, a floating signifier loose in the semiotic system of their plot; an actor in search of a role, a character in search of an author. One of them asks, "How'd he get mistaken for George Kaplan when George Kaplan doesn't even exist?" Hitchcock is playing with multiple layers of self-reflexive irony here: how does Archibald Leach get mistaken for Cary Grant? How does Cary Grant get mistaken for Roger Thornhill? The power of the auteur—or of the Professor—lies in his ability to "will a suspension of disbelief" in the audience, as Samuel Taylor Coleridge famously put it[34]; it lies precisely in the ability to create misprisions in the mind of an audience.

Language works by one thing (signifier) getting willfully mistaken for another (signified); conventional narrative cinema works by one thing (the face of the star) getting willfully mistaken for another (a character). Hitchcock emphasizes this irony in what is perhaps his most self-reflexive film, because it points to the power of fiction, or of the ideal, to determine reality, to underwrite the ordinary, when the reverse is generally taken for granted. It also provides a commentary on the relationship between art and commerce. A better question for these latter-day gods might be: why wouldn't George Kaplan exist? After all, we created him. In what seems prophetic of the looming Vietnam War, Hitchcock emphasizes in this scene the dehumanizing distance between these Cold Warriors and the violent realities of the battlefield (a point that Kubrick would pick up on and run with in his depiction of *Dr.*

Strangelove's War Room). This critical and emotional distance allows them to view human beings as nothing more than characters, signifiers, or pawns, depending upon which analogy one prefers. When one of these bureaucrats glibly points out that the only real casualty that has occurred so far is that the real Townsend has been killed, one of the men at the table shrugs it off as the inevitable "collateral damage" of any war, hot or cold: "C'est la Guerre," he states as casually as one might state, *c'est la vie*. A colleague sitting next to him in this two-shot replies, "It's so horribly sad, how is it I feel like laughing?" This line sums up the tragicomedy of Hitchcock's satire and the tone of this film in its combination of guilt with the illicit pleasure that Jonathan Greenberg calls "the double movement of satire."[35] Who doesn't love a good spy story as long as the characters getting killed are not too real or too killed?[36]

"What do we do?" asks the only woman at the table, Mrs. Finlay (Madge Kennedy), to which the Professor replies, sounding a bit like a Beckett character, "We do nothing." Like the deist idea of God-as-watchmaker, setting His creation in motion and then stepping aside, the Professor advocates letting the plot they have wound up run its course and resolve its own inconsistencies, never mind the fact that an innocent man might die (he even goes so far as to call it "good fortune" that their fictional decoy has become a live decoy, that fiction has miraculously become reality). He rationalizes this decision by arguing that their real agent, the one for whom George Kaplan was created as a red herring to divert attention from, might be exposed and compromised and even killed if they intervene (later in the film, Thornhill will protest directly to the Professor: "I'm an advertising man, not a red herring!", a winking one-liner that belongs alongside the famous "Gentlemen, you can't fight in here, this is the War Room!" in *Dr. Strangelove*, for its ironic punch). Again, Mrs. Finlay challenges the strategy of "doing nothing" by asking a question: "How long do you think he'll stay alive?" To which the Professor replies: "Well, that's his problem." Hitchcock suggests that the authors of historical destiny are concerned with the big picture, the metanarrative of history, not with the fates of individuals. As the author of this particular narrative, the Professor seemingly cares more about his fictional creation than the thorn-in-his-side, Thornhill:

> We didn't invent our non-existent man and give him the name of George Kaplan, establish elaborate behavior patterns for him, move his prop belongings in and out of hotel rooms for our own private amusement. We created George Kaplan and labored successfully to convince Vandamm that this was our own agent hot on his trail for a desperately important reason… If we make the slightest move to suggest that there is no such agent as George Kaplan, give any hint to Vandamm that he's pursuing a decoy instead of our own agent, then our agent working right under Vandamm's very nose will immediately face suspicion, exposure and assassination, like the two others who went before.

In other words, they created George Kaplan for an audience in order to manipulate its emotions and distract from the reality right under its nose, like an ad-man might create an image to sell a product, or like an expatriate Englishman might create a persona, or like an auteur director might create a MacGuffin for his own "desperately important reason." Hitchcock ends this scene with another high-angle long shot of these five unassuming figures sitting at their conference table, determining the fate of an individual who is not even aware of their existence, implying, perhaps, that there is a power even higher than them, determining their actions. Mrs. Finlay says, "Goodbye Mr. Thornhill, wherever you are…"

Thornhill's status as a floating signifier signifying nothing, thus potentially signifying anything, which troubles the metanarrative of the Cold Warriors back in Washington, is most directly alluded to in Ernest Lehmann's dialogue between Thornhill and Eve Kendall (Eva Marie Saint) on the Twentieth Century Limited bound for Chicago. This scene develops Hitchcock's satiric themes through the double-entendres revealing an immediate duplicity in their discourse between the revealed and concealed, the known and unknown, a duplicity that determines the inevitable romantic attraction between the film's two leads, the former undercutting the latter.[37] Upon being seated at her table in the dining car, after she has inexplicably helped him escape capture by the police, Thornhill asks if Eve would recommend anything. She recommends, "The brook trout. A little trouty, but quite good." Perhaps a self-referential nod to Thornhill's status as red herring, and the fact that this whole story is a bit fishy, but still satisfying, her remark pleases the ad-man, who knows a good slogan when he hears one, and he replies: "Sold."

After the waiter takes his order, and alluding again to the comparative self-reflexivity of Thornhill's diegetic notoriety and Grant's extradiegetic status as star, Thornhill notices Eve staring at him intently: "I know. I look vaguely familiar." "Yes," she says. "You feel you've seen me somewhere before." She nods and murmurs assent, to which Thornhill-Grant delivers the punchline: "Funny how I have that effect on people. It's something about my face." That paradoxical "something" about faces is a prominent theme in Hitchcock's Cold War satire; faces can simultaneously reveal and conceal their significance. The movie star stands out from the crowd by design and he is supposed to have a face that is attractive even when writ large on the big screen; the mandate for Americans in the wake of McCarthyism was to blend in, to conform. Grant's image appeals to the fantasy of being recognized without the threat of being singled out for scrutiny and judgment. The star is exceptional in his appearance, but he is nothing more than image; the spy is exceptional in his ability to manipulate his appearance, which is a container for the information he carries. With apologies to Marshall McLuhan, the star is the message in Hitchcock's satire of image-obsessed American culture in the Golden Age of television.

The innuendo and double-entendres of the dialogue, although perhaps practically necessary to elide the censors in one of Hitchcock's favorite games, also provide a commentary on the duplicity of Cold War discourse as it manages what information is revealed and what is concealed, maintaining a separation between official and unofficial or secret narratives. After giving Thornhill her name, age, and marital status—like a prisoner of war listing the identifying statistics of name, rank, and serial number—Eve lies: "Now you know everything."[38] Thornhill tries to assume an alias, but Eve immediately sees right through it, "You're Roger Thornhill of Madison Avenue, and you're wanted for murder on every front page in America. Don't be so modest," she says. There's always a fine line between fame and infamy in Hitchcock's films, a claim that also applies to the world of espionage. After reassuring him that she has no intentions of turning him in because of his "nice face" (who would throw Cary Grant back into the sea?), and because it is going to be "a long night" and she doesn't "particularly like the book [she's] started"—a subtle jab on Hitchcock's part at those who privilege literature over the nice faces of film—Eve implies that Thornhill should stay in her room with her. "Do you know what I mean?" she asks, as much to the audience as to Thornhill, telegraphing the double meanings of the dialogue. "Yes, I know exactly what you mean," he answers, but does he? Do we? Later, when they are both in Eve's room, Thornhill points out that there is only one bed and says, suggestively, "it's a good omen, don't you think?" They continue kissing and fate—raised by the use of the word "omen"—seems to be leading them to this bed, but, when Thornhill asks her, "You know what that means?" Eve interprets the signs for him: "It means you're going to sleep on the floor," leaving no doubt who is in control of the diegesis in this romance.[39]

The duplicitous dialogue between Thornhill and Eve on the Twentieth Century Limited is a kind of linguistic dance, each party testing what the other knows. In the dining car scene, she pulls out a cigarette and he produces a matchbook with a logo spelling out his initials: R.O.T. "That's my trademark: Rot," he says. "Roger O. Thornhill," she replies, "What does the O stand for?" "Nothing," he says with a shrug.[40] Stanley Cavell writes, "In a Hitchcockian context this means both that this man knows that the advertising game (and the modern city generally that it epitomizes) makes up words that are rot but also that it would be rot to think this is all he means" (252). Read as an allegorical figure in a satirical reading of this film, he is the rot at the heart of an image-obsessed American culture that the bland façade of 1950s conformity carefully concealed. Does this suggest that *North by Northwest*, in spite of its allusion to *Hamlet*, is really more *Macbeth*? A Cold War "tale / Told by an idiot, full of sound and fury / Signifying nothing" (Shakespeare 5.5.26-28)?

This also makes Thornhill the personification of a MacGuffin. "My best MacGuffin," Hitchcock told Truffaut, "and by that I mean the emptiest, the most non-existent, and the most absurd is the one we used in *North by Northwest*...the MacGuffin has boiled down to its purest expression: nothing at all" (99). In fact, there is another MacGuffin, a pre-Columbian statue which, we eventually find out, is full of microfilm, and George M. Wilson believes this film in the statue is the "emptiest" McGuffin Hitchcock refers to in his conversations with Truffaut: "The crucial object at the heart of all this movie's hallucinatory action, the goal that locks the opposing forces in loony Cold War conflict, is no more and no less than a piece of the stuff that movies are made of" (1171). the microfilm functions as a metonym for the film we are watching, and this interpretation certainly makes sense as the ultimate self-reflexive moment into which all of the others dissolve, the revelation that, no matter how many layers you peel back, there is nothing there. This is an interpretation that recalls Karl Marx in spirit if not in tone from *The Communist Manifesto*: "All that is solid melts into air, all that is holy is profaned, and man is at last compelled to face with sober senses his real conditions of life, and his relations with his kind" (10). Except that there are two McGuffins in this film, and Hitchcock may have been referring to Roger "Nothing" Thornhill in the above quote. Ultimately, how one interprets Thornhill—whatever significance we project onto this empty signifier—will determine what significance one finds in this Cold War satire.

    Later, after they have moved to her compartment and are beginning to make love, Eve says, "I ought to know more about you." "Well, what more could you know?" asks Thornhill. "You're an advertising man, that's all I know." "That's right," says Thornhill. Unlike when Eve claims that we "know everything" while holding crucial information back, the identification of Thornhill as an advertising man really is all you need to know about him and in fact all there is to him as he is defined by his job; what you see is what you get, image is reality in post-war America. If the microfilm is a metonym for *North by Northwest*, then Cary Grant as Thornhill is a satiric metonym for mid-century America. As "nothing," Thornhill obviously can signify anything; he has turned his status as empty signifier into an advantage. "You're very clever with words," Eve tells him. "You can probably make them do anything for you. Sell people things they don't need, make women who don't know you fall in love with you..." "I'm beginning to think I'm underpaid," he responds.

    When a porter arrives to clean Eve's room, interrupting their lovemaking, Thornhill hides in the washroom where Hitchcock takes the opportunity to develop the ironically comic juxtaposition of large and small that is a hallmark of much literary satire (think Gulliver amongst the Lilliputians in Swift's satire of his age). Checking his appearance in the mirror (his face is, of course, the location of his identity and his most valuable commodity), Thornhill notices an absurdly tiny shaving brush and an absurdly tiny razor. Hitchcock pays off this bit of comic business at the end of the sequence when Thornhill escapes the train—with Eve's help—disguised as a redcap porter. When the man he stole the clothes from informs the detectives waiting on the platform that their man is disguised as a redcap, they begin rushing through the crowd looking into the face of every redcap they see; another example of how Hitchcock's film functions as a commentary on the double-bind of Cold War conformity in the 1950s: homogeneity is the desired cultural status quo, but if everyone looks the same, then how does one identify the enemy? How does one distinguish the individual from the masses?[41]

Having evaded detection, Hitchcock cuts to Thornhill standing at another mirror in the men's room of the train station with shaving cream covering his lower face, disguising his appearance to the detectives that pass in the background. This is followed by a brief dialogue-less sequence in which a fat man shaving at the sink next to Thornhill notices the absurdly tiny razor and, in a sequence that practically functions as an homage to the silent comedies of Chaplin or early Laurel and Hardy (and Hitchcock's own roots in the era), "The man looks down at the razor and his face takes on a baffled expression. He and Roger resume shaving. Roger cuts a narrow path down the middle of his upper lip and stands back to survey the results. He looks a bit like Hitler or Chaplin," Naremore notes, connecting the visual incongruity (iconic face of Cary Grant on the big screen with the tiniest of razors) with an implied ideological incongruity—tragicomedy—in his transcription of the continuity script. The coincidence of Hitler's tragic mustache looking the same as Chaplin's comic one, an incongruity that Chaplin himself exploited in *The Great Dictator* (1940), underscores the fine line between comedy and tragedy and the persistence of fascism haunting the shadows of the Cold War (a persistence that Kubrick and Peter Sellers also explore in the character of Dr. Strangelove himself).

The juxtaposition of large with small has already, of course, been established through visual cues such as the extremely high camera angles that make Thornhill look like an ant. This signals Hitchcock's intention to use such extreme juxtaposition to comment on the relationship between the individual and Althusserian ISAs or, even more generally, the larger forces of historical or narrative superstructures guiding our destinies. This is nowhere more apparent than in the juxtapositions of Thornhill's face with the impossibly large, iconic faces on Mount

Rushmore. The first time we see the monument, Hitchcock dissolves from a close up of Thornhill to the faces on Rushmore, which briefly superimposes his face over the monument. Thornhill of the skyscrapers, the advertising man and avatar for consumer capitalism, the straw man under attack in an open barren field, the matinee idol double-crossed by a femme fatale, the floating signifier swept up into the alphabet soup of Cold War intrigue, must become an American hero to rescue the damsel in distress.[42] The individual is hailed, plucked from the masses; the hero is called upon to be part of something larger than himself: "I don't like the way Teddy Roosevelt is looking at me," Thornhill says after looking through a tourist telescope while the Professor sits nearby, retorting: "Perhaps he's trying to give you one last word of caution, Mr. Kaplan: Speak soft and carry a big stick." Roosevelt represents the opposite of what Thornhill has been up to this point; Teddy, the rough rider and icon of American rugged masculinity, was a man of action, whereas Thornhill, the advertising executive and icon of an unresolved Oedipal complex, is a man of words, but he will have to cross that line to achieve apotheosis. The implication here is that Grant, who has become Thornhill in all of his manifestations, will have to become what Roosevelt symbolizes: the hero that America, and Hitchcock's film, needs. What, however, might this signify in a reading of the film as a satire of the Cold War?

Going back to Molière, Voltaire, Swift, and Pope, modern satire usually advocates for mediation and moderation by exaggerating extreme positions and demonstrating the ruthless absurdity of their absolutism, thus serving as a caution against the dangers of binary and hierarchical thinking. As I have suggested here, Hitchcock achieves this in *North by Northwest* through doubling, scale, and ironic juxtaposition. The doubling of identities both diegetically—Thornhill/Kaplan—and extra-diegetically—Thornhill/Grant—creates two levels of commentary, cinematic and metacinematic. Thornhill/Kaplan/Grant is also juxtaposed with Townsend/Vandamm/Mason, which exposes their similarities more than their differences, not to mention all of the metadramatic jokes in their exchanges that foreground the concept of identity as symptom of performance. Hitchcock extends the doubling through the narrative repetition of similar sequences. So, for example, Eve's staged assassination of Thornhill in the cafeteria at the base of Rushmore reflects and comments upon the "real" assassination of the "real" Townsend when Thornhill has him paged at the UN.[43] The scene in the Townsend house at the beginning of the film is reflected in the scene in the Frank Lloyd Wright styled house near Rushmore (a juxtaposition that, itself, suggests tensions in modern America) at the end. If Vandamm and his collaborators were the interlopers in Townsend's traditional estate, then, at the end, it is Thornhill who infiltrates Vandamm's modern house—a vision of a potential future America—to rescue Eve, who has become a rather conventional damsel in distress by the film's climax. Whereas the Townsend estate represents old money and old institutions of power centralized in the American northeast, a more conventional pre-World War II America, the Wright-design house, and its South Dakota location, represents more futurist and modern ideals like harmony with the environment through organic design and a more expansive, if not necessarily more democratic, north by northwestern dissemination of power.

Hitchcock also forces comparison between symbolic geographies, signifying different ideas of America in the 1950s: Manhattan is contrasted with the empty fields of the crop duster sequence, as discussed earlier, and both of these geographies contrast with Mount Rushmore as a monument to the past and to America as an idea. It is fitting that everything builds to the climactic scene of Vandamm's henchmen chasing Thornhill and Eve, in pursuit of the statue filled with microfilm, across the faces of these four giants, providing the most striking juxtaposition of large and small, of history and the individual, in the film. Nadel notes the central importance of scale in Hitchcock's scheme here: "If the shot from the top of the UN makes Thornhill look microscopic, the shots on Mount Rushmore make the national icons look grotesque, suggesting that in this second struggle the significance of the two key objects has been radically redefined by a world of pervasive duality: the two Kaplans, the two Townsends, and the double agent, Eve" (175). The demands of the plot demand that the "pervasive duality" be resolved. Thornhill, no longer an empty signifier scrambling across a waste land, an empty flat field, threatened by an anonymous death from above, Thornhill is now Cary Grant, star of the silver screen and hero of this movie, scrambling across the monumental symbol of what he is called upon to protect and defend, interpellated into an ideological subject to serve the American way of life as personified on a personal level by Eve, the double agent who is, discouragingly, no longer the femme fatale, but the conventional damsel in distress and the future Mrs. Thornhill (he proposes while they dangle from the monument!) appropriate to the marriage plot of traditional comedy.[44] Vandamm's henchmen pursue, and Thornhill throws one of them to his death and, as Eve slips and he rushes to grab her by the hand, he calls upon the nearby Leonard to help them. Leonard picks up the statue and begins to step on Thornhill's fingers, but suddenly he is shot by the Professor's men—the cavalry has come to the rescue in this postmodern Western, or *deus ex machina* if one prefers the reading of the Professor and his men as the Olympian gods authoring the destiny of our heroes.

"That wasn't very sporting," says Vandamm who is now in their custody, "using real bullets."[45] Games and play reflect and influence reality and work, art reflects and influences life, and cold wars become hot.[46] Through these ironic and comic juxtapositions, Hitchcock explores bigger thematic binaries: action and words; sanity and madness; and, especially, the individual and history. Now safe, Thornhill pulls Eve up and, in a match cut that relocates them on the Twentieth Century Limited almost as if the episodes between the two scenes on the train were just part of a crazy dream, Hitchcock completes the traditional marriage plot of comedy in a speedy dénouement, by having Thornhill pull Eve up onto their nuptial bunk, the redeemed first couple of the American paradise regained, an Adam and Eve for a modern America. "Oh, Roger, this is silly!" Eve says as though commenting on behalf of the audience. "I know," Roger says, "but I'm *sentimental.*" Are we to take Hitchcock at his word here? That the warmth of sentiment is necessary to thaw the modernist mind of winter described by Stevens? Could Hitchcock be suggesting something as trite as love being the source of a genuine identity, or authentic signification, and that being concerned with tending our own gardens, as another satirist, Voltaire, suggested at the end of *Candide*, is what we should concern ourselves with and not with forces that are above and beyond our control? This is certainly more hopeful than the dark ending of Kubrick's *Strangelove* a few years later, when hope became harder to come by as the stakes of the Cold War escalated.

Alternately, however, the self-reflexivity of Hitchcock's film calls attention to the trite artificiality of such an ending, seeming to suggest, more cynically, that we are at the mercy of forces beyond our control, forces that do not have our best interests in mind because from their perspective we are pawns on a chessboard or data points on a graph, forces both historical and biological that determine our destiny for us. This ambivalence should come as no surprise to those familiar with Hitchcock's films. "[T]he satirist," Greenberg writes, "experiences the classic ambivalence between enjoying an illicit desire and experiencing guilt over that enjoyment" (6). The last shot of the train going into a tunnel—a shot that Hitchcock himself identified as a phallic symbol—seems to undercut any absolutely sincere reading of Thornhill's last line. Let's also not forget that Thornhill is an ad-man, a creation of Madison Avenue, and exploiter of sentiment on the altar of expedient exaggerations. Hitchcock might be suggesting that the Cold War is a zero-sum game, and that's ultimately what the O stands for.

Notes

I would like to thank Charles Bradshaw and Mattie Davenport for reading over earlier drafts of this article and providing me with invaluable feedback and criticism.

1. Hitchcock himself downplayed the "seriousness" of this film when compared to its immediate predecessor, *Vertigo* (1958): "*Vertigo* and *North by Northwest* don't have much in common and weren't produced in the same spirit....*North by Northwest* is an adventure film, treated with a certain levity of spirit. *Vertigo* is much more important to me than *North by Northwest*, which is nevertheless a very entertaining film" (qtd. in Domarchi and Douchet 177).

2. The first of what Naremore calls the "four essential features of...the modernist or 'artful' suspense story" is "Skepticism toward established legal and political institutions" ("Spies" 9). The same claim is generally made as a defining claim of postmodernism (e.g., Jean-François Lyotard's identification of its defining characteristic as a distrust of all "grand narratives").

3. Frye identifies Comedy with spring, Romance with summer and Tragedy with autumn. For his discussion of Irony and Satire as the Mythos of Winter, see pp. 223-239 in *Anatomy of Criticism*.

4. Stanley Kubrick would up the ante on this question just five years later with his dark satire of Cold War angst and futility, *Dr. Strangelove; or How I Learned to Stop Worrying and Love the Bomb* (1964).

5. This is also the point on which the satire of Kubrick's *Dr. Strangelove* turns.

6. For an analysis of the dialectical tension that Hitchcock perfects in his mature style through the alternation of dialogue-heavy scenes with sequences of "pure cinema" in *Vertigo, Psycho*, and *The Birds*, see my article "The Difference Between Crows and Blackbirds: Alfred Hitchcock and the Treason of Images" in *PostScript: Essays in Film and Humanities* 34:2/3 (2015), 53-70. Ironic juxtapositions and contrapuntal structure are hallmarks of Hitchcock's late style. He does it to produce horror in the three films above, but the same methods produce comedy and evoke the absurd in *North by Northwest*. Comedy cut by anxiety and the absurd might describe the general feeling about the Cold War in 1959.

7. Leitch genders the color symbolism, arguing that these cool colors "are associated with male figures" and "are the colors of masculine and institutional authority, represented by the world of Madison Avenue shown briefly at the opening of the film and the twin bureaucracies of government and criminals" (208-09). He points out that, in contrast, "[t]he film's maternal figures are all associated with red, rust, and earth tones" (208).

8. Christopher D. Morris notes that "[t]he abstract grid also illustrates spacing, or écart, one of the many metaphors Derrida uses for the constitutions of language in self-division as a condition of legibility. This grid precedes the introduction of any semantic content (here, Mies van der Rohe's Seagram Building); finally, the human, or the crowds of New York City, is constituted only as a reflection on the grid and thereby subordinated to its spacing" (45-46). He suggests that discourse orders reality and gives it meaning, but that meaning is self-divided, dual, which can only be discovered through the deconstruction of binaries; for example, beginning with this opening scene, "the deconstruction of the public/private distinction" (48).

9. This movement from high to low, from big picture to little detail, is a favorite structural device of Hitchcock's as part of his general contrapuntal style. For example, the long, overhead crane-shot that moves from high-angle, extreme long shot to extreme close up of a key in Ingrid Bergman's hand in *Notorious* (1946), or the long tracking shot in *Young and Innocent* (1937) that moves through a crowd up to the band playing in blackface, terminating in an extreme close up of the drummer's twitching face.

10. As George M. Wilson puts it, "In *North by Northwest* we quickly learn that even the legions of the nondescript are pockmarked with secret agents, assassins, and deceptive blondes" (1164).

11. Naremore does an excellent job of succinctly articulating "Hitchcock's technique...[which] depends upon a careful manipulation of two formal extremes: the

purely subjective shot/reverse shot, focalized through a character; and the purely objective shot, often positioned from a 'bird's-eye vantage, looking down on a scene. Again and again, his films veer back and forth between an uncanny private perspective and a schematic, godlike omniscience" ("Spies" 13).

12. Eliot's poem "The Hollow Men" (1925) refers to the men who have come of age between the world wars as "hollow men," as "stuffed men / Leaning together / Headpiece[s] filled with straw" (ll.2-4). These straw men reflect an age that, from Eliot's point of view, lacked the faith and conviction of earlier ages. The modern age, for Eliot, was marked by a moral-less malaise, and hollow men are a kind of living dead, denizens of a modern world that seemed to lack definition, coherence, and moral direction: "Shape without form / shade without colour, / Paralysed force, gesture without motion" (11-12). Roger O. Thornhill, or R.O.T., the empty signifier floating across the American landscape fits the mold as a latter-day variation of Eliot's hollow man.

13. In addition to Eliot's wasteland imagery from poems like *The Waste Land* (1922) and "The Hollow Men," I am also reminded of Robert Browning's description of the "gray plain all round: / Nothing but plain to the horizon's bound" in *Childe Roland to the Dark Tower Came* (lines 52-53). The visual correspondence with these literary intertexts serves to underscore a reading of Grant as a modern, existential variation on hero and quest archetypes.

14. Beckett's play premiered in France on January 5, 1953, and had its American premiere three years later in 1956, three years before the release of *North by Northwest*.

15. The title itself, with its possible allusion to *Hamlet*, encourages such interpretations. In his excellent deconstructive analysis of the film, Morris notes, "As a statement of 'mere direction,' the title thus implies the possibility of slippage of meaning, referentiality without content, signifier without signified. It suggests a parallel between compass points and language: both may generate the illusion of precise denotation within arbitrary and self-referential systems" (44).

16. Keats defined "negative capability" as "when man is capable of being in uncertainties, Mysteries, doubts, without any irritable reaching after fact & reason...with a great poet the sense of Beauty overcomes every other consideration, or rather obliterates all consideration" (43).

17. J. Hillis Miller articulates the irony upon which this conception of being-in-the-world turns: "being is a pervasive power, visible nowhere in itself and yet present and visible in all things. It is what things share through the fact that they are. Being is not a thing like other things and therefore can only appear to man as nothing, but it is what all things must participate in if they are to exist at all" (qtd. in Bloom 62).

What the O Stands For

18. *Mad Men* ran on AMC from 2007-2015. It followed the exploits of advertising executives on Madison Avenue in the 1960s exploring some of the same thematic ground as Hitchcock does through Thornhill, such as the formation of identity between being and performance, a negotiation of the past with the future. Don Draper (Jon Hamm) is a man who has constructed a new life for himself by appropriating the identity of another, dead, man. One of Draper's favorite aphorisms, not unlike Thornhill's "expedient exaggerations," is, "If you don't like what they're saying, change the conversation."

19. Immediately following this line, Roger asks his secretary if he looks "heavy-ish" to her, then tells her to "put a note on my desk in the morning: think thin." Like Stevens's Snow Man, Roger believes that one must first imagine or "think" a state of being before achieving it: "one must have a mind of winter." In other words, imagination precedes existence.

20. As Naremore puts it, "Hitchcock and Lehman poked fun at the CIA, subtly linking its activities to the 'expedient exaggerations' and image-making techniques of Madison Avenue" ("Spies" 11).

21. Harold Bloom refers to Stevens's perspective in "The Snow Man" as "[p]rotectively impersonal, as though holding oneself at arm's length, one appeals to the ethos of Fate, to the necessity of having a mind of winter" (60).

22. Althusser uses the term *Ideological State Apparatuses* to distinguish institutions that subjugate primarily through ideology from *State Apparatuses* (SA) that subjugate primarily through direct, violent suppression: "the Repressive State Apparatus functions 'by violence,' whereas the Ideological State Apparatuses function 'by ideology'" (142-43).

23. Indeed, this is the primary theme of most of Hitchcock's films in the 1950s, especially, *The Trouble with Harry, The Wrong Man,* and the two films immediately before and after *North by Northwest*: *Vertigo* and *Psycho*.

24. Hitchcock was famously opposed to the vogue of method acting in the 1950s and '60s. Originated by Stanislavky and brought to America by Lee Strasberg in the 1930s and '40s, it achieved mainstream, institutional status with the prominence and influence of the Actors Studio in the 1950s. The method entailed emptying out—or at least sublimating—all aspects of one's own personality in order to fill it with the psychological reality of the character one was playing; it is the Snow Man approach to acting methods.

25. The name Thornhill itself is suggestive in the context of the film's plot: Thornhill becomes a thorn in the side of these, presumably, communist conspirators. By the film's end he will have made a mountain (Mount Rushmore) out of a molehill by

thwarting their plot to escape the country with state secrets on microfilm hidden in a figurine. Comic and ironic juxtapositions of large and small, visually and linguistically, are a significant part of Hitchcock's pattern here.

26. "Everyone likes the idea of Cary Grant," Kael writes. "Everyone thinks of him affectionately, because he embodies what seems a happier time—a time when we had a simpler relationship to a performer" (645). On the fictional status of "Cary Grant," "Once told by an interviewer, 'Everybody would like to be Cary Grant,' Grant is said to have replied, 'So would I'" (O'Connor).

27. Naremore goes so far as to argue that "Grant 'coauthored' *North by Northwest*." As he puts it, "Our constant awareness of his stardom is enhanced by Hitchcock's lifelong interest in the paradoxes of theatricality and identity, and by Lehman's story of a person who is created out of nothing" ("Spies" 5).

28. Notably, Hitchcock provides this information to the audience, but not to Thornhill. This kind of dramatic irony as an element to build or accentuate suspense is a favorite device of Hitchcock's. For just one significant example, see his previous film, *Vertigo*, in which he informs the audience of Judy Barton's guilt and complicity in covering up the murder of the real Madeleine Elster well before Scottie Ferguson figures it out for himself.

29. See Nadel, pp. 66-67 for just one example.

30. Michael Griffiths corroborates the position of authority of this agency and its similarities in tactics and strategy to the world of advertising, blurring the boundaries between business and government: "Thornhill's role in the spying and counter-spying of the film is controlled and manipulated by the surveillance of the Professor's own agency (in both senses), which further implicates the application of marketing expertise in governmental tactics."

31. As Leitch observes, "Thornhill's middle initial, which stands for nothing, might just as well stand for Oedipus" (210). Not only is Thornhill a deconstruction of the Hollywood star, the Cold War spy, and Hitchcock's own trope of the Wrong Man, he is also a deconstruction of the archetypal hero going back to the Greeks.

32. Griffiths elaborates on the relationship between the professions of espionage and advertising: "the schizophrenic language of advertising agencies brings this 'middle or high level manager' to the attention of an American Cold War spy agency that would exploit and transform his expertise to intervene in the political export of commodified 'secrets.'"

33. Another headline next to the image of Thornhill holding the knife that killed Townsend reads, "Nixon Promises West Will Remain in Berlin."

34. From Chapter 14 of his *Biographia Literaria*: "my endeavours [in *Lyrical Ballads*] should be directed to persons and characters supernatural, or at least romantic; yet so as to transfer from our inward nature a human interest and a semblance of truth sufficient to procure for these shadows of imagination that willing suspension of disbelief for the moment, which constitutes poetic faith" (492).

35. Writing on satire in the context of literary modernism, which he describes as "very nearly the same thing," Jonathan Greenberg identifies what he calls "the double movement of satire: on the one hand, the satirist speaks for a community, exaggerating, and ridiculing his target in order to urge reform; on the other, he is a renegade who enjoys the subversion of traditional values, delights in his own aesthetic powers, even savors the cruelty he inflicts" (7, 9). Citing Freud, Greenberg describes how such "contradictory impulses work in concert: the moral pretenses of satire do not simply contradict but in fact make possible its aggressive sources of pleasure. In satire, moral outrage and sadistic pleasure have the same stimulus" (5). Naremore makes similar points specific to *North by Northwest*, reading the film intertextually through "espionage fiction"—"a type of entertainment that sometimes lives a double life, supporting patriotic agendas even while it explores a Kafkaesque borderland between the individual subject and the authoritarian state"—to the nexus of late modernism and satire to an understanding of Hitchcock's film, which is "a highly self-conscious example of such narrative duplicity, poised neatly between a heroic adventure story and a nightmarish scenario in which personal identity and the sense of 'knowable community' are threatened with dissolution" ("Spies" 7).

36. Winking at fiction's ability to skirt the either/or, all-or-nothing, logic of life and death, Thornhill later tells the Professor: "I've got a job, a secretary, a mother, two ex-wives and several bartenders that depend upon me, and I don't intend to disappoint them all by getting myself *slightly* killed."

37. The struggle of an individual against the inexorable nature of fate (in this case the socio-political forces waging the Cold War) is one of the film's major themes. The train itself becomes a metaphor greater than the phallic joke Hitchcock makes with the film's final image. Always bound to follow the predetermined lines laid out by the tracks, it represents the extent to which fate and the pressure of external forces determine our actions and decisions. The narrative inevitability of Grant and Saint coming together and instantly being attracted to each other—two accidental spies—is another layer of this theme of fate versus will.

38. If James Stewart, an American everyman, plays a man who knows too much in Hitchcock's remake of his own film, then Cary Grant, an American ideal, is the man who knows too little!

39. Eve herself is a mystery at this point and draws power from her ambiguity as a signifier, as John Orr notes: "The train scenes actually define Kendall/Saint for us more clearly when we know not who she is, than do the final scenes where she reveals herself as working for CIA boss Leo G. Carroll....To find out who she 'really' is, is to limit the openness of possibility. For she is what she has become to us, watching her as the action unfolds" (36). This reinforces the idea that emptiness is a source of power here; if one's meaning is not predetermined, then one's potential remains unlimited.

40. Cavell also notes the multiple significations of the O: "The 'nothing' or naught, in the ROT monogram equally appropriately stands for origin, so its simultaneous meaning is that the actor is the origin of the character and also the origin of what becomes of himself or herself on film. The further thought the human self as such is both an origin and a nothing is a bit of Cartesianism that is conceivably not called for in the context of this film" (252).

41. There is much commentary on the reinscribing of heteronormative values in *North by Northwest*, usually focusing on the implications of some kind of homosexual relationship between Vandamm and Leonard, grouping communists generally with other social "undesirables." Robert J. Corber's excellent essay, "'You wanna check my thumbprints?': *Vertigo*, the Trope of Invisibility and Cold War Nationalism," reads this lingering McCarthyism as a subtext of *Vertigo*. Corber describes how the emphasis on conformity and the fear "the invisible subversive" guaranteed a perpetual state of fear and paranoia by grouping communists and homosexuals together in the general category of unAmerican, causing "many Americans ... to believe that they could trust no one, not even members of their own families" (302).

42. When Thornhill again meets up with Eve, Vandamm, and his henchmen in the auction scene, Vandamm says to him, "Seems to me you fellows could stand a little less training from the FBI and little more from the Actors Studio." Thornhill quips that "the only performance that will satisfy you is when I am dead." "Your very next role," Vandamm promises. "You'll be quite convincing, I assure you." Thornhill's witty reply to this line is telling: "I wonder what subtle form of manslaughter is next on the program? Am I to be dropped into a vat of molten steel and become part of a new skyscraper? Or are you going to ask this female to kiss me again and poison me to death?" The first option makes clear Thornhill's equivalence to the building façade of the opening credit sequence as a personification of what Manhattan represents. The second option makes clear Thornhill's equivalence to Grant, the star who acts as surrogate for the viewing audience and the threat of the female to the star as femme fatale. That threat—Eve as femme fatale—will become partner and lover, however, in one of Hitchcock's many ironic reversals.

43. I put real in scare quotes here because, although they are real within the diegesis, the real Townsend is, of course, not really Townsend, but played by an actor (Philip Ober) who does not really die. Unraveling the multiple layers that Hitchcock has woven together here can almost drive one mad or "tease us out of thought," as Keats put it on contemplating a Grecian urn.

44. Hitchcock conflates the narrative with the metanarrative, the big with the small, history with the individual, through the merging of dual romance plots, as Nadel notes:

> In terms of national issues...intimacy is symbolic and romance is metonymic. Love of country is, by definition, only possible as a member of an impersonal mass, while love of an individual requires making that individual distinct from and larger than the general populace. Politics and (hot or cold) warfare subordinate the individual to the greater good, the 'big picture,' while romance turns the big picture into a backdrop for the expediently exaggerated desires of a few privileged individuals. The romantic couple represents metonymically all the true lovers in the population, while the nation represents symbolically a love greater than individual desires. (173-74)

45. The development of the business with Eve's gun is pure Hitchcock and it becomes another metaphor for an empty signifier, first spied in Eve's purse by Thornhill when he believes that she is working for Vandamm, and then functioning as a red herring for both Vandamm and the audience when she "shoots" Thornhill. Then later, at the Wright house, Leonard demonstrates to Vandamm that Eve is actually a double-agent by demonstrating that her gun, which she used to "kill" Kaplan/Thornhill, fire blanks: "It's an old Gestapo trick," he says in perhaps another allusion to the lingering Nazi shadow over the Cold War, "Shoot one of your own people to show that you're not one of them." Finally, Vandamm's housekeeper holds Thornhill at gun point in an attempt to allow Vandamm to escape with Eve and the statue, but it is, once again, Eve's prop gun. The comic reoccurrence of this gun and the way that Hitchcock and Lehman use it to thwart audience expectations every time makes the shock of Leonard "really" being shot all the more significant.

46. The scene at the auction, where Vandamm bids on the statue with the microfilm and Thornhill catches up with his enemies (which includes Eve at this point) has a lot to say about the relationship between art and life, but it is beyond the scope of this essay. See Nadel's discussion of this scene (172-77) or Michael Griffiths's excellent essay "Production Values: Fordism and Formalism in *North by Northwest*."

Works Cited

Allen, Richard and S. Ishii-Gonzalès, editors. *Alfred Hitchcock: Centenary Essays*. BFI Publishing, 2000.

Althusser, Louis. *Lenin and Philosophy and Other Essays*. Translated by Ben Brewster, Monthly Review P, 1971.

Bloom, Harold. *Wallace Stevens: The Poems of Our Climate*. Cornell UP, 1977.

Cavell, Stanley. "North by Northwest." *A Hitchcock Reader,* edited by Marshall Deutelbaum and Leland Poague, 2nd edition, Blackwell, 2009, pp. 250-63.

Coleridge, Samuel Taylor. "From Biographia Literaria." *Norton Anthology of English Literature*, Vol. D, 9th edition, edited by Stephen Greenblatt, et. al., Norton, 2012), pp. 488-99.

Corber, Robert J. "'You wanna check my thumbprints?': *Vertigo*, the Trope of Invisibility and Cold War Nationalism." Allen and Ishii-Gonzalès, pp. 307-16.

Domarchi, Jean and Jean Douchet. "An Interview with Alfred Hitchcock." Naremore, pp. 177-85.

Eliot, T. S. "The Hollow Men." *The Complete Poems and Plays: 1909-1950,* Harcourt, 1980, pp. 56-59.

Frye, Northrop. *Anatomy of Criticism: Four Essays,* Princeton UP, 1990.

Greenberg, Jonathan. *Modernism, Satire, and the Novel*, Cambridge UP, 2011.

Griffiths, Michael R. "'Production Values: Fordism and Formalism in *North by Northwest*." *Postmodern Culture*, vol. 20, no. 3, 2010, n.p. Project Muse, muse.jhu.edu/article/444708.

Kael, Pauline. "The Man From Dream City—Cary Grant." *For Keeps: 30 Years at the Movies*, Dutton, 1994, pp. 619-47.

Keats, John. *Letters of John Keats*. Edited by Robert Gittings, Oxford UP, 1970.

Leitch, Thomas M. *Find the Director and Other Hitchcock Games*. Georgia UP, 1991.

Marx, Karl and Friedrich Engels. *Manifesto of the Communist Party. Basic Writings on Politics and Philosophy*, edited by Lewis S. Feuer, Anchor Books, 1959, pp. 1-41.

Morris, Christopher. "The Direction of *North by Northwest*." *Cinema Journal*, vol. 36, no. 4, 1997, pp. 43-56.

Nadel, Alan. "Expedient Exaggeration and the scale of Cold War Farce in *North by Northwest*." *The Cambridge Companion to Alfred Hitchcock,* edited by Jonathan Freedman, Cambridge UP, 2015, pp. 161-179.

Naremore, James, editor. *North by Northwest*: Alfred Hitchcock, Director, Rutgers UP, 1993.---. "Spies and Lovers." Naremore, pp. 3-20.

O'Connor, Dale. "Cary Grant Biography," imdb.com.

Orr, John. *Hitchcock and 20th Century Cinema*, Wallflower Press, 2005.

Shakespeare, William. *The Tragedy of Macbeth*. Edited by Nicholas Brooke, Oxford UP, 2008.

Stevens, Wallace. "The Snow Man." *The Collected Poems of Wallace Stevens*, Vintage, 1990, pp. 9-10.

Truffaut, François, Alfred Hitchcock and Helen G. Scott. *Hitchcock*. Simon and Schuster, 1967.

Wilson, George M. "The Maddest McGuffin: Some Notes on *North by Northwest*." MLN, vol. 94, no. 5, 1979, pp. 1159-1172. JSTOR, www.jstor.org/stable/2906570.

Žižek, Slavoj. "The Hitchcockian Blot." Allen and Ishii-Gonzalès, pp. 123-40.

"*Ceci n'est pas une Allemagne*": On the Treachery of Images and the Deconstruction of Hitchcock's Thriller in *Torn Curtain*

By Robert Dassanowsky

Of the very few Hitchcock films that were deemed critical misfires in their time, or have been perpetuated in cinema culture as inconsistent to the point of affecting the director's reputation, only *Torn Curtain* (1966) has been widely dismissed on the assumption that its maker had all but walked away from a mediocre backlot production over which he had lost control. The unsuccessful chemistry in coupling the year's most popular box-office stars Paul Newman (as American missile scientist Michael Armstrong) and Julie Andrews (as his assistant and fiancée) as forced on the production by Universal, whose salaries "amounted to more than half the film's total budget" (Truffaut 331), and the departure of close colleague and iconic composer Bernard Herrmann, as well as the director's supposed insecurities born of a difficult experience with *Marnie*, have been well discussed and debated. Moreover, critics underscore a confused or insincere narrative and a too-obvious backlot/process photography look that seems to dismiss the innovative stylistic growth found in the director's previous three films, particularly when measured against new waves and counter-cinemas of the time. The dismissal of the film, as some re-examinations now agree, was myopic even for a "film of compromises" (Mogg 2012), given its deeper philosophical and symbolist qualities.

Restating the unique fire and ice symbolism (also heat and cold; red and white) in the film and its generally agreed upon success with indirect lighting, Ken Mogg locates the use of Schopenhauer's concept of Will (Armstrong), themes of democratic representation (the resistance in the bus), and the "desperate reachings out for help" and the "sufferings in silence" (of the East Germans and then Armstrong and Sherman) in the work that add up to a film obviously "ahead of its time…or at least far more experimental than is often noted" (Mogg 10). This late epiphany emphasizes the self-reflective, abstract, and subversive qualities in *Torn Curtain*, despite the studio's meddling with the Armstrong character's intended moral quandary in favor of a simplistic Pax Americana adventure. Dominique Païni plainly asks:

> if anyone fully grasped the significance of the fact that Hitchcock was a contemporary of Marcel Duchamp? After all, the latter's work contains more Symbolist elements--and is also more conceptual—than that of any other 20th century artist. The films created by the "master of suspense" are, first and foremost traps that gradually draw the viewers gaze into descending spirals, thus undermining our concept of reality. (381)

Robin Wood suspects Hitchcock's subversion of his traditional audience-pleasing formula in *Torn Curtain* as a strategy that buoyed his risky tropes when he admits to treasuring "the richness of individual sequences while finding the whole disturbingly hollow" (225). David Sterritt insists that through his final film in 1976, the "actual extent of his independence waxed and waned, but no Hollywood filmmaker enjoyed more consistent creative control" (327), thus denying the axiom that Hitchcock was unable to deal with both script and specific acting "problems." There may well have been a crisis of confidence smoldering from the *Marnie* unpopularity (surely based on another critical misreading of Hitchcock expanding his vocabulary), but what the director wanted to convey with *Torn Curtain* was so dense with statements on social and political control that he must have realized that no elegant melodramatic form would be able to provide a satisfactory cushion for his narrative and cinematographic meanings. The fact that he accepted two lead performers who were wrong for the parts, or at least needed far more coaching, resolved the problem of structure. They would be the thinnest possible conduit on which to hang his important statements, and he would manipulate them to show their true sense of confusion with the project, and let the Kafkaesque, even surreal world that Hitchcock had dropped them in overrun their star personas, until they became abstract cyphers of a postwar amorality and elitism he had warned the world about as early as *Lifeboat* (1944).

Hitchcock took what he got from Universal and used it against their desire to have him create the ultimate Cold War espionage saga that dealt with real bullets (Soviet communism, divided Germany, a direct examination of the arms race) as opposed to the stand-in world domination threats of fantasy madmen and organizations that were nearly everywhere in the entertainment cinema of the 1960s. The studio omitted key aspects of the film's narrative points (Gromek's brother; the possible alternate ending in which Armstrong tosses the stolen formula) that would have made the lead characters more emotionally approachable to an audience that was to have felt not only the inhumanity of the setting and its victims, but also a moral quandary about nuclear weaponry. Yet much of what exists has made critics and audiences uncomfortable with the film's irony, the lack of a moral hero, and a heroine who soon jettisons her moral indignation, and with the fact that the curtain of the title is one that goes both ways.[1]

Donald Spoto's Orphic analysis arrives at the point that "the film is so firmly rooted in an ad hoc political situation (now no longer compelling) that the characters tend to be ciphers" (359). Why are the ad hoc situations of the other political conflicts long past in Hitchcock, particularly interwar Europe and the US threatened by Nazism, or World War II itself, directly compelling, while the still viable possibility of nuclear confrontation is not? In a comparison with a contemporary patriotic thriller like *Argo* (2012), which relates the deception staged to rescue Americans in Tehran during the US hostage crisis in 1980 and resists the kind of moral questions intrinsic to *Torn Curtain*, Mogg relates that "[s]everal Hitchcock films, by contrast, raise the subject of patriotism in order to show how it—patriotism—conceals or encourages affronts to individual life or well-being" (Mogg 10). Is it then because the subject deals precisely with something that reaches beyond the director's unique symbolist experiences to something that can happen, was and is unwinnable, and which ultimately favors no side in placing the world in an apocalyptic "fire and ice" that *Torn Curtain* continues to alienate? This was, after all, Hitchcock's mature and intellectual strategy to trounce the fantasy of the spy film craze with an anti-James Bond, and also to once more examine the woman sacrificed to the patriarchal power structure, as in *Notorious* (1946) and *North by Northwest* (1959). How can Hitchcock have gone both too far and not far enough in *Torn Curtain*, and can it be read as a metafilm or abstract construction on the director's own thriller tropes, his anti-war sensibilities, and the imitative spy film?

Forced to cleanse the narrative's intended backbone of moral ambiguity in Cold War attitudes that Hitchcock had obviously hoped to examine, he instead went the experiment route—as in *Rope* (1948) or *Rear Window* (1954)—with a deconstruction of the traditions of his oeuvre, which were summed up in *Marnie*, to tease out the aspects of cinematic deception, personal dislocation, political dystopia, and the role of art as a reflection of cinematic and social illusion and as an intertext for meaning. Of course, Hitchcock shoulders the blame for certain aspects that were forced out of the film. The most prominent deletion is Armstrong's meeting with Gromek's brother at a factory tour following his killing of Gromek and the intense guilt leads him to understand the political/personal/gender chauvinism that has driven him. Hitchcock refers to *Secret Agent* (1936) and its problems with a lead character that does not want to commit a killing he was ordered to do, and the "public couldn't identify with a hero who was so reluctant to carry out his mission" (Truffaut 313). Nevertheless, the director praises the scene as "quite effective," because the aim of *Torn Curtain* as for *Secret Agent* was to question the concept of a "hero" and the self-conscious incitement of an audience into taking politically-charged sides, the very basis of any overt propaganda film.

The puzzle of *Torn Curtain* manages to absorb and showcase its uneven and often intentionally crude quality as Hitchcock's most audacious metacinematic statement in his career. It can be read as the director's re-vision of his messages on the theatricality of politics, the transitory state of reality and identity, and the artifice of authoritarianism that reach back through his war period films to *The 39 Steps* (1935), including his attempt at Viennese Film, and which inflected his noir tributes to German Expressionism, to surrealism, and even his brief work at the Decla-Bioscop (later UFA) Studio. This allowed him to discover the culture of Berlin in the 1920s as well as the forces that would want to expediently deal with postimperial Germany's real and

On The Treachery of Images 111

perceived problems through scapegoating, the mythology of heroism, and ethnic/social masking, as Billy Wilder similarly experienced between his life in Vienna and Hollywood.[2]

Torn Curtain's Manichean struggle set in an illusory world of constant mirroring and doubling, from the narrative and its character constellation to the intensely artificial Universal Studio "New York Street" backlot setting representing "East Germany," mixed with the film's opening scenes shot in Denmark, which then also carefully season the studio footage as stand-ins for "East Berlin," make the film a unique trial: it is a self-conscious spy film built on the inversion and degeneration of Hitchcock's traditional structure. The message of political danger and individual identity in *Torn Curtain* is precisely about the visual "treachery," as surrealist painter René Magritte suggested for his famous painting of a pipe. It is a flat illusion that cannot even approximate reality. Nothing is more than it seems, indeed, it is far less, yet the danger is found in accepting the simplistic equations without question. On another level, *Torn Curtain* manages a powerful and intentionally fragmented statement on the illusory quality of freedom, democracy and safety in the deceptive games of the Cold War, and its own unique application of Hannah Arendt's "banality of evil."

This chapter will investigate the multifaceted metafilmic strategies Hitchcock utilizes to compensate for and exploit *Torn Curtain*'s inherent production problems, while he "renounces the [thriller] film genre he built up for thirty years," given its devaluation through plagiarism and caricature in the spy film glut of the 1960s (Truffaut 327). Four levels of experimentation and deconstruction and their interaction provide the keys to the symbolism in the film: 1) a relatively simple travelogue model as the basis for the film's form reveals the intentional artifice that makes up Hitchcock's "false" Germany, the topos GDR, and the film itself; 2) the mise-en-abyme structure which carries the film's superficial message in a repetition of the characters' action/reaction; 3) doubling and reflections as a strategy to deny cinematic totalism, evoke perspectivism, and relativize the concept of the Other; 4) finally, the self-reflexive use of art, artistic references and performance.

In 2000, the Museum of Art in Montreal offered *Hitchcock and Art: Fatal Coincidences*, a unique show attempting to trace Hitchcock's mise-en-scene and overall visions and philosophy throughout his career to movements and iconic imagery in modern art. The director began his career as a title card designer and later became an avid art collector. His films from the silent era onward were reactions to movements in painting and the influence of those movements on continental film. Most obvious is Hitchcock's absorption of German Expressionism, which directly influenced the haunting chiaroscuro and noir quality in all his films. His more comic works are no less formalistic and indeed have a classical, timeless quality because they are at the very least dark operetta, influenced by Austrian silent films and the stylized early sound Viennese film of Willi Forst and Walter Reisch, beginning with the Franz Schubert biopic *Leise flehen meine Lieder/Softly My Songs Entreat* (Austria 1933), which was remade as a highly successful British film, *Unfinished Symphony* (UK 1934). This manifests itself wholly in only one Hitchcock film, the musical *Waltzes from Vienna* (1934), based on a 1930 Austrian stage musical focused on Johann Strauss Jr.'s composition of the Blue Danube Waltz. Although Hitchcock considered this the nadir of his early career, and admitted that he did it to keep working despite his lack of ability with musical film, it nevertheless provided the artistic and technical roots for future film: "Ironically, it was in a film usually considered his least characteristic that Hitchcock made his most explicitly personal declaration of his artistic credo" (Ness 117), much like the problematic *Torn Curtain*. Moreover, the basic fact that the Sarah Sherman character, for all her blandness as played by Julie Andrews, is the most realistic, humane, and moral character in the film, a gender concept Hitchcock developed throughout his oeuvre, which began with this troublesome musical film set in Vienna: "in this film for perhaps the first time, Hitchcock gives the woman the power of will and mind" (Yacowar 165). The experimentation in *Waltzes from Vienna* is also credited by Charles Barr as the basis for the director's later accomplished set pieces involving music performance (127). Hitchcock used this film to explore the potential of the waltz, which he used as a musical device that carried intent and meaning (perhaps in reference to the poetic realist quality of Vienna in Forst and Reisch) or supplemented perilous aspects in *The Lodger* (1927), *Suspicion* (1941), *Shadow of a Doubt* (1943), and *Strangers on a Train* (1951). In *Torn Curtain*, it distracts Professor Lindt (Ludwig Donath) and makes it possible for Sarah Sherman to become an almost operetta-like diversion from Armstrong and Donath's private conversation by flirting and dancing with the painfully infatuated Professor Manfred (Günter Strack).

What has been largely ignored in the analysis of this film is its blatant statement on art/performance and its disruption that goes far beyond the chaos Armstrong causes at the ballet for the purposes of escape from the Stasi (state security police). Most of the narrative, which is set in a backlot and "painted" setting representing East Germany, is cinematically interpreted by Hitchcock as sheer public performance once the welcome of Armstrong at the airport press conference is replaced with mistrust and scrutiny. The country is intentionally represented by awkward stage tropes, obvious set pieces, and soundstage design, and by characters suggesting melodramatic cliché, but with embedded symbolic or allegorical references to both Soviet totalitarianism and German Nazism. Moreover, settings for art viewing, creation, or direct involvement make up a significant portion of the film's time and space, underscoring the film's overall concept of multidirectional performance and examples of obvious artifice both diegetic and non-diegetic.

Returning to Magritte's *Treachery of Images*, *Torn Curtain* performs as a consciously artificial metafilmic exercise that renders the entire shell of the narrative, not just the East German missile formula desired by America, a McGuffin, with several ruptures from emotionally and intellectually important vignettes that stand out from the seemingly intentional simplicity and triviality of the film. These ruptures, all of which include the scenes directly dealing with art and performance, call awareness to the self-consciously constructed Marxist identities of the Eastern Bloc and Hitchcock's vision of the "worker's paradise" of East Germany or the GDR (German Democratic Republic). In *North by Northwest*, there is no such man as the fictional Kaplan. He is a ruse for one ideology to capture the promoters of another. In *Torn Curtain*, with its obvious illusion of democracy, modernity, social and cultural well-being, and the constant schizoid presence of the double (two Germanys, two Berlins, two political blocs, two Europes, two scientists, two missile projects, and so on), there is no such country as East Germany beyond the film-set political strategy and its cinematic capsizal by Hitchcock.

Elizabeth Bronfen has investigated the particular use of process photography and rear projection across Hitchcock's oeuvre as "part of the overall stylistic arsenal through which he displays his central concern with artifice as well as external and internal staging, so as to distinguish between characters caught in a theatricalized world and those caught in internal projections" (Bronfen, "Abstract"). In *Torn Curtain*, however, this concept is deployed to render the entire film a fantasy on place, time, and substance in an approximation of a destination, with Armstrong and Sherman as sleepwalkers, a reading beyond the "Hell" which Donald Spoto and other critics have found in the (Catholic) Hitchcock's use of "fire and ice" and the demonic topic of the final Tchaikovsky ballet. It displays openly the film's problematic artifice as the filmic "reality" of the GDR and as a fictional film of that "reality." The self-conscious nature of commenting on cinema transcends the exploration of the spectator/object trajectory of *Rear Window* to true metafilmic proportions. Here, a jarring, almost hallucinatory mix of rear projection with on-location shots and backlot action, against both realistic landscapes and oddly defined matte processing, are without the sense of subtlety Hitchcock delivers in previous films. Nevertheless, it is an aesthetic choice and quite intentional given the constant doubling and suggestions of artifice in the film and in its portrayal of East Germany.

This false double applied to a state (the GDR as opposed to the truer representative of a sovereign postwar Germany, the Federal Republic of Germany or FRG) and a walled-in city—East Berlin—is also an expansion of the (false) resurrection trope in *Vertigo*. One can suggest both sovereignty and culture as performance, but here it is intentionally simplistic and imitative. The film does not display the vivid anti-communism that the studio obviously would have preferred for the sake of an "American hero," but rather Hitchcock's philosophical rejection of the Cold War, totalitarianism in general, and the targeting of the Other. Jean-Luc Godard would attempt something similar by reducing the world to the absurd and apocalyptic images of a deconstructing cinema in *Weekend* (France 1967) the following year, while Hitchcock does somewhat the opposite by placing the ill-fitting aspects of his traditional cinema onto the absurd realism of Cold War *Weltanschauung*. One can also see confluences between Hitchcock's tropes as floating signifiers and the meta-style of *Torn Curtain* as abstraction with Michelangelo Antonioni's "Hitchcock film" of photographic/cinematic delusion aligned with abstract modern art in *Blow-Up* (UK/Italy 1966).

Hitchcock's Travelogue and the Mise-en-Abyme

Beyond Bond and its spoofs and imitations, Torn Curtain also took on the more respectful Hitchcockian thrillers such as Mark Robson's The Prize (USA 1963), based on the novel by Irving Wallace, with Paul Newman and North By Northwest's Ernst Lehman as screenwriter, about an imposter physicist at the Nobel Prize Awards, which suggests elements of Hitchcock's The Lady Vanishes (1938) and North by Northwest; or Martin Ritt's adaptation of John le Carré's The Spy Who Came in from the Cold (UK 1965), a gloomy staged East German defection narrative that rejected the fantasy qualities of Bond with outright despair, and managed to find both popular audience and critical acclaim. Hitchcock was fascinated with high-level British defection to the Soviet Union and what effect it might have if told from the point of view of a spouse following the defector:

Hitchcock's initial plans for his "realistic Bond" film centered around a scientist who defects to Russia and the impact this has on his wife. In November 1964, he wrote to Vladimir Nabokov in the hope the Russian émigré novelist could be persuaded to write an original screenplay. Hitchcock told Nabokov, "The question I'm really interested in is what would be the attitude of a young woman, perhaps in love with, or engaged to a scientist who could be a defector" (Kapsis 95).

While such an angle is significantly reduced in the role given to Julie Andrews in Brian Moore's original script, the Irish-Canadian author was known for his realistic and sympathetic depiction of females in his novels' film adaptions, and he managed to populate Torn Curtain with supporting roles depicting the plight of women under communism: the variously flamboyant, bitter, and pathetic Polish Countess Kuchinska adrift in the faceless East Berlin landscape (Lila Kedrova); the stoic farmer's wife (Carolyn Conwell) who helps Armstrong (Paul Newman) kill the secret policeman Gromek; a widowed medical scientist at Leipzig's Karl Marx University, Dr. Koska (Gisela Fischer), who is depicted as an intelligent physician, a caring mother, and one opposed to the GDR dictatorship but who may not necessarily be an anti-Marxist; and the arrogant, self-absorbed, politically opportunistic Soviet prima ballerina on tour (Tamara Toumanova), who obviously understands how to exploit the communist regime as a virtuosic performer and informer.

Despite the thin construction of Andrews' Sarah Sherman character, she does have morality on her side as she blatantly rejects the East German examination on what she may know about the American Gamma 5 project. She tearfully embraces Armstrong in relief as she ultimately comprehends the deception and theft he is perpetrating for America. Armstrong learns to respect, not just love Sarah Sherman and to understand that he needs her in his life. Furthermore, it is her humanity and loyalty that give him his direction. She even protects or saves him several times in Leipzig and as they attempt to escape East Berlin. Moore's script, polished and even retailored as it was by Keith Waterhouse and Willis Hall, still manages to create memorable aspects of female self-reliance and personal strength.

The narrative structure and the character constellation seem intentionally uncomplicated to the point of too easily allowing the audience their hunch that Paul Newman would not be cast as a true defector. The spectator's concentration is instead on how his performance will allow support of the character, on why he would claim to be a defector, and how he can be so icily dismissive of his fiancée played by an actress freshly defined in the audience's mind as Mary Poppins and anti-Nazi novice-turned-beloved-step-mother, Maria von Trapp. Andrews' hair color, usually blonde to light brown, is given a dark ash tone and she is seen in earth-tone-colored wardrobe to deny any suggestion that she is a "Hitchcock blonde," with the exception of the low cut white cocktail dress she wears to attract attention of the professors at the Leipzig University party. She appears to embody the director's code of the white garment as a virtuous and gracious guest, but she is now fact a manipulative danger to Professors Lindt and Manfred.[3]

The director insisted the film is "divided into three sections and its movement follows a logical geographical course" that Hitchcock actually took before making the film (Truffaut 309). From the arrival in "East Berlin" onward, however, the film becomes a subtle parody of propaganda—a travelogue or a tourist brochure in which the GDR presents itself in its social, political, educational, technical, and daily life. We begin at the modern East Berlin airport and witness the press and media, followed by the security apparatus and their "friendly" welcome to visitors, even ones from the West, beginning with the hotel sequence in which Professor Manfred concerns himself with Sarah Sherman's dreary room, pointing out its spaciousness. The brochure of the famous Alte Nationalgalerie (Old National Gallery, constructed 1866-76) promotes its neoclassical architectural beauty and its priceless collection of Neoclassic, Romantic, and Biedermeier era German works, as well as later German and French Symbolist pieces. These priceless examples raise another question about intentional fakery in the film, given that the entire interior and its artistic holdings are matte processed—are paintings themselves. Armstrong's dash through the empty museum to escape Gromek demonstrates the ease of access for the tourist, especially the odd exit, which is a simple, unguarded and unalarmed back door, recalling the fictional back alley door of the flower shop which allows Scottie (James Stewart) to spy on the obviously aware Madeleine in *Vertigo*. Both doors signal the banal world on the outside of these containers of fantasy and beauty—suggesting that a cinema theater is such a space as well—but Hitchcock refuses to let the visual pleasure linger.

Continuing the travelogue, we visit a communal farm and relate to a farming couple and visit their modest cottage. Armstrong and Sherman might also have travelled to the industrial sector of the GDR to attend a meeting with a factory foreman (Gromek's brother in the excised scene), who displays his satisfying position as worker and his pride in family. East Berlin gives way to Leipzig and the Karl Marx University, displaying its multicultural student body gained through socialist educational outreach to African and Asian countries. Moreover, the large lecture halls are open and accessible, as are members of the medical staff, represented here by an unexpected female physician, underscoring Marxist gender equality. The comradery among an international presence of academics is shown in a gathering hall, complete with libation and dance music.

That buses run on time, as it was said the trains once did under Mussolini, is demonstrated during the "double bus" service into East Berlin, and unexpected infelicities (such as a thwarted robbery by Soviet army deserters and the outburst of Frau Mann's xenophobia) are of no true consequence to the spectatorial tourist. Wandering through East Berlin, we witness the clean, studio set streets, the orderly deportment of the masses at empty stores, the post office, a travel agency, and a shop filled with new model television sets broadcasting news programs about the GDR. A visit to an elegant concert hall to watch a ballet by a Czech company and featuring a famed Soviet prima ballerina ends this narrative tour.

Hitchcock's travelogue is underpinned by the film's overall stylistic pastiche quality of rear projections, the backlot public spaces and the matte processed interiors, which intentionally fail to normalize the GDR for the characters and the film spectator. As was the custom at the time, television news programs would regularly blank out West Germany on its map behind the announcer, which is apparent from the television broadcast in the East Berlin shop window. The map sans West Germany (there is only a white space where the state should be) is therefore the very basis of the GDR's creative interpretation of un-reality, and the director's application of this illusion to his own filmic GDR is pure Hitchcockian irony.

For the director, this "topos GDR" is the greatest connection between politics and performance in his entire oeuvre, and it is doubled as well by the indication that what represents this false Germany in the film and the travelogue structure which underpins much of the narrative cannot be accurately produced by a studio backlot and sound stages. There are intentional cracks in the surface of the filmic impersonation that remind the audience of the multi-layered artifice here and originally give us the POV of Sarah Sherman, who must decide what is real and what is a sham. Among the most prominent examples of this are the poorly executed, ruined facades outside the large window of the modern Stasi headquarters interior and the slightly New York feel to the backlot East Berlin, which connects with Gromek's desire to let Armstrong know he lived and went to "night school" in New York as a possible refugee from Nazism—or is this wholly a performance intended to draw out the truth about Armstrong? His connection with New York interrupts and also supports the false reality of this film with a reference to another illusion, that of traditional Hollywood cinema, through Gromek's admiration of Edward G. Robinson and his references to gangster films. This conflates his role as Stasi man with the focus of his admiration, equating the GDR state security police and their methods with gangsterism.

The actual transmission of the film's drama and its meanings—about geopolitics, society, gender, class, capitalism, socialism, and, finally, the hardly unpacked concepts of Cold War and nuclear options—is not found in the traditional narrative. Instead, the travelogue for Armstrong and Sherman hosts a collection of *mise-en-abymes*, which descend from heraldry, as in the miniature replica of the shield within the large shield, and which has been common in literary embedding but only much more recently so in film. Brian McHale's study of postmodernist fiction identifies the "nested representation" as "one of the most potent devices in the post-modernist repertoire for foregrounding the ontological dimension" and thus the fictionality of the diegesis (124). Hitchcock might have learned it from the emblematic embedding first used by Andre Gide or even conjured up a concept of it himself.[4] Postmodernist literary critics disagree on how or when the embedded representations are inferior to the "primary, diagetic narrative world," with the outer form being "real" and the textual *en abyme* considered less real, but the crucial aspect is that these embeddings represent the narrative as a synecdoche in which a small part can carry "as much significance as the whole that contains it" (Ron 130). Or as Kaja Silverman considers such a "condensation," "the part stands for the whole" (91).

Dissected, the episodic adventures of the film are clear embeddings that reiterate the basic overall plot emblematically and in a specific condensation. The mise-en-abyme chain begins in the second part of what Hitchcock considers is a tripartite structure and is ordered along the basic quest/chase narrative thusly:

a. The "hunt" for Armstrong at the Alte Nationalgalerie with the figurative help of the museum itself—both its architectural structure (with influence from Hitchcock and his fictional hallways) and, on a metaphysical level, its art.

b. The killing of Gromek with the help of the farmer's wife.

c. The interrogation at the Karl Marx University in Leipzig with the help of Professor Lindt

d. Armstrong's confession and plea to continue on the hill behind the university with the help of Sarah Sherman.

e. [The excised visit to the factory and meeting Gromek's brother?]

f. The formula theft from Professor Lindt and escape with the help of Dr. Koska.

g. The imperiled resistance bus ride with the help of Herr Jacobi and most of the "passengers."

h. Lost and found in East Berlin with the help of Countess Kuchinska.

i. The ballet performance with the informant prima ballerina, and the escape with help of the ballet itself and the stage manager.

It is certainly not coincidental that these emblems in repetition of the essential overarching narrative of action/endangerment met with assistance to complete the task and/or escape, carry the most successful and powerfully humanistic aspects of the film. They are sutured to a general narrative cover of a simplistic chase plot meets travelogue that harks back to Hitchcock's earliest espionage films and the wartime thrillers. In this way, Hitchcock manages to investigate the artifice of the GDR mirrored by the artifice of the Armstrong representation, and both nations' insistence on scientific and moral superiority, as a statement on the absurdity of the Cold War.

Doubles and Distorted Reflections

Clearly, Hitchcock must have Walter Benjamin's definition of fascism as the aestheticization of politics in mind in resisting the blatant jingoistic piece the film might have been given Universal's (ineffective) tinkering to make Paul Newman and his cause superior to anything else in the film. The setting of *The Lady Vanishes*, in which a multivalence of perception undercuts even the precise location of the "enemy," would become the root of Hitchcock's anti-totalitarian commentary. The opening credits of the film introduce a snowed-in Alpine resort, but with a closer look at the "aerial" establishing shot of this landscape (a model or still) obscured somewhat by the graphics, it is clear that we note a train station at what appears to be the snow-covered roofs of barrack-like structures—of a military or even a labor camp. It is only as the action begins with the arrival of passengers attempting to find lodging in the overcrowded hotel that the Alpine-flavored set suggests culture and life rather than the hint of imprisonment and death of the establishing shot. This sort of dualism continues through the director's World War II films, in the guise of characterizations: the erudite, supposedly anti-war gentleman Stephen Fisher (Herbert Marshall) in *Foreign Correspondent* (1940), who admits his cover for a more organic loyalty to his British-born daughter, and rather than cause more mayhem, even attempts to rescue people from the plane shot down in the ocean by the his people; or the evil foreign agent Frank Fry (Norman Lloyd) in *Saboteur* (1942), who kills the close friend of the aircraft factory worker Barry Kane (Robert Cummings). By the end of the coast-to-coast pursuit in order to clear Kane of the crime, Hitchcock has made Fry so mortal that the audience does not want to see him fall from the Statue of Liberty, as he ultimately must in punishment of his murderous crime. The high society New York benefit that Kane and Pat Martin (Priscilla Lane) stumble into during the chase is equally unexpected and ironic—many of the attendees are American gentry and also subversive fifth columnists for the sake of money to preserve their outmoded and twisted notions of American elitism.

Hitchcock claims his final war film, *Lifeboat* (1944), was intended to rally the Allies together against the German resoluteness, and has often been misunderstood as a war propaganda film, or even one "siding with the Nazis" (Hark 296). It was made when there was no longer much need of an anti-German film, given the state of the Allied march across a shrinking Nazi Europe, and should be examined instead as a philosophical exercise. In a microcosm of the postwar world, the American/British front are obvious winners of this war, but will the Allies continue to hold to a Judeo-Christian sense of morals, or will the resulting global power and superiority lead to an ends-justifies-the-means philosophy that fed genocidal Nazism and which is hinted at by the class conflict, racism, and the uncomfortable "extermination" statement at the conclusion of the film? The evil for Hitchcock is not the single German survivor and his manipulation of the passengers on the lifeboat, although he frames this in a teasingly noir manner. He is doing what they should expect of him and what all in his place might do—attempt to sail the boat away from "enemy" waters to save himself. Again, Hitchcock dispels jingoism to make the German truly comprehensible if not sympathetic. *Torn Curtain*, which even in its title suggests a vulnerability undercutting the totalizing principle of the Churchillian Iron Curtain, attempts to show a communist state and its artificial quality, but does not give higher moral ground to the equally deceptive American representative.

Christopher D. Morris insists that "deconstructive study reads the film as a narrative of the illusion of mutual understanding, one that puts into question political, ethical, and religious distinctions" (54). But he also suggests that *Torn Curtain* might well be a satire with an underdeveloped script. Given the mismatched studio tools by which Hitchcock was to shape the film, it becomes another experiment in examining the personal and the national façades and the Cold War performances of both sides—an ideological *Rear Window*, if one will—in which the spectator is again challenged to comprehend reality's relationship with cinema and illusion. Hitchcock overloads the film with doubling and doubles that float like empty signifiers above his critical sympathy for the subjugated East German characters, but his dismissal, perhaps also influenced by his Catholic rearing, of a Soviet colony of the GDR and its pretentions to be the sole representative of the Germany Hitchcock must have remembered from the 1920s leads him to consider the GDR an impostor.

The most discussed and appreciated scene, or mise-en-abyme, of the film has been Hitchcock's reach back to his own past landscapes inhabited by theoretical enemies of democracy to create an intertextual double with the Crofter's wife (Peggy Ashcroft) from *The 39 Steps*. Remade into a woman who may well be a farmer herself, but is only masquerading as the wife of the tractor riding American intelligence agent (Mort Mills) who dictates Armstrong's path, she appears less modern GDR and far more a timeless and exploited symbol of man's inhumanity to woman. Like the original, she risks her own safety to help save the foreigner. Gromek, who has followed Armstrong to her cottage and knows he is there to contact the underground pi organization, bullies him physically and with fragments of dialogue from Hollywood gangster films. It is, however, the scene between Armstrong, Gromek, and the farmer's wife where the Hitchcock of *Psycho* and *The Birds* reemerges to remind the audience they are not seeing a soulless spy film, but to witness what most other spy films bely—the immense difficulty and time it takes to kill a man. It is accomplished slowly and deliberately with a great deal of audience POV and without music, and becomes the inversion double of the open space terror of the Prairie Stop in *North by Northwest*. Here it is not the dangers that can arise in a free, open society, but in those that are walled in. Unlike the spy films of the era utilizing East Germany as a location, there is never an establishing shot of East Berlin, the Brandenburg Gate, or, most importantly, the Berlin Wall. Hitchcock's wall is an abstract one. The claustrophobia of psychological oppression can be anywhere, much as the agoraphobia caused by the vulnerability of the seemingly endless barren horizon at the Prairie Stop indicates that true freedom is an existential and psychological comprehension, not necessarily a physical one.

The symbolist attack on historical evil that brought Germany to its division is acted out in the death of Gromek by gas in the kitchen oven—his flailing fingers in the faces of his two killers as they struggle to hold him in the belly of the stove are reminiscent of Harry Lime's (Orson Welles) hands hopelessly reaching for escape from punishment for his crimes through the locked Vienna manhole grating in *The Third Man* (UK 1949). Uncomfortable, no doubt, to German audiences at the time, the scene was generally avoided in international critique, but Hitchcock finally does give credence to the inescapability of the past regardless of the performance of the present, as Gromek's black leather coated Stasi redux of the Gestapo dies in the way that millions were killed in an earlier incarnation of German totalitarianism. Hitchcock "fully intended the farm house's gas oven to evoke Auschwitz," and Mogg adds that "it was in just such tranquil surroundings as those of this [East] German farm that some of the extermination camps operated" (24). Recall the aerial shot of the Alpine hotel that suggests the appearance of a labor camp in the opening title credits of *The Lady Vanishes*, the illusions of continued civilized culture that came with the Nazi term "resettlement," and the orchestras and bands that greeted the cattle cars at their extermination camp destination.

Hitchcock's indications in *Torn Curtain* that the dictatorship of the GDR as set up by Stalin might have been too easily patterned on Nazi Germany was a point that was avoided in the contemporary critique of the film, despite spy films and thrillers that dealt with fictional neo-Nazism in West Germany or Austria.[5] Hitchcock's specific view was unique to film but not to academia, even from behind the Berlin Wall. East German-Jewish writer, diarist and cultural figure Victor Klemperer, who survived the Holocaust and held an academic post at the GDR University of Leipzig, collected propaganda and jargon that drew a strong similarity between Nazism and GDR/Soviet communism in his studies LTI (*lingua tertii imperii*, or language of the Third Reich, 1947) and in the posthumously and post-GDR published LQI (*lingua quarti imperii*, the language of the Fourth Reich, 1995). His diary, *The Lesser Evil*, written secretly between 1945 and 1959, compared life in the GDR to Nazi Germany, and described its leader Walter Ulbricht as a personality cult figure similar to Stalin or Hitler. The three volume diaries which began in 1933 were not published until 1995-2003 (Klemperer; Johnson).

The ultimate twist on Holocaust revenge allegory of Gromek in the gas oven comes later in the film when we learn that Herr Jacobi (David Opatoshu), an anti-GDR resistance leader obviously intended to be Jewish or of Jewish extraction[6] (as is the actor himself), is in charge of a "people transport" in this Germany, and in a bus used to access freedom and not in a train bound for his execution. Frau Mann, an obviously trusted member of Jacobi's group and with similar convictions, becomes the eptiome of hysteria and scapegoating, accusing Armstrong and Sherman for the problems that beset the bus *en route* to Leipzig because they are Americans. As Robin Wood asserts, the audience should realize at this point that these Americans are endangering these German lives "to enable Michael [Armstrong] to take back to America a formula that may destroy them all" (204). Certainly, Wood reflects precisely on the anti-heroic nature of Hitchcock's spy drama (or ideological suspense film?) which is opposed to the political propaganda the studio would have liked to see: grateful Germans that have not forgotten the American liberation from Nazism, and the notion that East Germans must naturally wish to side unquestioningly with any American against their own culture, people and identity, whatever the cost. Today, the reaction to Frau Mann in screenings is somewhat different.[7] It is clear to the spectator that she reacts this way for fear of being caught and tortured by the security police, but her distress is understood as more of an indication that xenophobia that may rise anywhere, even in this selflessly committed group, and in spaces the American couple and an audience might well identify with.

As previously mentioned, one of Hitchcock's most important doublings in this film is the character of Gromek's brother (also played by

Wolfgang Kieling), who Armstrong meets just after the killing in a tour of an East German factory. There he briefly gets to know a gentle and hardworking man with a family, and the guilt apparently overwhelms him and gives a clearer meaning to his actions and hesitancies. Without this source, however, Armstrong's reactions later in the film have been criticized as unmotivated, selfish, or vague. This cut was at the heart of the film's disgust at playing into a war of differences based in suppositions and manipulations. Kubrick would satirize the rationalization of irrational Cold War games two years earlier in *Dr. Strangelove or: How I Learned to Stop Worrying and Love the Bomb* (1964), with differing values in the absurd amount of "megadeaths" that can make nuclear annihilation allowable and patriotic. A deleted part of the original script that would have totally shifted the psychological development of the main character was apparently the act of Armstrong tossing away the slip of paper with the formula he saw in Professor Lindt's office and which nearly cost Armstrong, Sherman, and certainly others their lives. Hitchcock's unused ending, in which a scientist realizes he is not a spy or a military man, but works for the good of all people, would have literally unplugged the moral questions intentionally troubling the film, and perhaps placed the work in a roster of ironic and philosophical anti-war films that include Renoir's *Grand Illusion* (France 1937) and Kubrick's *Paths of Glory* (USA 1957).[8]

Land der Dichter und Denker:[9] Intertexts with Low Art, High Art, Total Art

In discussing the transactions between "spectator and the world of art" in Hitchcock's films, Brigitte Peucker asks "why is it in Hitchcock's *Torn Curtain* pivotal scenes take place in aesthetic spaces—in an art museum and in a theater in which a ballet is being performed? How are artifice and illusion related to diegetic reality?" (202). She follows with an intricate examination of the museum sequence in the film, comparing it to the museum moment in *Blackmail* (1929) in which the villain falls through the glass dome of the British Museum, which presents "in another register the imbrication of art and death that informs the earlier part of the film's narrative" (Peucker 206). Peucker proceeds to discuss the film's inventory of the neo-classical façade and the interior which provides framing, so to speak, of this portion of the narrative. She takes on Berlin's Alte Nationalgalerie (Old National Gallery) as a maze for Armstrong's disappearance, and reiterates that filming in the GDR was impossible during the Cold War and that the image of the museum after we see a photograph of it on the tourist brochure is "more painting than photograph" (Peucker 206).[10] Additionally, the path Armstrong takes in the museum did not exist and was altered and added for the film. This is the single attempt at suturing the film's GDR to a representation of an architectural historical landmark: the East Berlin Airport is a generic façade; we see nothing of the city's landmarks either in the first visit nor in the escape; the Leipzig University architecture is first ornate, then represented by the red brick modernity of its stand-in, the Los Angeles campus of the University of Southern California, but mostly obscured. The interior of the Alte Nationalgalerie is not only reconstructed to suit the film's chase sequence, but also its very holdings, which we glimpse as Armstrong rushes by them, are paintings of these masterworks. The visual collision of a three-dimensional man rushing past matte processing and painted studio floors (Grafe 5), which in an overhead shot reveals a mosaic pattern of an octagon with several concentric circles, creates a hypnotic sensation with the omniscient POV of Armstrong running from the sound of the Stasi agent's approaching footsteps.

The central perspective beginning with the propaganda shot of the neo-classical museum on the brochure, then transferred to the "live" entrance for Armstrong, is, as Peucker claims, the rigidity of the communist state emblematized in the oppressiveness of this central perspective.[11] It is the reflection of the very first image of the GDR we in fact see—the monumental and equally symmetrical rectangular steel and glass façade of the airport which welcomes visitors and the spectator to the visual oppression—but it also quotes the inhuman scale of modern capitalist America as telegraphed in the imprisoning crosshatch of steel on glass suggested in the title credits and opening shots of *North by Northwest*. There, however, we eventually see the reflection of the sky and a diverse and busy city. The supposed large glass facade of the East Berlin airport buidling, with a shadowy painting of a reflected skyline in the distance: suggests both theatrical backdrop and static illusion.

In the Alte Nationalgalerie, Armstrong is being hunted by the secret police, while the image of artistic expression and particularly the age of Enlightenment and beyond hang in a totally empty space, which fails to communicate anything of the art and its ideas to anyone. As Armstrong rushes by them, the desire for freedom and safety is reflected in the mute, unexamined paintings and sculpture. The high art cultural aspect of the GDR is deemed untrue in this hollow space, and Armstrong may seem to equally misuse the art as a brief refuge on the way to a murder. But the killing of Gromek is one leveled against totalitarianism, and not one warranted just for the sake of Armstrong's selfish mission of intellectual theft.

Of course, the killing of Gromek is also an intertext with art, as its very act, as explained earlier, is not only emblematic of the Holocaust but also roots the scene in the folk tale, *Hansel and Gretel*,[12] in which Gretel thwarts the attempt of a witch to cook her and her brother Hansel by shoving her in the oven instead. The German farmer woman is constructed along the lines of Hitchcock's selfless secondary female characters, often abused, always wise, and who help the leading male character out of a dangerous situation that could put her into equal peril. Here, she is translated into an aged but no less determined Gretel, who utilizes a gas oven to help Armstrong, her so-called "brother in victimization," kill Gromek silently.

Armstrong doubly "performs" for the faculty in the amphitheater classroom at the university in Leipzig—about the reasons for his defection and what he would bring to the GDR project, but also regarding his lack of knowledge regarding the sudden disappearance of Gromek. It is the unknowing Sarah Sherman who refuses to perform and remains steadfastly loyal to her national/political identity. To keep the ruse from collapsing, Armstrong takes her from the room and the crowd to a grassy hill behind the university, a trope of the couple isolated in nature that Hitchcock has used with various differentiations in such films as *Suspicion, Spellbound, To Catch a Thief, North by Northwest, The Birds*, and so on. Alain Bergala considers these to be elements of key episodes of Genesis that haunted Hitchcock throughout his career and "served both as textual (narrative) and visual matrices for his plots. He would restage these episodes in an entirely personal manner. The expulsion from the Garden of Eden is the basis of his couple in nature trope, and in *Torn Curtain*, as in other films, Adam and Eve are shown at a distance, making agitated gestures on a hilltop in the garden, from which they are soon to be expelled" (Bergala 111-12). In *Torn Curtain*, however, the Edenic story is reversed: "a duplicitous Adam who has assumed a false identity…is the one who tempts Eve to taste the fruit of knowledge," and this "paradise" must be escaped (Bergala 122). The image of the couple on the hill is reminiscent of fifteenth century Italian paintings of Adam and Eve being chased from the Garden of Eden; Bergala points specifically to "Massacio's fresco in the Brancacci chapel in Santa Maria del Carmine, Florence (1425) and Fra Angelico's Annunciation altarpieces at the Prado in Madrid (1430-32) and at the Diocesan Museum in Cortona (1433-34)" (116). He also considers how the insertion of this powerful but usually unexpected trope breaks the continuity of the films, but it is a voyeuristic concept for an omnipotent camera eye (and the spectator) that both withholds and teases out the truth.

Hitchcock must have also known neo-classical and Romantic German literature in which these Edenic moments between lovers represent the "third space" (neither his nor hers; neither urban nor rural; neither heaven nor hell) in which not only the truth between the lovers will out, but the very quality of humanity is shown to be good, as in Heinrich von Kleist's 1807 novella, *Das Erdbeben in Chili* [The Earthquake in Chile], in which the survivors of the 1647 Santiago earthquake come together in the countryside as kind and caring humanity, even embracing a young couple that had been sentenced to death for their illicit relationship and child. Such Edenic moments are found in Goethe, Schiller, and Kleist in particular, who emphasizes irony in all his works and, as with Hitchcock after him, offers an unexpected twist ending that refocuses the narrative.[13]

Another artistic interlude—one that allows a cameo by a previous Hitchcock film, so to speak, *Waltzes from Vienna*—is the party for the new arrivals that offers dancing, and Sherman begins her "performance" by flirting with Professor Lindt and dancing with the omnipresent and infatuated Professor Manfred to allow Armstrong an opportunity to connect with Lindt. Suddenly the music switches to Johann Strauss Jr.'s sensual *Wiener Blut* (Vienna Blood Waltz), and Lindt excitedly announces "a Viennese Waltz" and is carried away by the melody, closing his eyes and conducting the music with his table knife. Suddenly he ruptures his own romantic reverie with a non sequitur, recalling that his sister was knocked down by a bus in Vienna. The ugliness of everyday life quickly dispels any notion of artistic elevation. A small fracture, surely, but yet another one in the list of art that is ignored, interrupted, altered, or dislocated in some way throughout the film.

One referential shot at the university bears closer examination in this context. When the loudspeakers announce the search for Armstrong during his meeting with Lindt after Gromek's body has been found, it launches the student body into a chaotic scramble to find a man they would not even recognize. Hitchcock particularly focuses on a modern staircase with students rushing up and down its steps. It recalls Oscar Schlemmer's 1932 *Bauhaus Staircase* painting, in which energetic and focused students (and one male dancer en-pointe) utilize the airy, geometrical and utilitarian modernity of the design school to get to their various artistic tasks. The painting was completed the year that the National Socialists closed down this second school in Dessau (the first had been in Weimar—both sites would be part of the GDR after 1949) as part of their campaign against so-called Marxist modernity and degenerate art. Enacting this reference in what is itself a reenactment of the government-controlled atmosphere of the Leipzig Karl Marx University, it becomes a parodic and politically critical interpretation of the original: the students have none of the individualistic creative spirit of the Bauhaus; the rational calm and even grace of the figures in the painting is replaced with a film image of a disoriented but frantic mob hunt for an enemy of the state; and the so-called modernity of Walter Gropius and the Bauhaus is unwanted in the GDR. Regardless of its designers' victimization by the Nazis, the formalist style was denounced as a "hostile manifestation" by the future Stalinist leader of the state, Walter Ulbricht, in 1951 (Bauhaus blog), and the GDR opted instead for brutalist concrete slab architecture.

A deeper statement on humanism arrives with the twisted reflection of the Polish Countess Kuchinska and the haughty, self-serving opportunist that is the "black" prima ballerina. The obviously poor and socially isolated countess, a critical sympathetic reframing, surely, of Jean Giraudoux's 1945 stage satire, *The Madwoman of Chaillot*, is disgusted with the Marxist world and its poverties and its abuses of what was obviously for her a "humanizing" traditional class culture (she approaches

Sarah Sherman speaking English and then French). She decorates her old tailored suit (complete with a collared shirt and man's tie, as was in vogue during the 1930s and '40s) with a colorful floral scarf to personally dispel the monotone of the surroundings. She wears gloves, pearls, a broach, and an old hat with a veil pinned to it, scraps of haute bourgeois coding as an elitist statement of protest against the false "equality" of the babushka- and-shift wearing proletarian women crowding the streets and standing in line for meagre offerings at unidentifiable, empty store fronts. They stare at her, or even worse ignore her, as if she were mad. Her mild pressure on the needy and exposed couple lost in East Berlin after the events at Leipzig University is peculiarly coquettish for a woman her age, but Hitchcock has frozen her in time, trapped as a witness to history, as if she were encased in the amber so prized by the Polish aristocracy. One can easily imagine her backstory—the impossibility of remaining in communist Poland where Stalin's NKVD undertook to murder over 22,000 members of the Polish military, the intelligentsia, and traditional society and cultural leaders at Katyn Forest in 1940, and where her very presence in a strongly repressed state that for the most part continued to remain subversively loyal to Catholicism and Poland's identification with Western Europe would be a danger to anyone that associated with her. In the GDR, her bourgeois appearance and behavior would be somewhat covered by her foreignness and the Soviet desire to display liberation from fascism and Nazism in particular in the Warsaw Pact brotherhood, which would protect her from any apparent anti-Polish sentiments made by hostile East Germans. She lures the couple into a café to negotiate her "terms" as her self-consciousness and obvious bipolarity form a virtuosic performance ranging from tear-stained joy to crumpled disgust. When her request for the best coffee they have is rejected by the indifferent waitress, she confesses to them that "the liquid" will be "undrinkable," and she further shows them that half of the cigarette she intends to smoke is empty paper, props for a play. She is a woman without a country.

The Soviet ballerina is Hitchcock's distortion of the countess, a woman who, like the Soviet satellite states, has no historical depth, true past, or connection with any world except the immediate political one that has made her survival and importance possible. Arrogance and cruelty seem to be her only character traits, to the extent that her astringent, aquiline face is a human caricature of a Disney witch and stands in opposition to the countess' pink-rouged roundness and grandmotherly softness that still bears the wide eyes of a young beauty, now made weary by sadness and time. The star of an art form considered a great Soviet achievement to be set in the people's pantheon along with Olympic athletes, nuclear scientists, and cosmonauts, she should stand on the same level with Professor Lindt, but Hitchcock gives him independent and even critical thought and is much harder on the artist that learns nothing from her art, and in fact cares so little for it that she can spot the "enemy" in the audience as she performs on stage in a difficult ballet version of Tchaikovsky's 1876 symphonic poem based on Dante, *Francesca da Rimini*. Rather than insist on a parallel of Armstrong and Sherman with the foolish and later damned couple in the Dante piece, as Spoto suggests, the originally planned piece, Maurice Ravel's impressionistic 1912 *Daphnis et Chloé* ballet, based on a Greek erotic romance, tells quite a different love story: a young man and young woman, raised by different step-parents, fall in love but experience different adventures and threats (including suitors for Chloé and an instructive and possessive lover for Daphnis, as well as the kidnapping of both by pirates), until they find their true parents and identities and can share their destined love through marriage (Sullivan 222; Pomerance 227 n27).

It is therefore the ballerina that is marked as a damned creature by the Dante/Tchaikovsky dance, not this couple, particularly as she subverts her performance with ideological fanaticism born of opportunism. Hitchcock has always warned against the ease in which politics and performance cross, from *The 39 Steps* onward, and the symbolic mix of art and politics in this balletic moment, where the latter is concealed by the former—she never stops her performance, but integrates her policing action in the dance and offstage—represents another crucial moment of impersonation in the film. Here, Hitchcock, who has linked us to the couple's POV for the function of the thriller, also expects us to loathe the ballerina for her behavior. Unlike Professor Lindt, whose explosive conclusion of his meeting with Armstrong is to protect his own formula from theft, the Ballerina is deemed indefensible, and to add injury to her (Soviet) misuse of art, she strikes once more on the boat as the self-appointed executioner of the escaping couple.

In a moment of sheer panic to find a way to escape the police-surrounded theater, Armstrong focuses on the artificial flame on stage and finds his voice, as did Jo McKenna (Doris Day) in her primal scream at Royal Albert Hall in *The Man Who Knew Too Much* (1956), both disrupting a complacent but potentially deadly order with the protest of a single person's voice. Not only does this echo Hitchcock's "memory" of Nazism through the GDR in the film, it is of course tied to Gromek's gas oven death, and the ballerina's witch-like countenance, but also to the metafilmic game of the narrative. Just as Magritte's pipe and cinema, the flame is fake— crepe paper fluttering in a fan—yet its suggestion of burning is just as powerful as if it were real.

Was wird hier gespielt?

Christopher D. Morris understands that "Hitchcock's Derridean world of empty communication, both frightening and droll, is epitomized when his main characters leave a post office in East Berlin and stand by the shop window of an appliance store where behind them, on a television screen, appears this untranslated line of German: 'Gespräche ohne Nutzen' (futile talk)" (54). The message is also a direction for the spectator from a filmmaker who has always remained a powerful, silent director at heart and emphasizes the value of the image in his "pure cinema" montage. Professor Lindt responds to the "truth seeking" questions and verbal jousting of Armstrong by shouting at him (and us), "Learn!" as he scrawls an unintelligible formula on the board that might as well be an artistic design, possibly teaching the spectator the authority of creative intellect and the respect owed that achievement. It might well be Hitchcock advising the studio heads the same before he slams down the proverbial storyboards to protect his own plans for this film.

The largest "torn curtain" is the Lyotardian concept that the grand narratives of history have failed. Jean-François Lyotard argues that we have ceased to believe that narratives of this kind are adequate to represent and contain us. He indicates that the grand narrative may indeed never have been a unifying concept or one of monolithic value. Instead, postmodernity is characterized by an abundance of micro and personal narratives. Lyotard proposed this in 1979, but the implosion of

Hitchcock's "grand" cinematic formula in the 1966 film suggests both the director's understanding that his style has waned with the iconoclastic quality of 1960s film, particularly in the spy genre, and that business as usual was also an absurdity in a destabilized, bi-polar Cold War world on the verge of a confrontation that used fantasy as its security. The nuclear deterrent concept of M.A.D., or Mutual Assured Destruction, which so absurdly presents the rescue of the world by bringing it to an unresolvable opposition, is at the root of *Torn Curtain*'s unintelligible communications. Talk is futile here among the floating signifiers and the spins of two ideological spheres doubling, reflecting, and rivalling one another on the brink of nuclear war. If *North by Northwest* insisted on the problems of communication in an America of cross-hatched connections and steel and glass modernity that celebrates the height of individualism, capitalism, and rationalism, this film places that rationalism and personal identity in question. And so this film suggests with more complex tools the Lyotardian condition already functional in *Rear Window*. There is diversity and variety, but only the imagination of a grand narrative—for the film's diegesis or for the experiment with the protagonist that enacts the cinema/television-spectator relationship. Hitchcock's interest in art, on the other hand, provides the true signposts in *Torn Curtain*. It is a return to the purity of subjective creation and its interpretation in a film in which the director has had to resolve the discordances of its production but maintains his original message through experimental form, destabilized visuals, and the intertextuality of creation.

During the Leipzig to East Berlin resistance group bus ride, an unscheduled stop must be made to pick up a real passenger, an elderly woman with baggage who is hustled aboard so that the escorting Vopos (Volkspolizei or People's Police) that rescued the bus earlier from Soviet army deserters do not get suspicious. She is outraged at the how she is pushed aboard, and when her money for the fare is rejected, she scans the filled space and in a state of bewilderment asks: Was wird hier gespielt?" (What is being played at here?). The question is apt for every level of this film as it is for its targets. Stanley Kubrick has said, "We are not interested in photographing the reality. We are interested in photographing the photograph of reality" ("Interview"). *Torn Curtain* approaches that paradigm in its concern with artifice as it deconstructs the director's thriller and disrupts the safety and clarity of the spectator's voyeurism, even with the studio's interference, into a statement on the Cold-War, national representation, film creation and art, and morality that verges on counter-cinema. It serves as the director's abstract *performance* of a Hitchcock thriller, in an effort to escape the making of a traditional one.

Notes

1. Spoto had already hinted at the "themes of journey and displacement" framed by false pretenses from the side of the United States and Armstrong's selfishness (355).

2. There are quite a few parallels in cinematic approaches to identity, social construction, irony, and moral/ethical questions that Wilder and Hitchcock share given reflective elements of their backgrounds, their relationships with their origins, with Germany, class, and gender that should be explored systematically. I offer a slim introduction into the possibilities in "Home/Sick: Locating Billy Wilder's Cinematic Austria."

3. "I did not have to act in *Torn Curtain*. I merely went along for the ride. I don't feel that the part demanded much of me, other than to look glamorous, which Mr. Hitchcock can always arrange better than anyone. I did have reservations about this film, but I wasn't agonized by it. The kick of it was working for Hitchcock. That's what I did it for, and that's what I got out of it" (Maxford 31).

4. James Vest locates evidence of Hitchcock's "Francophilic tendencies" in *Strangers on a Train* and *I Confess* and writes that the "apparent motiveless killing" in *Strangers* is "a representation of a nonchalant *acte gratuit*, as described by Gide and Camus" (371).

5. For example, *The Quiller Memorandum* (1966), *The Salzburg Connection* (1972), *The Odessa File* (1974), *The Boys from Brazil* (1978), and so on.

6. The German surname Jacobi (from the Biblical name Jacob or Jakob) tends to be historically associated with Jewish families.

7. An unscientific but still pertinent poll taken from the reaction of several screenings of the film to my advanced undergraduate film students and film faculty.

8. Charlotte Chandler writes: "There was an ending written for *Torn Curtain*," Hitchcock said, "which wasn't used, but I rather liked it. No one agreed with me except my colleague at home [his wife Alma]. Everyone told me that you couldn't have a letdown ending after all that. Newman would have thrown the formula away. After what he has gone through, after everything we have endured with him, he just tosses it. It speaks to the futility of all, and it's in keeping with the kind of naivete of the character, who is no professional spy and who will certainly retire from that nefarious business" (285).

9. "The land of poets and thinkers" is a phrase referring to Germans and Germany that originated in different formulations from varied literary figures (Johann Musäus, Saul Ascher, Jean Paul, Wolfgang Menzel, Madame de Staël, and others) during the early nineteenth century. It reflected the importance of the German language, culture and art that had firmly established itself in Europe and beyond in the previous century and also a new German nationalism which was awakened by Napoleon's wars and desired the creation of a unified German state.

10. Peucker refers to Steven Jacobs' information that "only the doorway and the pillars were constructions" (58).

11. Neo-classicism was also the basis for the gargantuan architectural style of Nazi Germany, and the philosophy of the era of the Enlightenment which is associated with neo-classicism in art, architecture and literature was often utilized to valorize the "rationalism" of Nazism in its cinema and literature.

12. A German romantic period fairy tale published by the Brothers Grimm in 1812.

13. Following the Edenic idyll in Kleist's *Erdbeben*, the rescued couple and a baby are brutally killed during a mass in a surviving cathedral as the congregation seeks scapegoats for God's wrath.

Works Cited

Barr, Charles. *English Hitchcock*. Cameron and Hollis, 1999.

Bauhaus in East Germany: The Formalism Debate. www.smow.com/blog/2016/12/bauhaus-in-east-germany-the-formalism-debate/#Bauhaus DDR_8/.

Bergala, Alain. "Alfred, Adam and Eve." *Hitchcock and Art: Fatal Coincidences*, edited by Dominique Païni and Guy Cogeval, The Montreal Museum of Fine Arts/Mazzota, 2000, pp. 111-25.

Bronfen, Elisabeth. "Screening and Disclosing Fantasy: Rear Projection in Hitchcock." *Screen*, vol. 56, no.1, March 2015. doi.org/10.1093 screen/hjv004.

Chandler, Charlotte. *It's Only a Movie: Alfred Hitchcock, A Personal Biography*. Applause, 2006.

Dassanowsky, Robert. "A Reasonable Fantasy: The Musical Film under Austrofascism (1933-38)." *Colloquia Germanica* 4, 2013, pp. 319-40.

---. "Home/Sick: Locating Billy Wilder's Cinematic Austria." *Journal of Austrian Studies*, vol. 46, no. 3, 2013, pp. 1-25.

Firth, Catriona. *Modern Austrian Literature through the Lens of Adaptation.* Rodopi, 2012.

Foreign Correspondent. Directed by Alfred Hitchcock, performances by Joel McCrea, Laraine Day, Herbert Marshall, George Sanders, and Albert Bassermann, Walter Wagner Productions/United Artists, 1940.

Grafe, Frieda. "Verblichen, die Farben der DDR: Hitchcock's Palette und Rohmer als Vermittler." *Filmfarben. Ausgewählte Schriften,* vol. 1, Brinkmann & Bose, 2002, pp. 85-97.

Hark, Ina Rae. "Hitchcock Discovers America: The Selznick-Era Films." *A Companion to Alfred Hitchcock,* edited by Thomas Leitch and Leland Poague, John Wiley and Sons, 2014, pp. 289-308.

"Interview with Jack Nicholson," *Stanley Kubrick: A Life in Pictures.* Directed by Jan Harlan, Warner Brothers, 2001.

Jacobs, Steven. *The Wrong House: The Architecture of Alfred Hitchcock.* 010 Publishers, 2007.

Johnson, Daniel. "A New Life and a New Tyranny." Review of *The Lesser Evil: The Diaries of Victor Klemperer, 1945-1959.* www.telegraph.co.uk/culture/books/3603547/A-new-life-and-a-new-tyranny.html.

Kapsis, Robert E. *Hitchcock: The Making of a Reputation.* U of Chicago Press, 1992.

Klemperer, Victor, *The Lesser Evil: The Diaries of Victor Klemperer, 1945–1959.* Translated by Martin Chalmers, Weidenfeld & Nicolson, 2003.

The Lady Vanishes. Directed by Alfred Hitchcock, performances by Margaret Lockwood, Michael Redgrave, Paul Lukas, May Whitty, and Cecil Parker, Gainsborough Pictures, 1938.

Lifeboat. Directed by Alfred Hitchcock, Performances by Tallulah Bankhead, William Bendix, Walter Slezak, John Hodiak, and Mary Anderson, Twentieth Century Fox, 1944.

Maxford, Howard. *The A-Z of Hitchcock: The Ultimate Reference Guide.* Batsford, 2003.

McHale, Brian. *Postmodernist Fiction.* Routledge, 1989.

Mogg, Ken. *The MacGuffin: News and Comment,* 10 Nov. 2012, the.hitchcock.zone/wiki/The_MacGuffin:_News_and_Comment_(10/Nov/2012).

---. *The MacGuffin: News and Comment,* 17 Nov. 2012, the.hitchcock.zone/wiki/The_MacGuffin:_News_and_Comment_(17/Nov/2012).

---. *The MacGuffin: News and Comment,* 24 Nov. 2012, the.hitchcock.zone/wiki/The_ MacGuffin:_News_and_Comment_ (24/Nov/2012).

Morris, Christopher D. "*Torn Curtain's* Futile Talk." *Cinema Journal,* vol. 39, no. 1, 1999, pp. 54-73.

Ness, Richard, R. "Hitchcock and Melodrama." *A Companion to Alfred Hitchcock,* edited by Thomas Leitch and Leland Poague, John Wiley and Sons, 2014, pp. 109-25.

North by Northwest. Directed by Alfred Hitchcock, performances by Cary Grant, Eva Marie Saint, James Mason, Jessie Royce Landis, and Leo G. Carroll, MGM, 1959.

Païni, Dominique. "Forms and Rhythms. *Hitchcock and Art: Fatal Coincidences,* edited by Dominique Païni and Guy Cogeval, The Montreal Museum of Fine Arts / Mazzota, 2000, pp. 379-81.

Peucker, Brigitte. "Aesthetic Space in Hitchcock." *A Companion to Alfred Hitchcock,* edited by Thomas Leitch and Leland Poague, John Wiley and Sons, 2014, pp. 201-18.

Pomerance, Murray. *An Eye for Hitchcock.* Rutgers UP, 2004.

The Prize. Directed by Mark Robson, performances by Paul Newman, Edward G. Robinson, Elke Sommer, Diane Baker, and Micheline Presle, Roxbury Productions/MGM, 1963.

Ron, Moshe. "Restricted Abyss: Nine Problems in the Theory of Mise en Abyme." *Poetics Today,* 8, 1987, pp. 417-38.

Saboteur. Directed by Alfred Hitchcock, performances by Priscilla Lane, Robert Cummings, Otto Kruger, Alan Baxter, Clem Bevans, Frank Lloyd Productions/Universal Pictures, 1942.

Secret Agent. Directed by Alfred Hitchcock, performances by Madeleine Carroll, Peter Lorre, John Gielgud, Robert Young, and Lilli Palmer, Gaumont, 1936.

The Shining. Directed by Stanley Kubrick, performances by Jack Nicholson, Shelley Duvall, Danny Lloyd, Scatman Crothers, and Barry Nelson, Hawk Films/Warner Brothers, 1980.

Silverman, Kaja. *The Subject of Semiotics.* Oxford UP, 1983.

Spoto, Donald. *The Art of Alfred Hitchcock: Fifty Years of His Motion Pictures.* Anchor Books, 1992.

The Spy Who Came in from the Cold. Directed by Martin Ritt, performances by Richard Burton, Oskar Werner, Claire Bloom, Sam

Wanamaker, and Rupert Davies, Salem Films/Paramount Pictures, 1965.

Sullivan, Jack. "Hitchcock and Music." *A Companion to Alfred Hitchcock*, edited by Thomas Leitch and Leland Poague, John Wiley and Sons, 2014, pp. 219-36.

The 39 Steps. Directed by Alfred Hitchcock, performances by Robert Donat, Madeleine Carroll, Lucie Mannheim, Godfrey Tearle and Peggy Ashcroft, Gaumont, 1935.

Torn Curtain. Directed by Alfred Hitchcock, performances by Paul Newman, Julie Andrews, Lila Kedrova, Hansjoerg Felmy, Tamara Toumanova, and Ludwig Donath, Universal Pictures, 1966.

Truffaut, Francois. *Hitchcock*, revised edition, with the collaboration of Helen G. Scott, Simon and Schuster, 1983.

Vertigo. Directed by Alfred Hitchcock, performances by James Stewart, Kim Novak, Barbara Bel Geddes, Tom Helmore, and Henry Jones, Alfred J. Hitchcock Productions/Paramount Pictures, 1958.

Vest, James M. "French Hitchcock, 1945-1955." *A Companion to Alfred Hitchcock*, edited by Thomas Leitch and Leland Poague, John Wiley and Sons, 2014, pp. 367-404.

Waltzes from Vienna. Directed by Alfred Hitchcock, performances by Jessie Matthews, Edmund Gwenn, Fay Compton, Esmond Knight, and Frank Vosper, Gaumont, 1934.

Yacowar, Maurice. *Hitchcock's British Films*. Archon, 1977.

Espionage and Humanity: The Cold War in Hitchcock's *Topaz*

By Walter Srebnick

The Cold War is never far in the background of Alfred Hitchcock's post-war films. It often permeates their narratives and his characters' lives with an undefined, free-floating fear. In his later espionage films, such as *Torn Curtain* (1966) and *Topaz* (1969), this fear is connected with the terror of nuclear annihilation and is an explicit, immediate presence shaping the narrative, the characters, and even the visual imagery. Nowhere is this more evident than in *Topaz*, his adaptation of a 1967 Leon Uris novel about the spying that helped resolve a Cold War nuclear conflict between the US and the Soviet Union favorably for the United States: the Cuban Missile Crisis of 1962 (Uris).

Like other of the director's later films, *Topaz* is a better, more interesting work than earlier reviewers and critics give it credit for. It has a sweeping suspense narrative and many characters that keep the viewer engaged throughout. However, *Topaz* remains a problematic and not entirely satisfying film partially because of its relationship to the source novel, the time of its release, and its representation of this particular moment in the Cold War: a terrifying standoff between the two nuclear adversaries. Despite an attempt to transcend the book's mean-spirited and heavy-handed anti-communism and present a more sympathetic view of the characters and their relationships, Hitchcock remained limited by his source. As a result, the film does not sufficiently escape the novel's labored characterization and plot devices, even in the longer DVD version that I will discuss, with its different ending from the original release.

The film villainizes the Russians and the Cubans in stereotypical terms, while America and American values and what America perceived as its Cold War interests receive a more even-handed and nuanced treatment. As a result, the full humanity and complexity of the characters and their relationships on both sides are often compromised by the limited trajectory of the plot and its dominant ideology. This becomes evident in the way the narrative and the characters develop and in the film's visual language that is sometimes in conflict with its verbal language. The finished film thus seems not to have fulfilled the director and screenwriter's professed intentions to create a rich human drama with a poignant "story" at its center. These shortcomings were also exacerbated by the historical context of what was happening abroad and at home in Cold War America at the time of the film's production in 1968 and release in 1969: the disastrous Vietnam War and the growing anti-war movement and counterculture.

Topaz in the Vietnam Era

Topaz is unique among Hitchcock's espionage films in that its subject matter is based on an actual event: the Cuban Missile Crisis. While it fictionalizes that event as had the Uris novel and places the theft of secret documents by agents working for the US at the center of the espionage narrative, it stays remarkably close to the broad outline of what actually happened in 1962. A French spy ring did work for the Russians very much like the one that in the film is called *Topaz*. Even several of the main characters, such as the French spy Andre Devereaux and Juanita de Cordoba, his Cuban counterpart and love interest, were modeled after real people: an actual French agent and allegedly Fidel Castro's sister Juanita Castro (McGilligan 683). Hitchcock's use of newspaper headlines to provide a contemporary American historical background for what occurs in the film further reinforces a sense of verisimilitude. But the seven years between the actual events and the release of Hitchcock's film had produced great changes in American culture, and particularly in attitudes toward the Cold War, changes that were then firmly at odds with the film's portrayal of the United States and its foreign policy. While the contemporary American press and public had in 1962 overwhelmingly supported American actions during the Cuban Missile Crisis and the stand taken by the young president John F. Kennedy, by 1968 the American public and the media had turned against the Vietnam War. By that point Vietnam defined America in the Cold War and by 1969 the country was challenging not only America's position in Vietnam but also the Cold War itself. A corresponding challenge to

Espionage and Humanity 141

America's Cold War interests in the cinematic narrative would have made *Topaz* a more interesting film.

At the time of the Missile crisis in 1962, Vietnam and the conflict there were little known to the American public, even though the US had helped install an unpopular anti-communist regime in the south of the country. By 1969, however, an escalating war in Vietnam had become a national crisis that had weakened not only America's position abroad, but support for the Cold War and American anti-communism at home. The Vietnam War was strongly connected to President Lyndon Johnson, and by 1969 to Richard Nixon, rather than their predecessor, John F. Kennedy, from whom Johnson had inherited the war and who had actually first committed the US to pursuing it militarily. In 1962, the Cuban Missile Crisis, however, was identified more with Russian aggression than with a failing US policy or with Cuba, which was viewed as the underdeveloped communist puppet of the Soviet Union from which that aggression could proceed. At the time, Americans credited Kennedy with staring down Premier Nikita Khrushchev and the Russians and with resolving the Missile Crisis in America's and the world's best interest, a view that *Topaz* appears to confirm (Gaddis 75-78).

Even years later Americans continued to associate Kennedy with the Missile Crisis rather than with Vietnam. So while the public, and movie audiences in particular, had been more than willing to support the government's Cold War policy in Cuba in 1962, by 1969 in the case of Vietnam the opposite was true; in fact, in some circles Vietnam was now positively associated with Cuba, and both countries were seen as underdog, underdeveloped nations that were being challenged by a powerful antagonist: the US. This perception undoubtedly impacted the film's reception then, both with reviewers and audiences. The Vietnam War and criticism of the American Cold War foreign policy position as the "world's policeman" in that conflict and elsewhere became, I believe, the elephant in the room in theaters throughout the US, even though it was not acknowledged explicitly in reviews (McElroy). Most contemporary reviews considered the film a weak effort by Hitchcock, and two reviews in particular, Vincent Canby's positive notice in *The New York Times* and Richard Corliss's harsher account in *Film Quarterly*, called out what they saw as the film's political conservatism (Canby, Corliss). By 1969, the 1962 Cold War anti-communist sensibility of the film was an anachronistic throwback—one more likely to be rejected than supported.

US policies toward Vietnam and Cuba were in many ways analogous: both policies had more to do with its conflict with the Soviet Union than with its relationship to either of these small countries. The Soviets had supported both the North Vietnamese Viet Minh and the southern Viet Cong beginning in the post-war period and afterwards, just as they had earlier supported the Chinese and Korean communists. At the same time, first President Harry Truman in the late 1940s, and then Dwight Eisenhower had supported and bankrolled the French military effort to hold onto Vietnam as a colony, fearing that the fall of Vietnam to the communists could have a domino effect on other nations nearby (Gaddis 130-134). And in 1960, the Russians gained an unanticipated Cold War victory much closer to American shores, and a strategic ally, when the Cuban Revolution turned Marxist under Fidel Castro and embraced the Russians as their mentors and protectors. Within a short span of time Cuba became aligned with the Soviet bloc, and Soviet aid and military equipment flooded into it. In 1962, the Cuban leader allowed the Soviets to place their nuclear weapons in his country pointed at the US (just as the US had earlier convinced Turkey to allow American missiles pointed at the Soviet Union on its territory).

In both Cuba and Southeast Asia, the chief Cold War conflict at stake was actually the ongoing struggle between the two nuclear superpowers. In fact, American critics of the Vietnam War and the antiwar movement saw the war as having little to do with American interests, except in a very marginal sense, and some saw analogies between our policy in Vietnam and our policy toward Cuba. In both countries the US had a history of supporting corrupt interests and dictators, such as the Diem family and Batista, who had little popular support and less concern for the interests of their people. This policy was justified by the American Cold War concepts of containment and the domino theory that supposedly "contained" communism and prevented these countries and their neighbors from falling like "dominoes" in line with the communists. Ironically, just five years after the release of *Topaz*, *The Godfather: Part II* (1973) would set some of its most important scenes in the politically corrupt Cuba of 1959 and suggest that the left-wing revolutionaries overthrowing the Batista-like dictator were heroes.

Espionage and Humanity

In essence, 1969 America was mired in a tragic military conflict that called into question the US position in the Cold War, a crisis affecting and changing American culture. The release of *Topaz* late in 1969 came after the North Vietnamese and the Viet Cong's Tet offensive of 1968 and their subsequent coordinated nation-wide assault on American and South Vietnamese positions. These attacks had convinced most Americans that a military solution was impossible, and events such as the My Lai Massacre of innocent civilians in 1968 had undercut American claims to the moral high ground, which it seemed to have had in the 1962 crisis. In reaction, anti-war protests reached their peak throughout the country at this time, particularly on college campuses. There left-wing student movements proliferated and college dorm walls were covered with pictures of the North Vietnamese leader Ho Chi Minh, and the Cuban revolutionaries Che Guevara and Fidel Castro, both of whom actually appear in *Topaz* through archival footage.[1]

A Hollywood effort in 1968 to create a film supporting the war, *The Green Berets* starring John Wayne, was widely considered fraudulent, hooted at by theater audiences, and mocked by reviewers, one of whom called it "unspeakable," "stupid," "rotten," and "false" (Adler). At the same time, Hollywood was producing films that reflected and applauded the growing contemporary counterculture and its anti-war values, particularly in films such as *Butch Cassidy and the Sundance Kid*, *Alice's Restaurant*, *The Graduate*, and the explicitly anti-war *M*A*S*H*. So, in essence, *Topaz* was being released to an American audience much less willing to accept American espionage, or espionage done in the name of America's Cold War interests or anti-communism, in the positive, uncritical terms that it would have seven years earlier.

How sensitive Hitchcock was to these political and cultural changes in relation to the Vietnam War is hard to determine; certainly screenwriter Samuel Taylor was and tried to get Hitchcock to shape the narrative into something much closer to John le Carré's *The Spy Who Came in from the Cold* (1963) that had been adapted as a highly successful film by Martin Ritt in 1965. Taylor's goal, which he felt the director shared, was to show "that the Cold War, and spying, and power politics, destroys lives" (McGilligan 693), which le Carré's novel and Ritt's film had done so poignantly. Taylor had given *Vertigo* (1958) a rich human dimension, which the original screenplay lacked when he took over as screenwriter, by adding the grounded female character Midge and by weaving into the narrative specific San Francisco locales whose historical resonance impacts the characters' lives. On *Topaz*, however, he came to the project too late. He took over the writing from novelist Uris at the last minute, and was composing dialogue and scenes just before they were shot and even before the entire cast was selected (McGilligan 686-90; Nadel 187-88). As a result, one of the things lost in the process was what Taylor frequently referred to as the "story" of a Hitchcock film, as opposed to its "plot," or narrative events. In *Vertigo* the story is a man's attempt to recreate a beloved woman for whose death he feels unbearable guilt: the plot, however, is much more farfetched. In *Topaz* there is a great deal of plot covering at least four settings, each with its own cast of characters and most of it believable, but relatively little "story." This by itself made the project daunting for a director and a screenwriter who had in their previous collaboration focused on a narrower tableau with a richer human core. If *Topaz* had not had so sprawling a plot, the "story" might have concerned how a spy, Andre Devereaux, helps solve an international crisis and perhaps saves the world, but in the process ends up sacrificing people he loves, relationships he treasures, and his own happiness. All of this happens because he allows himself to subscribe to Cold War values and alliances that are themselves tainted. This is in fact what Hitchcock's suggested was his own sense of the film, though it became diluted during the process of making it.

Hitchcock's actual announcement of the project on May 3, 1968, came at the historical moment "between the assassinations of Martin Luther King, Jr., and Robert F. Kennedy, and just days after Lyndon Johnson's declaration that he would not run for a second full term as president" (Spoto 499). Hitchcock was aware of the significance of this last event, and perhaps its relationship to the unpopularity of the Vietnam War. He was not totally divorced from politics: he had been one of the speakers at an inauguration event for Johnson in 1964, and in 1968 he even played on Johnson's word "run" when announcing *Topaz* as his upcoming project as if he expected his audience to have Johnson's words in mind. Yet he insisted that his film would "emphasize not political but emotional realities" (499), ones that would create the kind of "story" that Taylor suggested was at the heart of the director's best work. But perhaps Hitchcock's lack of sensitivity to political realities actually undermined the emotional realities he hoped to foreground in the project. In both the novel and the film versions of *The Spy Who Came in from the Cold* these Cold War political realities are articulated very candidly in geopolitical terms by "Control," the spymaster who sends the protagonist Alec Leamus on his mission:

> The ethic of our work is that we are never going to be aggressors....Thus we do disagreeable things, but we are *defensive*....I would say that since the war—our methods and those of the opposition—have become much the same. I mean you can't be less ruthless than the opposition simply because your government's policy is benevolent, can you now? (le Carré 15-16)

In that film ruthlessness takes precedence over benevolence on both sides, and the story concerns the way Leamus decides that his human values are more important, and actually goes to his death for them, after being betrayed by both sides. In *Topaz*, however, a film produced three years farther into the Cold War, the human realities that would have made for a "story" suffer, largely because the film seems committed to making the Americans and their operatives come off far better and less ruthless than their communist opponents, particularly in visual terms.

Topaz as Visual Ideology

To have created a film about the personal and emotional realities of the espionage that resolved the Missile Crisis in the favor of the US, without tipping the human balance in favor of the US, would have meant making a different film than the one Hitchcock produced, one that would have presented the politics and espionage closer to what Control articulates above. The director had hoped to repeat the success he had had earlier with a film such as *Notorious* (1946), an espionage thriller with complex characters and relationships at the heart of the narrative. But in the view of novelist Uris, Hitchcock did not understand how much espionage had changed since the earlier film. According to Uris, who had been the film's first screenwriter, the director had little insight into the "political complexities" that now existed (McGilligan

385). Despite several commentators who assert that *Topaz* exposes the terrible human toll of espionage and the Cold War (Wood, McGilligan, Krohn, Walker), the film never deviates far enough from the novel's ideological position to do so convincingly. Much of the human toll is too easy to ascribe to the ruthlessness of communism, or the communists. From the outset the film's emphasis is on political plot intrigue and the superiority of the cultural and ethical position of the West and its standard of living, particularly the United States. While the human and personal are forefronted in scenes such as those involving the Kuzenov family, Andre Devereaux and his wife Nicole, and Andre and Juanita, Andre never seems to be sufficiently caught between his personal and political worlds, and is never critical of the Americans or their position. This American/Western bias becomes evident from the opening credits in Moscow's Red Square and a May Day military parade, effectively the film's first political scene.

The credits play over this scene with its dull colors, military music, and a banner with images of Marx, Engels, and Lenin that fills the screen in a reverse tracking shot that sets the ideological tone. Titles inform us we are about to see Alfred Hitchcock's *Topaz* from the novel by Leon Uris, but the next information on the screen shows how much Uris and his values are still present in the film's Cold War stereotyping. Samuel Taylor later lamented the lack of sufficient narrative depth and substance in the source (Spoto 503), but here he bears responsibility too for some of the rhetorical excesses: "Somewhere in this crowd is a high Russian official," a prologue title informs the audience, "who disagrees with his government's show of force and what it threatens. Very soon his conscience will force him to attempt an escape while on an apparent vacation with his family." The binary opposition set up at the opening is very revealing: the threatening "force" we see here at Red Square in this display of military might and elsewhere is all Soviet, while "conscience" leads Kuzenov, a high Soviet official, shortly later to defect to America and to the Americans because of what they stand for. As the leader of the free world, the US, it is implied, employs force only "defensively," to paraphrase Control, when it must, but to different ends as the ultimate arbiter of "conscience" and freedom in the world.

The opening sequence in Copenhagen, which in a familiar Hitchcock manner identifies the place and the date (1962), reaffirms the conflict

Espionage and Humanity

between the Soviets and the US through a contrast that visually parallels the opening dualism about "force" and "conscience." This is apparent in the disparity between the way the Russian and American embassies are represented as well as the agents connected to each. The wire fence and mirrors that define the Soviet embassy with its prison-like demeanor as it is shot from above contrast dramatically with the open, spacious, and fenceless American embassy. Menacing agents people the Soviet embassy, one of whose threatening visage in close up in a mirror is the first human face we see. Two Russian operatives and a dowdy glamorless woman then trail the three Kuzenovs—father, mother, and daughter—as they exit the embassy in a long left to right single tracking shot on their way to a porcelain factory. (The woman's appearance becomes more glaring in light of the beautiful, superbly groomed French women we will see in the rest of the film.) The delicacy and precision of the escape is underscored by the delicacy and precision of the porcelain in the factory from which daughter Tamara Kuzenov makes her phone call. In contrast to its Soviet equivalent, at the utilitarian US embassy the handsome, paternal John Forsythe as Mike Nordstrom answers the phone firmly, but reassuringly, in a close-up at his desk. Over his right shoulder there is a photo of John F. Kennedy, the symbol of conscience and freedom who will resolve the missile crisis, as Nordstrom details for Tamara Kuzenov the scenario for her family's escape to freedom. Clearly, even when the dialogue is more neutral, Hitchcock begins the film with Cold War visual clichés in order to define the different sides and their respective values.

This contrast is dramatically extended in the actual escape outside the Den Permanente department store, as the ruthless, brutal Russian agents make the threat they represent very real in a show of "force." They draw and aim their handguns at the would-be defectors and then at their retreating car with the three Kuzenovs and Nordstrom inside, only to be thwarted by the swift maneuvering of the "defensive" Americans. Even an errant bicycle that upends daughter Tamara on the way to the car to freedom gives the Americans agents the opportunity for an extra moment of suspense-filled heroics as they help her up and block the Russians. Once the Kuzenovs are on the plane that will bring them to freedom just outside of Washington DC, it is the American Mike Nordstrom who shows the concern and sensitivity associated with freedom for young Tamara's scratched knees and female pride when he asks the pilots to radio ahead for two different sizes of nylons as the plane rises into a promising sunset on its way to the US.

In general, however, the dialogue seems to attempt a more even-handed human portrait of each side, more than the visual narrative, even before Andre Devereaux makes an appearance in the film. While actual Soviet policy believed an intransigent, dictatorial, even cruel, modus operandi in their espionage and international security apparatus was necessary for survival against the capitalist West, the Russians tried to present a more human face in their personal, diplomatic, and cultural dealings (Gaddis 29). Some of this is clearly reflected and embedded in the film's dialogue and screenplay. Kuzenov, the unsmiling defector and the sole Russian we see in any depth after the opening, reveals his humanity when he professes to be interested solely in sanctuary and protection for himself and his family, and harbors, as he maintains, a certain amount of understandable guilt for betraying his country. Yet his "liberators" taunt him just as cruelly as his compatriots might have an American defector in his position. When McKittreck, his interrogator, admonishes him for his reluctance to divulge secrets, the American threatens: "the way you are going you might find yourself on the steps of the Russian embassy." This statement seems to present the Americans as potentially as self-serving and ruthless as their Russian enemies, but the visual imagery of what the Kuzenovs are being offered tends to undercut and soften this verbal threat. They are housed in an impressive upscale Georgian mansion just outside of Washington where every one of their needs is attended to by helpful, caring servants.

Later when Boris Kuzenov balks during the interrogation, Mike Nordstrom, echoing McKittreck's earlier threat, immediately cautions him that: "If you had me in Russia and I wouldn't talk, what do you think would happen to me?" This warning is reinforced by the choice the Russian is later given between a new identity, a "business" he will be set up in, and a musical conservatory scholarship for Tamara, or finding themselves abandoned on their own after a month if he refuses. But the visual imagery all along undercuts such threats in the dialogue at moments such as when friendly agents give the Kuzenovs an impromptu tour of the Capital on their drive to the "safe house," demonstrating that this world with its symbols of freedom will be their new home.

Espionage and Humanity

Similarly, to sweeten the material possibilities of their defection, Tamara is later shown happily playing a piano, and in the adjoining room Mrs. Kuzenov is custom-fitted for a dress. Just like these images of consumerism, leisure, and opportunity, the "business" Kuzenov is offered smacks of free enterprise capitalism at its most optimistic.

One of the issues raised in the novel that becomes problematic in the film concerns this American setting and American values. Although the conflict at the center of the narrative involves the two major antagonists of the Cold War—the Soviet Union and the US—the protagonist who eventually enters the narrative to help resolve it is not an American. In fact, he enters the narrative after the Soviets and the Americans have been visually at the center of it. Why does Andre Devereaux, a French national and agent, agree to work for the Americans? What, simply put, is his motivation? In the book Uris attempts to solve this by making him a champion of NATO, a dedicated anti-communist, something of an Americanophile, and someone who loves his native country but does not trust its leadership. This leadership is epitomized in the novel by a President Le Croix, a clear stand-in for French President Charles de Gaulle, who was a strong critic of America. Unlike the stereotype of so many of his countrymen, the novel's Andre believes America's Cold War "defensive" position regarding the Soviet Union is the correct one and the only way to preserve freedom in Europe and the entire West. Rather than disdaining American culture, Uris's Andre loves almost all things American, particularly bourbon and baseball. So when there are indications of something suspicious going on in Cuba, Andre offers his services to Nordstrom even though it will strain both his personal and professional life. But Andre's "story" in the film never emerges beyond his role in the plot, and to a large extent the anti-communism the film seems to have preserved from the novel makes a story very unlikely. Just what does he believe, or what in his past, such as Scotty Ferguson's rooftop disaster in *Vertigo*, makes him take this assignment on?

In the film Andre and Mike Nordstrom are friends who enjoy the occasional drink or meal together and who cooperate with each other in the interest of their respective nations, but they realize where the personal and political come into conflict. The dialogue tries to make sense of their relationship at the same time as it emphasizes the personal toll of their work and the uniqueness of their relationship: "Mike," Andre insists, "you and I have done things for each other that no other agents in this town would do." Even when Andre's marriage is threatened by his taking on this mission for Nordstrom, their friendship and bond with each other never wavers, although Nordstrom acknowledges and seems sympathetic to the strain on Andre's marriage. But whenever there is an American policy issue at stake as we later see, it takes precedence for Nordstrom over their personal bond and his empathy, and he lets Andre know he is on his own. Similarly, when the narrative shows instances when the personal and intimate are threatened or compromised by the political, it reveals more strain than irreparable harm within relationships. When Nicole, Andre's wife, communicates her displeasure to Andre about his spying for the Americans and her cynical distaste for the Cold War in general, she asserts it is a struggle between the Soviets and America that France has nothing to do with and that Andre should have no part of. Taylor's dialogue makes this very clear: "Let the Americans do their own dirty work!" she insists. Nonetheless, she entertains Nordstrom graciously at dinner and even lets him know that she is fond of him. The sense in the film is that within the context of American culture and values, human relations can thrive or, if injured, can presumably be healed. Ultimately, the film shows that working for the US and being connected to its agents is working for the right side not only politically, or morally ("conscience"), but personally as well.

Andre's family also provides an interesting parallel to that of the Kuzenovs, who quickly learn all the benefits of joining the right side: this parallel between families gives the plot an element of structural coherence with Cold War overtones. At the head of both families are men who are high-ranking government officials, each with a wife and a daughter. Everything is in keeping with contemporary gender values. Nicole Devereaux is clearly the kind of social and fashionable wife that Mrs. Kuzenov yearns to become. Tamara Kuzenov would love to walk in Michelle Devereaux's shoes as well. Her father Boris has made his choice to defect partially in the interest of his family, and of Tamara in particular, and in the interest of the more material possibilities of freedom that the Western Devereauxs epitomize and that his wife and daughter aspire to. Andre, we will see in later scenes, is initially willing to sacrifice family interests to his espionage responsibilities for the Americans, especially at the peril of his relationship with Nicole. But,

Espionage and Humanity 151

like Boris Kuzenov with his priority of family, it is ultimately family in the person of his daughter Michelle and her young husband Francois that will later bring Andre back together with his estranged wife. This will be accomplished at the same time as the last element of the espionage plot is resolved, once again, in the interest of the right side.

The same sense of the "right side" emerges even more stridently in the visual contrast between scenes at New York's elegant and gracious St. Regis Hotel where the Devereaux family are staying, and where Mike Nordstrom recruits Andre for the US espionage mission, and the Hotel Theresa sequence that Hitchcock and Taylor constructed for the film where the Cubans first appear. Borrowing from an actual event, Fidel Castro's stay at the hotel during his trip to New York to address the UN in 1960, the Hotel Theresa sequence reflects the anti-communism that the novel projects and even its stereotyping. Unlike the soothing ambiance of the St. Regis, which projects an air of affluence, respectability, authority and stability (just like the mansion where the Kuzenovs are housed), the film's Theresa is run down and untidy and projects an air of instability and menace. Chaos and anarchy dominate the crowded hallway where Rico Parra, the high Cuban military official, has his room and holds court. Even before the spy Dubois makes his appearance, an establishing shot in the corridor shows it stuffed with people of all sorts and represents the Cubans and their delegation as lawless, slovenly, brutal, and ruthless—the last two of these qualities mirrors what we saw of the threatening Russian agents in the Copenhagen sequence. There is little humanity and less civility among these Cubans, as New York police, hotel personnel, minor functionaries in military fatigues, hangers-on, prostitutes, and even terrorists eager to bomb the Statue of Liberty crowd the halls.

The black florist/spy Dubois, who has an easy rapport with Andre as well as the Cubans, moves almost effortlessly down this hallway and among these people. He manipulates Rico Parra into a sham interview seemingly in the same way he was earlier able to manipulate Rico's secretary Uribe into giving him access to the secret documents in a scene we see soundlessly in close-up from Andre's POV from across the street. He only has to suggest that Parra's reluctance to grant him an interview for *Ebony* makes him "anti-Negro," an obvious communist stereotypical catchphrase, for the Cuban to capitulate and agree to both the interview and photographs: a ruse that will take Parra out of his room long enough for Uribe to remove the attaché case with the secret documents that Dubois will photograph. Extending the stereotypical communist rhetoric, Parra and his lieutenant Hernandez will later refer to Dubois warmly as "comrade" to demonstrate their communist egalitarianism.

But what adds to the ideological oversimplification of Parra's portrayal and is even more damning is what the audience sees of him: his coarseness and slovenliness, as his oily skin suggests that he has not washed for a while. This slovenliness is visually reinforced when Parra hands a document that is covered in grease from his half-eaten hamburger to a typist for copying. Adding to this sense of physical and moral disorder, liquor and beer bottles cover Parra's desk and he pours himself a drink before he notices that his document case is missing. A few moments later an enraged Parra confronts Uribe and Dubois in Uribe's hotel room and fires a pistol at Dubois as he flees down the fire escape to the street. Parra's actions reveal him here to be just as ruthless and murderous as the Russian agents outside of Den Permanente. In short, by the time we get to the supposedly more human and sympathetic Rico Parra during the Cuban scenes, Hitchcock's visual imagery far more than the dialogue has already represented him negatively as a stereotypical Cuban communist thug.

The Cuba Sequences: The Film's Emotional Heart

When the scene shifts to Cuba, Rico Parra is transformed into a character of obvious humanity and complexity in the context of his own country and his love for Juanita de Cordoba. This is the portion of the film where human passions and on-site espionage in Cuba simultaneously dominate the narrative. But the underlying contradictions of Andre's deep feelings never sufficiently match his roles and activities within the narrative as a spy. His "story" never emerges in this part of the film where it should. We first see Rico with his arm resting on Juanita's shoulder, she dressed dramatically in red as Andre arrives at her villa in a French embassy car. The tension between the two men is palpable, fueled by their jealousy over Juanita, whose loving gaze we see in extreme close-up directed at Andre. There is a triangle here, such as

Espionage and Humanity

is evident in some of the director's other espionage thrillers, particularly *Notorious*, and the visual imagery and the shot/counter shot convey this effectively. A similar triangle will emerge later in the film when Nicole Devereaux takes as her lover Jacques Granville, Andre's and her former compatriot in the French resistance and the current head of the spy ring *Topaz*. In addition to adding another element of plot coherence, this triangle gives rise to some of the wittiest and most human lines in the film, such as the banter between Juanita and Andre after Rico departs. She refers to Parra as her "landlord" whom she needs to placate, and Andre asks her if he had come to "collect the rent." She then counters to Andre: "And how is your wife?" This is an example of Samuel Taylor's comedy of manners at its best, and it serves to verbally accentuate the human drama of what is going on with its defusing playfulness, drama that is suggestive of a "story."

Andre seems to feel the competition of Rico, but he never betrays as much emotion as his adversary, or as Juanita—certainly not a sufficient intensity of emotion for his "story" to govern the narrative. By contrast, the humanity of Parra comes through clearly in his love for Juanita, and he seems like a different man than the slovenly, explosive brute of the Hotel Theresa sequence, a man governed as much by feelings as by political imperatives. He even backs off later largely because of his feelings for Juanita when she confronts him at her dinner with Andre and accuses him of jealousy when he tries to order Andre to accompany him back to Havana. These two forces in Rico—political imperative and emotion—converge most powerfully and movingly in the much-discussed scene in which he shoots and kills Juanita at the bottom of the staircase to save her from torture, one of the great staircase scenes in Hitchcock. But Rico's story is not the one that should have been central in this part of the film.

Like in *Notorious*, this section of *Topaz* also has repeated moments of kissing between Andre and Juanita, the important difference being that they occur at repeated intervals throughout the Cuban scenes and never approach the visual intensity of the single sustained long-take dinner scene between Ingrid Bergman and Cary Grant. That scene powerfully exposes the tension between what Grant is feeling for Bergman and the detached, vigilant political role he believes he must play. No equivalent tension between roles emerges for Andre's character in *Topaz*, despite Karen Dor's passionate portrayal of Juanita. There is almost a James Bond-like coolness to the suave Andre during these scenes. And rather than parallel political scenes that build up personal tension, such as those in *Notorious* between the Claude Rains character and the Nazis or those between Claude Rains and his mother, such scenes in the Cuban portion of the film devolve visually into Cold War clichés. The Cuban soldiers who accompany Parra are coarse, menacing, inarticulate, and brutal. The truckload of Russian technicians we subsequently see on their way to the port where the missiles are being unloaded are all stereotypically dressed uniformly in white shirts, caps, and dark trousers, and are singing a Red Army Chorus song. The later torture scene of the Mendozas, with the dead Pablo on Carlotta's lap in a kind of *Pietá* moment, adds visually to the brutality associated with the communist Russians and Cubans and undercuts any possibility of a more even-handed portrayal in the film.[2] Similarly, the recognition scene at the rally with Juanita, Rico, and Hernandez on stage that uses archival footage of an actual Cuban rally with Fidel Castro as the speaker about to deliver a polemical tirade and Che Guevara adjusting his beret is straight out of Cold War anti-Cuban propaganda and, as such, not a humanizing moment. It is also perhaps of some significance that as the Vietnam War dragged on, Fidel Castro made repeated references to the war in such speeches and often compared Cuba and its struggles with the US to those of the small Asian nation.

In these Cuban scenes Andre Devereaux is able to penetrate Cuba and move freely there as he does because he is French, and he can do so in a way no American agent possibly could. By extension, even his earlier successful spying at Hotel Theresa was based on his and Dubois' "Frenchness"[3] and not on their working ultimately for the US. But being French will only get him so far. His wife Nicole had earlier appealed to his French identity not only to keep him from doing the business of the Americans, but as a way of attempting to reaffirm their relationship, a scene that adds to the humanizing elements present in the film's dialogue. Even Juanita will question his being in Cuba at this moment when she says, "the French don't give a damn about Cuba!" And Rico Parra will challenge his actual identity and express his suspicions when he interrupts the romantic dinner Andre has with Juanita. France, French issues, and Andre's French identity will be at the center of the narrative in the film's last section, which moves to Paris. But when he is in Cuba, he is essentially an American agent of French nationality doing the bidding of America, and there is a strange disassociation of the various elements of his identity, particularly his motivation, that affects all of his human relationships. All he ever says about his motivation is, "I've got to see what the Russians are up to in Cuba."

What keeps the Cuban sequences from presenting effectively enough how human relationships are undermined by the demands of espionage is the way spying is depicted and prioritized in these scenes, especially in terms of Andre and his relationships. Hitchcock had never cared for *Topaz* as a novel to start with and had agreed to adapt it to the screen as the best of the alternatives properties offered to him by Universal. In accepting it, he said that he hoped to turn it into a "realistic James Bond film" to which the source novel and the Andre Devereaux character seemed to lend themselves (McGilligan 690). Yet, if this was his intention, there is simply too much Bond in Andre and the narrative, and by extension too little realism and feeling. In Martin Ritt's film version of *The Spy Who Came in from the Cold* the characters and settings are the antithesis of their glamorized counterparts in the Bond series. Even when he is being wry and cynical, Richard Burton's disheveled Leamus oozes emotion and visually inhabits worlds with all the grit of the actual places he travels to. Director Ritt also was working from a source that he could seamlessly quote verbatim in the screenplay, which Hitchcock could not.

In key scenes in Cuba such as those with Juanita, Frederick Stafford's Andre, Hitchcock's Bond equivalent, seems to have his feelings bottled up. Though lacking the cavalier emotional indifference to women of the actual Bond, he shows and expresses so little lasting feeling about Juanita's death as he flies out of Cuba that it is hard to believe he feels her loss very deeply. On the other hand, she, as played by Karin Dor, is the most expressive and poignant character in the film. Juanita cannot leave Cuba to save herself since it is her country, as she tells Andre, and she intends to live and die there: this is perhaps her "story."[4] But Hitchcock provided too much Bond-like visual glamour in these scenes, including the feeling of luxury that pervades Juanita's home and Andre's impeccable grooming as a kind of Bond stand-in. However, by the time the film was in production, James Bond as a symbol and Bond films had fallen out of public favor, according to Robert Kapsis in *Hitchcock: The Making of a Reputation*, because of the growing "antiwar mood of the nation as a whole and the counterculture" (105).

To continue the comparison, the extent of the gadgetry that we see involved in the successful transmission of secrets also seems to suggest too much Bond with its overreliance on gimmicky plot devices: the razor blades, typewriter keys and ribbon, even the comical touch of the camera in the cavity of the chicken Andre and Juanita will have for dinner, compound this sense of Bondian overload and detract from the more human conflicts in the narrative.[5] For example, in the wordless scene on the plane when Andre discovers inside the cover of the notebook the recently murdered Juanita has made for him the photo negatives of the Russian missiles being unloaded, he does so just after he has read her inscription, "With all my love, Juanita, October 1962." The espionage theatrics here diminish, if not overshadow, the depth of both what she has written to him and what the actor tries to show he feels at the moment, especially when a moment later we see in extreme close-up that he has to wet down the book's inner cover in the plane's bathroom to get to what is hidden underneath—clearly a greater priority at this point than his emotional response to the death of a woman he supposedly loved deeply. Feelings have been sacrificed here, not just a living human being, undermined by the Bond-like gadgetry and subterfuge. And while it is possible to argue that all of these emotion-denying gestures are the director's way of showing how much of what is human has been forfeited, the fact that the main character, Andre, moves on so seamlessly with his mission and personal life after her death suggests that the sacrifice was "manageable." One can only imagine how Richard Burton, who stars in *The Spy Who Came in from the Cold*, might have conveyed the emotion and sense of loss in this scene.

A French "Hero" of an American Crisis: Who Stands for America?

After the seemingly traumatic loss of Juanita in Cuba, Andre's composure is remarkably restored once he is back in Washington, but his stay there is short-lived. It is just long enough for him to learn from Boris Kuzenov crucial information about the existence of *Topaz*, the spy ring working for the Soviets at the highest level of the French government, before he is recalled to France by the same French government. But we know little about what Andre actually does for the government, and less about his personal history in France. By contrast, Andre's French background in the novel is very extensive and makes up more than a third of its length. Uris goes into great detail about Andre's past: his aristocratic heritage, his experience as a very young man in the resistance during the Nazi occupation, and his meeting with and falling in love with Nicole during the Second World War. It is perhaps the novelist's way of trying to provide Andre with a "story." Uris also details his version of the complexity of the free French position in the war and especially of the compromises and duplicity of its leadership under the egomaniacal De Gaulle figure, General Le Croix. The implication is that under Le Croix France nearly fell into the Soviet camp, as perhaps by extension in the real world under De Gaulle it might one day. Uris, in fact, attributes the creation of *Topaz* to the "terrible price [paid] for the early alliances with the French communists and the Soviet Union...born of La Croix's blind spot, his extreme abhorrence of the Americans " (Uris 274). The Second World War and Russia's Stalin come into the mix, and the French colonial experience in Vietnam and defeat at Dien Bien Phu are all woven into the novel and the characters' lives, bringing the Vietnam War into play in the narrative.

Perhaps the biggest contradiction within the film's ideology stems from its elimination of all of this French background as well as the novel's representation of the French attitude toward the US in its contemporary foreign policy, especially in relation to Andre. The film's Andre spies for the Americans and their interests in Cuba, and his behavior and actions seem totally allied with American Cold War values. While French history and interests are thus marginalized in Hitchcock's adaptation, if not actually eliminated, Andre's nationality is nonetheless problematic in the film considering what his motivation might be and what his personal interests and those of France are at its end. While he has to try to repair his relationship with Nicole, and is essentially vindicated in his confrontation with *Topaz* and its two French representatives, what his "diplomatic" future will be is left hanging as is what resolving the missile crisis and exposing *Topaz* will mean for

France. Again, this creates a sense of disassociation in the film's narrative and puts the emphasis on plot rather than "story."

The absence of a French narrative context until this point is also problematic as it pulls the narrative in still another direction. The way the film's multiple settings are handled is essentially unique in Hitchcock. Important characters are introduced in each new setting, as are significant and crucial new plot elements. The French spy ring, its exposure and destruction take center stage in the film's last section. In some ways, this structure is more appropriate to a novel than a film, which as Hitchcock asserted several times is closer to a short story. But Andre's motivation is clearly apparent once he is back in Paris, as exposing *Topaz* will restore not only his position with his fellow French diplomats but also his marriage.

The scenes of Andre's earlier contacts with his French superiors in Washington present him as a maverick outsider among his French colleagues, one who is said to lack "respect." This immediately makes him interesting, but it is never explained or developed in a way that would lead to significant characterological possibilities and "story." In the first encounter of Andre and his countrymen, the scene begins with a POV shot of a French general looking down from his embassy window at Andre arriving in his white American car: a French flag is situated prominently below the general to signal France's national and ideological perspective. When the general tells the other French official, Rene d'Arcy, that Andre is "too close to the Americans," d'Arcy responds that "his closeness has value." Clearly his fellow attaché sees Andre as a conduit of important information from the Americans, and d'Arcy praises him as "dedicated." But the words "close" and "closeness" in the dialogue are highly suggestive here, and an instance when the verbal and the visual are totally in synch. As Andre enters and keeps his distance literally at the other side of the room, signaling perhaps his lack of "closeness" and his alienation from his own countrymen, the general questions him about why he did not know of Kuzenov's defection before they did. Andre turns the question on him, responding with sarcasm that "the Americans didn't tell me," and adds the challenging and critical question: "How does Paris know. Did the Russians tell them?" This question about the source of France's information is the nearest we get in the film to Andre challenging France's Cold War position in relation to the US and the Soviet Union and is an implicit critique of France's closeness to America's adversary, and perhaps of the whole espionage enterprise. Like the general, Andre stands throughout this scene and seems, if not hostile, then ill-at-ease at being at his nation's embassy, and their interaction is conveyed in shot/counter shot: the two of them are never in the same frame. But at this point the audience is given no clue as to what his motivation is for this behavior, and little sense of who Andre is, or what he does for France, which is never clarified in the film.

The second confrontation with his French superiors occurs later in the film after Andre has returned from Cuba, and this time d'Arcy is angry and impatient with him for allowing his spying for America to supersede his commitment to France. In an overhead shot reminiscent of the earlier one, the sequence begins with Mike Nordstrom gazing out the window of Andre's Washington home as a black embassy limousine arrives and is seen from the American's POV. Significantly, Nordstrom is the first contact Andre has upon his return from Cuba. With annoyance, d'Arcy announces that Andre has been recalled to Paris on the next plane to explain his spying for the Americans. The physical distance between the two Frenchmen is now negligible as they are both shot in the same frame, visually signaling perhaps a new French focus for Andre and the narrative. After d'Arcy leaves, Andre tells the sympathetic Nordstrom that he will face a board of inquiry that will want to know why he went to Cuba, what he did there, who he did it for, and what he found out: a board of inquiry we never see. Andre's position with regard to France and his "Frenchness" are both challenged in this scene. But, unlike in the novel where he is literally a fugitive in his own country at the conclusion, there is never a clear sense of the extent of Andre's vulnerability or what he may be sacrificing with regards to this position or his stature in France.

Nordstrom plays a somewhat ambiguous and ambivalent role in the film's narrative, especially in his relationship with Andre. He is at once Andre's American espionage contact, and, as indicated, a friend. The two men even dress and groom their hair alike in a kind of strange visual kinship. In the last cited scene he tells Andre exactly what the value of his spying was to the US: that it directly confirmed what they learned about Russian missiles in Cuba from other sources, including U-2 satellites. Several commentators have suggested that Andre's mission thus provided no essential information, only what was already known, and was, in fact, an "act of folly" (Brill 186-87; Walker 135-36). But Nordstrom's words at this point make clear that verification of what they had learned elsewhere was essential in formulating and justifying the US response.

Nordstrom also is the direct link between Andre and Boris Kuzenov, whose information makes possible the exposure and dismantling of the Soviet spy ring *Topaz* in France, strengthening both the US in the process and the NATO alliance. However, Nordstrom is more a part of the plot and less of the story where Andre is concerned, and we do not learn of the existence of the titular spy ring until late in the narrative. The two issues of the Missile Crisis and the spy ring come together for Andre in the scene of his meeting with Nordstrom, McKittreck, and Kuzenov at the "safe house" mansion. He realizes that at the same time as he must explain and, hopefully, exonerate himself in Paris, exposing *Topaz* in the process, he must also keep silent about what he has done and uncovered in Cuba until the Americans can officially inform France and their other allies of their pending actions. At his moment of personal crisis, Andre realizes that the loyalty he has shown to the US and its Cold War interests will not be personally repaid by any loyalty to him from the Americans or from Nordstrom, in particular. "That is quite a job my friends," he replies ironically to their expectation that he will keep silent about what he has discovered in Cuba as he tries to protect himself and, by extension, his country. The dialogue underscores his sense of abandonment by the very people and nation he has sacrificed so much for: the words "job" and "friends" highlight the difficulty and injustice of his situation. Clearly he has demonstrated a greater sense of personal courage, loyalty, and "conscience" than his American equivalent Nordstrom, who remains noticeably silent. Thus Nordstrom never becomes more than an extension of America's Cold War interests and strategy, and Andre realizes at this point that he can't expect any more from him. It is moments like this that suggest what might have been developed into Andre's and the film's larger "story."

The visual representation of Kuzenov at this point in the film is also interesting in the way it seems to be playing up his condescension and arrogance, especially where Andre is involved. While the dialogue has him suggesting to Andre that the Frenchman should follow his example and agree to a comfortable asylum in the US after his mission, his gestures and demeanor go far beyond what he is saying. He now is imperiously smoking a cigar and offering coffee to Andre and the Americans with the hauteur of someone with an inbred sense of his own superiority. He has become the cliché of the turncoat and convert who has adopted the values and behavior of his former enemies in an exaggerated manner than suggests he has always lived them and is dealing with inferiors. It is another instance of the visual imagery overshadowing what could have been a more even-handed and human portrait of both characters.

The Personal is Political in Paris: Saving Andre and Nicole's Marriage

This is the last instance of America and Americans in the narrative. The rest of the film will focus on Andre, his marriage and family, France, and the French, and, to a lesser degree, the French position in the Cold War. The setting will shift totally to France and a set of new French characters, two of whom are important and central to the "*Topaz*" plot. America will only be a presence at the end in a discarded American newspaper announcing the resolution of the crisis. This section is about the spy ring Topaz and uncovering Columbine, its leader, but it is also concerned, as indicated, with restoring Andre's relationship with Nicole after his doomed affair with Juanita. At the end of the novel Nicole blames herself for Andre's having taken up with the Cuban woman and recognizes that Juanita has been the love of his life. She faults herself for not sacrificing enough for him and forgives his unfaithfulness. The film avoids this kind of melodrama, but it still makes the reconciliation of the couple the central human issue of its conclusion, and it does so economically and cinematically.

Hitchcock's need to end the film's narrative in Paris to resolve its espionage element also presented special challenges: a practical one, in that the French government and its culture minister André Malraux found the treatment of France and De Gaulle in the book deeply offensive and would allow filming on French soil only on the condition that what they considered objectionable be omitted (Spoto 501); and a production one, in that concluding the film in Paris was essential for resolving Andre's personal and professional situations. Hitchcock and Taylor tried to solve this problem of multiple settings by keeping the film and the relationships in the present and narrowing the focus of them to Andre's unraveling the espionage plot among colleagues known to him and restoring his personal relationships. This scene shift to Paris links again the erotic and espionage motifs that were present in the Cuban section, and the dialogue cleverly indicates this as one of the French government officials, Claude, quips that Andre has been having "an affair with the Americans." Andre extends this statement to include the exchange that both affairs and espionage entail: "When you have an affair, it's a two way street. You give a little; you get a little."

What is perhaps most remarkable in the final portion of the film is that Andre comes out of his passionate affair with Juanita and his mission to Cuba with his marriage if not unscathed, essentially intact, and with his family, which he seemed to have earlier abandoned, intact as well. At this point in the narrative, Nicole has left Andre, is living in Paris, and she has begun her own affair with their old friend from the resistance, Jacques Granville, who ironically turns out to be Columbine, the head of the Topaz spy ring. This is the second romantic/espionage triangle in the film in which the personal and political are intertwined and at odds with each other. In the earlier Cuban triangle involving Andre, Rico Parra, and Juanita, Andre played a duplicitous role politically as did Juanita, but each person was well aware of the conflicting personal/sexual bonds among them. Here it is Granville, their old friend, who plays the duplicitous role in the Paris triangle both personally and politically. For her part, Nicole is totally unaware that Granville is a spy and traitor and Andre, though he may be aware of his old friend's role as his wife's lover, never confronts either him or her on that account. Clearly, uncovering the fact that Granville is Columbine is more important than any kind of personal retribution, or even personal reassessment.

In fact, Andre's struggle to salvage his position, reputation and marriage necessitate his exposing the spies, particularly Columbine. To get to Columbine he must first confront and expose a spy whom Kuzenov has identified by name, Phillipe Jarre, a NATO economist whom Andre knows. To do so he enlists his son-in-law Francois, a journalist, to conduct a fraudulent newspaper interview with Jarre that is intended to expose the traitor. The scene between Jarre and Francois is one of the strongest dramatic confrontations in the film, with Jarre leaving his desk and the camera following him as he circles nervously around the room. Francois's phone call from Jarre's apartment to his wife and father-in-law is abruptly dropped, and daughter and father both panic. To find out what has happened to Francois, Andre and Michelle hasten to Jarre's apartment where they find Jarre dead on the street, but the only trace of Andre is his sketchpad with a drawing of Jarre. Significantly, the fear for Francois' fate inspires the moment of emotional connection, or reunion, between Andre and Nicole that reunites them; fortunately, Francois turns up at their apartment with only a flesh wound, an event that reconnects the whole family.

But the visuals of the scene at and outside of Jarre's apartment do little to give a balanced view, to paraphrase le Carré, of the horror and compromises on both sides in espionage. Jarre's body is found atop a park car and his bloody face shown in close-up, after he has been thrown from a window by ruthless communist agents in a scene suggestive of the *Pietá* torture moment in the Cuban section of the film. When Francois appears at the Devereaux's apartment, it is also clear that these same communist adversaries had tried to kill him. Again the violence is perpetrated by one side only, and Andre and Nicole are fortunate to have evaded the worst of it and to have been reunited so neatly.

In fact, when Andre and Nicole had first met at a cocktail party on his return to Paris, their estrangement was obvious in that their "kiss" was the traditional French touching of cheeks customary between friends or acquaintances, not lovers or spouses. However, at this point she runs into Andre's arms with tears in her eyes and embraces him passionately with her head on his chest. The fact that their daughter's husband and happiness will be saved after this alarming moment brings Andre and Nicole back together as a couple without any discussion. So while the passion of Andre and Juanita, "forged in the cauldron of espionage," as Uris puts it, cannot survive, this more domestic, marital, and familial connection will, despite what is happening in the world around them. Just as importantly, another family unit consisting of the two of them as parents and a married daughter and her husband has become a central priority of the narrative and been reaffirmed, with the younger generation's welfare taking most prominence, not unlike the situation of the Kuzenovs earlier.

The importance of relationships is further reaffirmed in the ending that Hitchcock preferred, which is the one currently on the longer version of *Topaz* on the Universal DVD. All three of the endings Hitchcock filmed dispose of Columbine, the Granville character, at the end. But while he dies in the duel and the suicide versions, in this one he survives and will be an exile in the Soviet Union at the same time as the audience is reassured visually that Andre and Nicole and their marriage will survive. Hitchcock especially liked this airport ending because Granville's escape to the Soviet Union was for him reminiscent of Cold War episodes such as the British double agents Kim Philby and Guy Burgess finding refuge in Russia where they lived out their days (McGilligan 693). The DVD ending is the only one that has both Andre and Nicole together in the same frame as a couple at the same time as Andre and Granville, once the best of friends, cynically bid each other "bon voyage" as they each board planes, with Nicole appalled that the traitor, her former lover, is actually getting away. As Granville is boarding an Aeroflot Soviet airliner, Andre and Nicole are off to Washington on a Pan American plane. Has Andre been restored to his role as a diplomatic attaché, or are they accepting the refuge that Kuzenov found for himself and his family in America and recommended to Andre? We don't definitively know. This ending is ambiguous, and only the ending where Granville commits suicide off-camera at his apartment actually contains a visual reprise of freeze frames of all of the lives sacrificed in this Cold War crisis to reassert the extent of the human lives that have been sacrificed. That was the ending that the released film had in 1969, and the one Samuel Taylor preferred as it reinforced the idea that political espionage sacrificed people's actual lives, not to mention their humanity and relationships, which he and Hitchcock had hoped to forefront in the film.

But from an artistic and humanistic point of view, none of the three endings is a totally satisfying resolution of the film's human relationships or pulls the film together enough to create what Taylor would consider a "story." This is unfortunate because *Topaz* has so much that is entertaining and that holds the viewer's interest throughout. Although it was possible to resolve the espionage plots on all major fronts—missile plot uncovered, nuclear war averted, French spies exposed—there is no satisfying resolution of the film's human relationships in terms of what characters have suffered or learned. In Aristotelian terms there has been no "anagnorisis," or moral or spiritual recognition that the audience can take away. At the end of things, Andre seems to have lost too little that was of ultimate value to him or truly suffered in the way that protagonists in the outstanding Hitchcock films do. Further, throughout the narrative either compelling characters have been killed off, such as Juanita, disposed of, such as Parra, or they have been reunited by a kind of convenient *deus ex machina*, as have Nicole and Andre. Usually at the end of a Hitchcock film, the afterlife of the surviving characters provides a rich imaginative and critical potential for the audience (think of *Vertigo* and *Marnie*), but no such rich afterlife can be found here. Andre and Nicole do not inspire the same level of interest or identification, as individuals or as a couple.

This is compounded by the fact that the political and human ambiguity of what characters have said throughout the film is not often enough in sufficient alignment with what is seen. At times, the dialogue and visual narrative seem to be in synch and show the contradictions and human toll of spying. But there are too many instances where, as I have argued, the dialogue's suggestions that both sides are equally responsible for the dehumanization caused by the Cold War are undercut by what appears to be a visual narrative unambiguously supporting the US, its material advantages, and its values. So, in essence, what the film could have been is compromised, or undercut, by the Cold War vision to which it ascribes, and the anti-communism it inherited from the novel mitigates what could have been a powerful story. Finally and significantly, what is achieved politically, and sacrificed for, by the principal characters through the espionage could not have had the same positive resonance with and reception by audiences at this point of the Cold War with the Vietnam War raging: a war that had less to do with Vietnam, a small marginal nation like Cuba, and more with America and its vulnerable prestige. To have created a work that was more even-handed and critical of both sides would have meant undercutting not only the fundamental vision and ideology of the novel, but perhaps of contemporary American foreign policy and, specifically, what was happening in Vietnam. Perhaps the film's final image says it best. We see an American newspaper left on a park bench near the Arc de Triomphe that reveals the final disposition of the crisis, with Khrushchev finally backing down and removing the missiles from Cuba. Maybe this discarded image is also Hitchcock's way of suggesting and acknowledging that the Missile Crisis and the Cold War will not only recede into history but be discarded from our collective memory.

Notes

1. This was somewhat before the worst excesses of the Cuban Revolution and its assault on civil liberties were widely acknowledged in left-wing circles.

2. Juanita's servants, who share her anti-Castro espionage values and activities, provide a kind of surrogate family for her that parallels the Kuzenovs and Devereauxs and adds another element of structural coherence to the plot.

3. Dubois is originally from Martinique in the Caribbean, a former French colony.

4. Ironically, Karin Dor had been a "Bond girl" two years earlier when she played Helga Brandt in the Bond thriller *You Only Live Twice* (1967).

5. By contrast, in *Notorious* there is the burnt chicken that Ingrid Bergman has intended for her dinner with Cary Grant that is never eaten because Grant is called away.

Works Cited

Adler, Renata. "Topaz." *The New York Times*. 20 June 1968.
Brill Leslie. *The Hitchcock Romance: Love and Irony in Hitchcock's Films*. Princeton UP, 1988.
Canby, Vincent. "Topaz." *The New York Times*. 20 Dec. 1969.
Corliss, Richard. "*Topaz*." Film Quarterly, vol. 23, no 3, 1970, pp. 41-49.
Gaddis, John Lewis. *The Cold War: A New History*. Penguin Books, 2005.
Krohn, Bill. *Hitchcock at Work*. Phaidon Press, 2003.
Le Carré, John. *The Spy Who Came in from the Cold*. Penguin Books, 1963.
McElroy, Wendy. "How America became the World's Policeman." *The Daily Bell*. 19 Mar. 2015.
McGilligan, Patrick. *Alfred Hitchcock: A Life in Darkness and in Light*. Harper Collins, 2003.

Spoto, Donald. *The Dark Side of Genius: The Life of Alfred Hitchcock*. Da Capo Press, 1999.
Uris, Leon. *Topaz*. McGraw Hill, 1967.
Walker, Michael. "*Topaz* and Cold War Politics." *Hitchcock Annual*, 2004-05, pp. 127-53.
Wood, Robin. *Hitchcock's Films Revisited*. Rev. ed. Columbia University Press, 2003.

The Unreliable Narrative in *Torn Curtain* and *Topaz*

Randall Spinks

Alfred Hitchcock's *Torn Curtain* (1966) and *Topaz* (1969) were likely influenced by Martin Ritt's successful film adaptation of John le Carré's *The Spy Who Came in from the Cold* (1965), a work that says of the Cold War, "a pox on both your houses." But wasn't Western capitalism, for all its faults, to be preferred to Communist regimes? Wasn't the former's dirty work the necessary evil of self-defense? Or is some wholly other question possible (a Hegelian *aufheben*), one that sublates or moves beyond both systems? Must rejection of actually existing capitalism automatically endorse the actually existing socialisms of the Cold War? Since these "realistic" spy films answered the James Bond fantasies begun in the 1960s, the context I wish to examine here is the one sociologist, political scientist and historian Charles Tilly proposed: the rise of the national state as a gigantic protection racket. Likewise, linguist, philosopher and historian Noam Chomsky maintains that not the sole, but the primary responsibility for all repression and atrocities perpetrated by both camps during the Cold War lies with Racketeer Number One, the United States. For, if winners write history, a consideration of Tilly's and Chomsky's frameworks questions the ideological system of the United States as, in effect, what literary studies calls an unreliable narrator. Hitchcock's Cold War films are embedded within such an ideological system even as the director inchoately questions it, not as a political dissident, but rather in his "apolitical," misanthropist persona. Hitchcock's more or less unwitting message thus proves the more powerful once it meets with a dissident reader response.

Dissident Counter Narratives

To better situate Hitchcock's Cold War cinema, it is necessary to spend time on narratives counter to the ones he seems to take for granted in his storytelling, like patriarchy's claiming, for example, that women's liberation leads to the breakdown of the family as the backbone of civilization. Where feminism indeed is concerned, consider how a *Torn Curtain* reversing the traditional gender roles in 1969 would strike audiences as absurd at the time. Women's representation in Hitchcock's films is well within mainstream expectations, though feminist critics have detected in his works inklings that patriarchal ideology does not completely work. In Hitchcock's films "it may be possible to argue," writes Tania Modleski, "that woman's story gets out, though weakened and distorted in the process" (100). Although Dr. Sarah Sherman (Julie Andrews) in *Torn Curtain* is, like her fiancée Professor Michael Armstrong (Paul Newman), a physics PhD, she is nonetheless merely his assistant. Michael refers to her as "Miss Sherman" to male colleagues who in turn call her "a beautiful girl." Hitchcock did set out to spin the yarn from her point of view.[1] She does a little espionage work of her own to discover that Michael has lied to her about flying to Stockholm. She follows him to East Berlin, heartbroken to discover his treason. Only behind the Iron Curtain does Michael learn his fiancée's middle name: Louise. "You should come to me for your information," retorts the Stasi chief, Heinrich Gerhard (Hansjörg Felmy). Paradoxically, her endangering Michael's mission enables it. Critics have noted that it is precisely her attractive presence that expedites Michael's meeting of minds with East German Professor Lindt (Ludwig Donath) in order to trick a secret rocket formula from Lindt's head before Michael and Sarah hasten their escape. This hardly does justice to Sarah's intellectual standing. Similarly, Andre Devereaux's wife Nicole (Dany Robin) in Hitchcock's *Topaz* had been a French Resistance fighter against Nazi occupation during World War II, her carbine proudly displayed on the mantle. But true to women's role after the war, she obviously has been relegated to homemaker.[2]

 Counter narratives indeed include those of gender, race (or caste), and socio-economic class since all are modes of both internal and external exploitation feeding the West's capitalist system. Both *Torn Curtain* and *Topaz* represent Hitchcock's first non-stereotypical depiction of people of color, if only briefly. Since the USSR had long propagandized the abominable race relations in the US, Hitchcock makes a point in *Torn Curtain* of showing black students in Leipzig's Karl Marx University.

The Unreliable Narrative 171

And in *Topaz* he showcases Philippe Dubois (Roscoe Lee Browne) from Martinique in a scene in Harlem. Before Noam Chomsky in the 1960s, it was indeed black dissidents who called out US ideology as the unreliable narrator of history, and they were subjected to the FBI's COINTELPRO program for it (*Necessary Illusions* 189). In 1966, for example, Kwame Ture (Stokely Carmichael) spoke to the Student Non-Violent Coordinating Committee (SNCC) at Berkeley arguing that African Americans must question how America got its wealth. Here he calls specific attention to exploitation external to the US: "I do not want to be a part of the American pie. The American pie means raping South Africa, beating Vietnam, beating South America, raping the Philippines, raping every country you've been in. I don't want any of your blood money" (Ture). Yet if Hitchcock's Cold War films omit overt references to such scathing critique of US foreign policy as Ture levels here, we may nonetheless be mindful of it as a frame of reference.

Hitchcock's films may seem also to take for granted the prevailing conservative-to-liberal narrative that the worst atrocities in the twentieth century, save for the Nazi Holocaust, are solely the responsibility of regimes claiming Marxist inspiration. Whatever was "Marxist" in Twentieth-century Communism, its actual, anti-Marxist failure was that it did not get beyond a deep history of Eastern Despotism, czarism, secret police, brute censorship, and powerful Strong Man traditions that cultural habit grants under constant threat of invasion across, say, easily-traversed Russian steppes. Naturally, Western imperialism reacted to and encircled the Bolshevik regime, exacerbating this autocratic version of Communism. But the US, for all its Magna Carta and Enlightenment traditions, emerged from World War II as the world's greatest power, and proved ingenious at camouflaging its own residual class-based authoritarianism, racism, sexism, secret police-like activities, censorship and sponsored global atrocities. Just as Hitchcock well knew the villain's ability to hide and be charming, the greater "Evil Empire" in international relations is that which can best afford a certain aloofness from its own coercions. But what of US exceptionalism, liberal democracy and free speech? Again, these are primarily the prerogatives of elites. For example, while elite Hawks and elite Doves in the 1960s debated the feasibility of prosecuting a noble defense of South Vietnam, both camps together were, Chomsky has argued at length, attacking it (*Necessary Illusions*

163; Year 501 28, 273; *Hegemony* 101, 104, 190; *Chronicles* 63-64). This is exactly the ingenious "conservative/liberal" range of debate in the so-called free press that has restricted citizens' ability to understand issues outside elite agendas.

Hitchcock's espionage films might be understood, then, against a pattern that dates back to 900 AD, according to Charles Tilly. In *Coercion, Capital, and European States* (1990), Tilly argues that modern European states grew out of feudal systems whereby rival lords consolidated land and power by exacting tribute from peasants as, in effect, a protection racket. By the modern era, "A state's essential minimum activities," writes Tilly, "form a trio: *statemaking...; warmaking...; protection.* No state lasts long, however, that neglects a crucial fourth activity: extraction: drawing from its subject population the means of statemaking, warmaking, and protection" (96). We could add a fifth according to Leon Uris throughout his novel *Topaz*: espionage. In the West espionage consists of rule-governed "intelligence gathering." Among the West's enemies, espionage consists of stealing secrets, planting misinformation, arranging deadly covert operations, and strategically murdering one's own agents. Hitchcock's *Topaz* seems to tow Uris's line, but the director's insistence on moral ambiguity may account in part for Uris's dropping out of the film project.

Torn Curtain and *Topaz* can therefore be understood as psychological projections onto the Eastern Bloc of the West's own expansionist designs in the Third World. Chomsky concurs with Tilly, insisting that the US engaged in propaganda called "the Red Scare" to suppress leftist-inclined social unrest at home. And after World War II it fomented the nuclear arms race not to protect itself from the Soviet Union so much as to threaten the Soviet Union. The Soviet Union's predictable self-defensive behavior would thus appear aggressive, expansionist and menacing (Chomsky, *Hegemony* 70-71). Indeed, we may recall the stock footage that opens Hitchcock's *Topaz*: the parade of Soviet military might in Red Square. In short, the US military-industrial complex enriched itself in the manner of a protection racket, coercing Americans to pay taxes for "defense" they would not otherwise approve. This was the culmination of a long pattern that Tilly analyzes in the "civilianization" of European states:

> As rulers drew more and more resources for war and other coercive enterprises from their local economies, the major classes within those economies successfully demanded more and more state intervention outside the realm of coercion and war. Over the thousand-year span we are surveying here, nevertheless, coercive activities clearly predominated. (97)

A very advanced version of that tension between "civilianization" (citizen demands) and the military provides a wider framework within which to read Hitchcock's two Cold War films of the 1960s.

Just as Hitchcock generates "necessary illusions" for art's sake, so also it would be important for social power structures to beguile us into believing "our cause" is just and good, that the greater evil lies without. Therefore, the major US media, the education system, and official government narratives may be regarded, literarily, as "unreliable narrators" of history. Indeed, argues Chomsky, state- and corporate-funded public relations, the major, corporate-owned media, the whole doctrinal system, in fact, have managed to ignore, obscure, disguise, dismiss, or minimize the global ravages of US policies that give rise to and exacerbate repressive regimes in response, regimes that the US can then point to as sources of "evil" rather than symptoms of history. Throughout his oeuvre, Chomsky explains that, in effect, the doctrinal system is like an Ego denying, rationalizing, or projecting onto Cold War rivals or subjugated populations its own violent, greedy, and power-hungry urges while using Orwellian language. "An attempt by villages to run their own affairs," Chomsky insists, "is 'violence,' and a brutal attack to teach them who rules is 'preventing violence'" (*Necessary Illusions* 120). If Chomsky's reversal of the prevailing narrative has any merit, it means that substantial US middle-class affluence has derived, on balance, from corporate looting around the world. By the 1960s Western Europeans and North Americans can be said to have been "bought off" by their wealthy rulers, or, more accurately, by the "System" itself, and then coerced into paying taxes as re-investment for future systemic looting. Chomsky speaks, then, of Western propaganda as the "manufacture of consent" (*Necessary Illusions* 16-17). Surely, for Hitchcock and his audience, there must be an eerie, underlying sense of guilt (or avoidance thereof) so often ascribed to Original Sin.

Torn Curtain: Ideology and Poetics

Hitchcock both deliberately and instinctively, or inadvertently, builds into his films just enough questioning of the doctrinal system to generate a subversive narrative pleasure, enhanced by film poetics such as color. In *Torn Curtain* a hurt and puzzled Sarah tails her fiancée Michael from the colorful free world to the drabness behind the Iron Curtain (Allen 225, 227, 229). In Copenhagen she passes colorful storefronts on her way to a certain bookshop to pick up a package addressed to Michael. Donald Spoto argues that *Torn Curtain* represents a mythological quest "to a hellish underworld where the predominant color is appropriately red, suggesting Communism and the infernal (or perhaps, more accurately, the purgatorial) fires through which Michael and Sarah must pass" (418). The poetics of color can turn subversive, however, once we examine Michael's motivations for the whole enterprise.

Consider indeed this "hellish underworld" as actually a projection of the American psyche dominated by the Ego of capital itself via film poetics. The Berlin Alte Nationalgalerie sequence is beloved of Spoto for its "pure cinema" (401). In that scene the gangster-looking security agent Herman Gromek (Wolfgang Kieling) shadows the American defector who will, in the next scene, out-gangster him. It is a halting chase of ominous, echoing steps (Gromek is never seen once inside) as Michael seeks to give his security guide the slip. Drawing on Theodor Adorno, Steven Jacobs comments on the phonological and etymological connection between "museum" and "mausoleum" (597). The scene conveys a paradoxical, nightmarish realism suggested by the black and white chessboard floor surrounded by process photography representing walls, columns and works of art (Jacobs 596). Surely, with such much-maligned effects in *Torn Curtain* (due to budget constraints and the restrictions on second-unit photography on location in East Germany), Hitchcock tries to make a virtue of necessity.

Ironically, the phony backgrounds come to frame the audience's learning the truth: Michael is a phony defector. He temporarily evades Gromek, leading to the scene on the tractor with the oddly Southwestern US-accented farmer (Mort Mills), an agent of the underground organization Pi. We think of the old joke about socialist realism: boy meets tractor; boy loses tractor. Boy reunites with tractor. Sarah had asked

Michael, "Aren't I of use to you anymore?" When her mere presence in East Germany happens later to entice Professor Lindt (Ludwig Donath) to meet with Michael off the record, perhaps only then in Michael's instrumentalist universe does his fiancée indeed come to stand in for his tractor. In any case, the rear-projection landscape behind Michael and the farmer on the tractor looms artificial. After appearing so callously to desert Sarah in order to commit treason, we learn to our relief (within the doctrinal system, of course) that Michael has not come to join the enemy, but to pilfer the same anti-missile missile formula that had been thwarted by Washington: Michael's pet Gamma Five project.

Of course, Michael's original motivation is not so much patriotism as self-aggrandizement. Interestingly, it is Sarah who must pass a loyalty test during the interrogation scene at Karl Marx University in Leipzig. It is her refusal to spill Gamma Five information that seems to open Michael's heart both to her and his country. He appears to divulge to her the true mission in long shot on the knoll, out of our hearing, in silent cinema. Their relationship heals (sealed with a passionate kiss behind shrubs) along with his apparently newfound patriotism. This may momentarily please a mass Western audience. But as Neil Sinyard observes, the scene is shot "against a patently and expressively fake backdrop" that undermines the patriotic theme (272-73). Yet here, unlike Hitchcock's spy masterpieces *The 39 Steps* (1935), *Notorious* (1946), and *North by Northwest* (1959), *Torn Curtain* reverts to a mere fetch-the-MacGuffin-and-escape plot absent the parallel, redoubling suspense about whether, or how, the leading woman and man will become a couple.

The "fake backdrop" idea calls to mind Hitchcock's oft-used prop, the newspaper. Pi operative Doctor Kosca (Gisela Fischer) contacts Michael Armstrong by tripping him on the stairs. In fact, the media and official history can be bizarrely skewed toward reinforcing a power structure about which Hitchcock is suspicious. In the infirmary she explains that her "organization must resort to bizarre means of communication." Cut to a newspaper, a significant juxtaposition. Is this Hitchcock's instinct that newspapers may also act as "bizarre means of communication"? Or that they may convey "bizarre" information, even if only by presenting limited facts absent greater context? In the cut we eavesdrop on the taxi driver's recognizing a news photo of the missing Gromek whom Michael has murdered. Straightaway the driver reports to Security Chief Gerhardt.

Over his German dialogue we see in silent cinema a flashback of the farm scene from the driver's point of view as Michael walks back to the farmhouse from his tractor ride. Gromek arrives on his motorcycle and follows Michael inside. Gerhardt, looking down at the newspaper on his desk and hearing only a small part of the driver's testimony, impatiently lifts the phone and speaks commands over the driver's ongoing and barely audible verbosity. Hitchcock thus emphasizes visual reinforcement of narrative details already known to the audience over superfluous dialogue. But the flashback also provides new information that stokes audience suspense: the Stasi is onto Michael. Is the taxi driver's flashback not analogous to dissident historians' role in supplying additional facts to original newspaper accounts and official history?

We must remember that in the modern age the state is dominated by big business's extolling individual entrepreneurialism, and that is not far from Michael Armstrong's mission. "Michael, going it alone," writes Raymond Durgnat, "exemplifies Western individualism" (372). That means using the state to protect corporations from popular objections to their externalizing costs to society. Or, conversely, advantage may lie in decrying the state, seeking "free-market" de-regulation. That in a sense is what Michael does when he loses his state funding and engages in a quest to regain that funding by transgressing state boundaries in order to pick Professor Lindt's brain. Both Armstrong and Lindt are impatient with the state when it threatens to obstruct their private pursuit of mathematical gain: "Yack, yack, yack," Professor Lindt complains against his own government's security precautions. Hitchcock positions Lindt high above his patriotic colleagues in the lecture hall. Both he and Armstrong engage in a kind of private-sector espionage.[3] Only in the chalkboard scene when Lindt realizes he's let slip a secret without an equal exchange does he sic the state on Michael.

Likewise, capital has ready access to the state, but there is no need for capital to be loyal in return. As Neil Sinyard points out, Michael is not motivated by patriotism but by physics for physics' sake. He engages in an ego duel with Professor Lindt in which Michael would not commit patriotic espionage but plagiarism (274). Michael goes rogue, casts his fiancée aside, murders Gromek, and puts many other peoples' lives at risk. Sinyard declares: "It is striking how Hitchcock lingers on those moments of chaos that the hero's actions and presence have provoked,...

the bus passengers scattering in panic...as the policeman opens fire." Countess Luchinska (Lila Kedrova) repeats, "My sponsors...," as she lies injured on the stairs, having helped [Michael and Sarah] escape," but they abandon her to "her surely unpleasant fate." Indeed, "[T]he American blunders in with his own self-serving agenda; does not have an exit strategy; and leaves chaos in his wake," Sinyard concludes, noting the parallel with the Vietnam War (273-74).

It is not surprising, then, why stories produced under capitalism might express longing for human connection. For capitalism by its nature subverts community and solidarity in favor of a self-serving, global upper class hardly loyal to any country or population that supports it. According to Spoto, the harrowing escapes from the Stasi and the cyclic structure of *Torn Curtain* (from cold sea back to cold sea) present "at once the meaning and...the meaninglessness of the mission. The meaning is in what Michael learns about his need for other people, particularly Sarah" (416). Given the roots of the national state as explained by Charles Tilly and the history of dominance of the state by powerful, private elites, the question should be whether those private elites are themselves patriots. Or do they use states as a means to further their own self-interests like Jacques Granville (Michel Piccoli) in *Topaz* or Professor Armstrong in *Torn Curtain*?

Indeed, *Torn Curtain's* ending questions the Cold War arms race that was most lucrative to certain private sectors. This is why so much was invested in "public relations" to convince taxpayers to fund it in the name of stalemating the Communist Bloc. Significantly, Michael Armstrong, played by the athletic Paul Newman, is no mere physics nerd, but arm-strong enough to stalemate Gromek, who "was trained by experts," while the farmer's wife (Carolyn Conwell) stabs Gromek once with a faulty kitchen knife and kneecaps him with a shovel before the tandem—after an agonizing struggle—manages to drag the hapless Gromek into the gas oven. And for what? Hitchcock had wanted originally to have Armstrong burn the formula stolen from Lindt at the end of *Torn Curtain* as an act of redemption, certainly clearing up "any notion that the hero was meant to be seen as acting out of patriotic motives." But Hitchcock either succumbed to commercial pressures or decided such a conclusion would repulse the audience (Sinyard 284). While Michael's later stopping mid-escape to scribble Professor Lindt's formula enhances the suspense, I suggest that Hitchcock opted for a more subtle way to subvert Michael's project should the final swim to safety soak the stolen formula into illegibility. The first thing Michael asks the Swedish rescuers is for a quick way to dry out passports and drivers licenses so the audience can hope the hard-won formula, too, might survive. But Hitchcock leaves this deviously unresolved. The final image is of Michael and Sarah snuggling beneath the blanket, not his triumphant salvaging of the MacGuffin.

Still, Hitchcock's films would ride the commercialization of Cold War fears while appealing directly to consumerism as well. In his classic examination of European art history, *Ways of Seeing*, John Berger observes that Western capitalism substitutes consumer choice for political choice (149). This is best exemplified in that form of consumerism known as travel, which the professional class in the West was enjoying by the 1960s. Travel serves not only as consumption pleasure but as also a token experience of upper-class prestige, complete with *savoir faire*. One travel element both *Torn Curtain* and *Topaz* have in common is colorful Copenhagen, the jumping off point for the defectors in both films, Armstrong to East Germany in the former and Boris Kusenov (Per-Axel Arosenius) to America in the latter.[4] In *Torn Curtain* we are treated to exotic travel as an adventure of puns on temperature. It seems the heat can fail on board a capitalist cruise liner (carrying physicists, no less) sailing a picturesque Norwegian fjord. Hitchcock structures *Torn Curtain* upon a binary of cold and fire, introducing us to the protagonists by juxtaposing the fork-in-the-ice of a water glass in the cruise liner's dining area with Doctor Sarah Sherman and Professor Michael Armstrong hotly fornicating under covers in their cold cabin. They will undergo a trial by cold (Michael's strategic distance from his fiancée) and fire, the harrowing escape from the dreaded Stasi during a performance of Tchaikovsky's *Francesca da Rimini* when the ballerina (Tamara Toumanova) spots the fugitives in the audience. She inadvertently dogs the hero couple's tracks throughout the film, helping the Stasi stay one step behind, and even has a machine gun fire upon them (so she thinks) at the end. From the simulated fire imagery on the stage (repeating the rocket engine fire in the opening credits) Michael has the desperate idea to falsely yell "Fire!" in a crowded theater.[5] Finally, they swim to safety in icy waters and are last seen huddling before a

The Unreliable Narrative   179

hot stove beneath a blanket sharing warm love. And they do it all (if the Hitchcockian pun is in order) by going "under cover." Similarly, the US used the Cold War as an excuse for hot wars around the world and as cover for sabotage operations against whole populations.

While Sarah is concerned with the couple's relationship at the outset, Michael is desperate to salvage his exalted career lest he be relegated to teaching undergraduate math. The scene in the Gentlemen's room of Copenhagen's Hôtel d'Angleterre has Michael feverishly unwrapping a textbook that conceals a double-coded passage. As is well known to Hitchcock students, the director often salaciously reveals plot secrets in privies. Michael locks himself in the stall and follows directions handwritten on the title page of *The Young Students Mathematics Refresher* to page 107 and a heading: "Circular Measure." We cut to what Michael sees. Where the small screen cuts off words or letters I leave blanks:

> Numerous problems en_c_ountered daily involve the use of c__ure. For the stude_n_t planning _t_o pursue further studies in higher ____this is especi_a_lly true. Examples oc_c_ur in all _t_he physical sciences: phys_i_cs, mechanics, engi_n_eering and astronomy. The relationship ____ diameter, _c_ircumference _a_nd area of a circle is not intuitively ob____ the relation_s_hip b_e_tween the perimeter, area and the sides of ____ and triangle. The number that defines the ratio _o_f the circum____ circle to its diam_e_ter cannot be expressed as the quotient of ratio___. Hence it is an irrational nu_m_ber and is re_p_resented by a symb _____ as follows.

The above appears briefly as the camera tilts and tracks or zooms into "The Greek letter π (pronounced "pie") is often used," until the circled π symbol almost fills the screen. Of course, π is the name of the underground organization in East Germany that will have to improvise Michael's (and Sarah's) escape. In the fragmented and adolescent cryptography of the book's introductory note, the underlined letters spell out "contact in case of emergency" (with some underlined letters out of frame). The emergency threatening both his romantic relationship and his mission will happen before Michael even lands in East Berlin because Sarah follows him onto his flight as what Gerhard calls "excess baggage," leading to a quarrel on the plane in front of the ballerina.

The visual words act as a silent film's inter-titles. And their message beginning with "Numerous problems encountered daily" and repeating the words "relationship" and "circle" is at least a three-fold mystery, an irrational 3.14159 ad-infinitum-fold mystery to be more exact, suggesting "numerous problems" that Michael will encounter as an amateur spy, and as Sarah's betrothed. He is thus one of the "young students" the introductory note addresses. This adds resonance to Professor Lindt's impassioned and impatient injunction to Michael during the chalkboard scene: "Learn!" he glowers.

Indeed, the scene is key to Hitchcock's commentary upon Western espionage: far from glamorous, it is of an excretory nature. Michael gingerly sets the book atop the toilet tank, using it as a desk. The low-angled camera and the lighting make of his craning neck a grotesque image of his monomaniacal quest, reminiscent of a similar shot of Norman Bates in *Psycho* as he cranes his neck to read Marion Crane's pseudonymous signature.[6] Michael writes, "CONTACT π IN CASE...." *on toilet paper*, no less. Again, we get an extreme close-up on the Greek letter magnifying the black ink on the white and gray-specked tissue. We cut to the next scene by way of an establishing shot of the Nimb Fountain garden before the boutique Nimb Hotel. The latter's façade continues the toilet paper's white-to-gray texture. The graphic match from toilet paper to the site of Michael's deceiving Sarah is also an intellectual match. Critics love to speculate on Hitchcock's cameos and their supposedly organic, though sometimes remote, associations with their respective films. The men's room scene takes place just off the lobby of the Hôtel d'Angleterre, a few feet from where, a couple scenes earlier, a baby in Hitchcock's cameo wets the director's knee. Perhaps we can infer a further link suggesting Hitchcock's attitude toward Michael's escapade.

Topaz and Public Relations

Nor was Hitchcock lacking a sense of irony about the interplay between cinema art, the motion picture industry, and media in general. In the mid-to-late 1960s he returned to the spy genre. Hollywood wanted to capitalize on the espionage trend in what had become, owing to the James Bond craze, a kind of operant conditioning. For further marketing effects, recall that the above cameo in *Torn Curtain* is accompanied by

Hitchcock's trademark theme music, Gounod's "Funeral March for a Marionette" from his popular television show *Alfred Hitchcock Presents*. Yet during his monologues he often recited scriptwriter James Allardice's sarcastic references to the show's commercial sponsors. This reminds us that the advent of radio, film and television in the twentieth century ushered in advertising and corporate Public Relations (affordable only to wealth-wielding elites) which have had a profound propagandistic effect in the doctrinal system, especially in light of Slavoj Žižek's oft-quoted remark that "we feel free because we lack the language to articulate our unfreedom."

This freedom/unfreedom binary accords with the way Hitchcock structured his films on doubles. It is one thing to use film to manipulate audiences' desires and values for box office (thus reinforcing the capitalist class system). It is perhaps another to "put the audience through it," as Hitchcock liked to say, in the sense of a rite of passage that opens minds. Yet by the late 1960s Hitchcock must have felt especially obliged to combine box office and art. For so much of his career this double motive mutually reinforced itself. In the late 1960s it threatened to cancel itself out. Rather dreamlike, Hitchcock's cameo in *Topaz* strangely condenses two different symbolic rites of passage. One is jet-setting: his arrival at La Guardia Airport. The other is being discharged from a hospital. A nurse conveys him by wheelchair. He stands abruptly, shakes hands with a man and exits screen right.

Another doubling occurs in *Topaz*'s opening sequence. We have the appeal to tourism at the same time as confrontation with the proverbial existential angst of the affluent professional class. We are made to identify with Soviet intelligence official Boris Kusenov, who is defecting to the Americans. In the Copenhagen ceramics museum, the Royal Porcelain Factory, where he has been pursued by Soviet agents, Kusenov peeps through blinds. A point of view shot skews the blinds unnaturally diagonal, invoking German Expressionism, to convey his anxiety about escaping safely with his loved ones.

But distortion, to invoke Chomsky, can be put into the service of political and consumerist propaganda. He and media scholars such as Mark Crispin Miller refer to Edward Bernays, who has been called The Father of Public Relations. Bernays, in his book *Propaganda* (1928), for whom the term has a neutral connotation, avers that:

> In almost every act of our daily lives, whether in the sphere of politics or business, in our social conduct or our ethical thinking, we are dominated by the relatively small number of persons who understand the mental processes and social patterns of the masses. It is they who pull the wires which control the public mind, who harness old social forces and contrive new ways to bind and guide the world. (Bernays 37-38)

For cinema art, think of the most famous set-piece in *Topaz* when Rico Parra (John Vernon) shoots Juanita de Córdoba (Karen Dor). We cut to the extreme high angle above the couple's embrace. As Rico lets her corpse drop slowly to the floor, her lavender robe fans out bizarrely (yet we believe it) like a pool of blood against the black-and-white chessboard tiles.[7] The effect was achieved by stagehands pulling wires that had been inserted into her garment, "a perfect example," writes Spoto, "of that curious union of the beautiful and the grotesque" (431). Thereby operating on our consciousness off-screen, Hitchcock and crew, yes, "pull the wires" of our experience in much the same way that elitists like Bernays argue that the masses need to be manipulated commercially and politically for the betterment of the social order.

The difference, of course, is that, in art for art's sake, Hitchcock calls attention to the universally sexual, submerging the political history and cultural logic on which the scene is principally based. Equally chilling are the preceding eye-line matches in this scene. Juanita's head jerks back at the pistol blast; she gives a little cough as her eyes fix into a wide death stare. This is Hitchcock's patented murder-as-lovemaking, orgasm-as-death, followed by the close-up of Rico's limply lowering the phallic gun beside his thigh. We cut to her corpse's "point of view" as the murderer gazes down at us. We cut to the murderer's point of view: her unseeing eyes staring up at us. We are beloved and lover, victim and murderer. As always, ironies abound in Hitchcock's morally ambiguous universe, and they turn out to be socio-political after all. Rico Parra, the former peasant, now a high-ranking official of the regime, had become the landlord of the finca (estate) Juanita had shared with her rich husband, a rico (rich man) who had evidently betrayed his class to become a hero of the Cuban Revolution. Of course, we may cynically surmise that he had foreseen on which side the revolutionary

The Unreliable Narrative   183

bread was buttered precisely in order to maintain his class position in a not-unheard-of interchange of capitalists and Communists. Juanita has been executed by a Rico for her treachery against the regime as well as in jealous revenge for her affair with the French agent working for the Americans, Andre Devereaux (Frederick Stafford), and with whom she was spying. Yet the execution is also a tender mercy killing to spare her from torture. Hitchcock often ensures that we feel a certain empathy with villains.

But again, we have US-projected guilt in a Shakespearean tragedy: "You make my country a prison," Juanita had just told Rico.[8] The standard narrative, the one advanced in Uris's novel, in fact, is that Fidel Castro's rule would have been identical regardless of the US response. Surely, the torture of the Mendozas in *Topaz* is emblematic. Insofar as the regime became the new employer of an employee population, I argue, the prison analogy rings true. It is just that the US had been the Cuban people's absentee landlord, employer, and jailer under the Batista dictatorship and wanted to go on as such. US elites felt betrayed by Fidel Castro. What the US government and media as "unreliable narrator" omit, according to Chomsky and the historians he draws upon, is the rest of the story: not just the failed Bay of Pigs invasion but the added effects of US-sponsored terrorism against Cuba and populations around the world.

I am arguing that we must view *Topaz* and the above iconic scene in particular in light of the following. No sooner was Fulgencio Batista overthrown in January 1959 than the National Security Council and the CIA began taking action for regime change. Guerrillas inside Cuba were armed and the CIA supervised incendiary bombing raids carried out by Cuban exiles based in the US. "We need not tarry on what the US or its allies would do under such circumstances," Chomsky remarks.:

> Cuba, however, did not respond with violent actions within the US for revenge or deterrence. Rather, it followed the procedure required by international law. In July 1960, Cuba called on the UN for help, providing the Security Council with records of some twenty bombings, including names of pilots, plane registration numbers, unexploded bombs, and other specific details, alleging considerable damage and casualties and calling for resolution of the conflict through diplomatic channels. (Chomsky, *Hegemony* 81-82)

After carrying out Eisenhower's planned Bay of Pigs invasion, Chomsky explains, John F. Kennedy's White House was hysterical over the loss of control of Cuba and the implications for all of Latin America. Kennedy "implemented a crushing embargo that could scarcely be endured by a small country that had become a 'virtual colony' of the US...He also ordered an intensification of the terrorist campaign:...Operation Mongoose" (*Hegemony* 82). Chomsky cites historian Piero Gleijeses' description of Operation Mongoose as "a program of paramilitary operations, economic warfare, and sabotage...launched in 1961 to visit the 'terrors of the earth' on Fidel Castro," in order to topple him (*Hegemony* 82).

The quoted phrase, Chomsky notes, is from historian Arthur Schlesinger, referring to the goals of President Kennedy's brother Attorney General Robert Kennedy whom the President had appointed to oversee the operations (*Hegemony* 284n20). Chomsky further conteds that:

> US terrorism against Cuba has been excised from the record in a display of servility that would impress the most dedicated totalitarian. In the media, Cuba's plight is regularly attributed to the demon Castro and "Cuban socialism" alone. Castro bears full responsibility for the "poverty, isolation and humbling dependence" on the USSR, *the New York Times* editors inform us, concluding triumphantly that "the Cuban dictator has painted himself into his own corner," without any help from us. That is true by virtue of doctrinal necessity, the ultimate authority. (*Year 501*, 149)

Given what Chomsky has analyzed at length throughout his career as the doctrinal or ideological system, including journalists' prevailing incapacity to see through the US government's evasions and Orwellian language, neither Uris who wrote *Topaz* the novel nor Hitchcock who adapted it to film could have known what later histories would reveal about US-sponsored terrorism, subversion, and other coercions launched against Cuba right up to the missile crisis.

Whether—like journalists attaining editorial levels by internalizing the values and worldview of ruling elites—Uris and Hitchcock were

The Unreliable Narrative

ideologically conditioned not to want to know is another question. "An admirer of John F. Kennedy," writes biographer Patrick McGilligan, "Hitchcock was fascinated by the American president's showdown with Castro and Khrushchev in 1962" (684). Uris and Hitchcock had, as always, only the official narrative written by corporate journalists acting mostly as dutiful stenographers of business and government elites spinning "necessary illusions" as a false backdrop for Hitchcock's Cold War films. As Raymond Durgnat suggests, "It is interesting to apply the paranoid logic of spy films to Hitchcock's films and wonder if he had been asked by the C.I.A. to make films which would keep the Cold War image alive in everyone's minds" (370).

If so, it is not, perhaps, without reservations. On his flight to Cuba, for example, we get Andre as a false backdrop to the news. We see him in a rather diffused, rear projection close-up while an actual *New York Times* front page for October 22, 1962 rises up before him in the frame, creating an obvious illusion that he is reading the newspaper. The right-hand column headlines loom up in the frame, "CAPITAL CRISIS AIR HINTS AT DEVELOPMENT ON CUBA; KENNEDY TV TALK LIKELY" and "Latins' Sympathy for U.S. Rises in Castro Dispute: Surveys Find Support for the Isolation of Cuba but Not for Armed Action—Caribbean Countries Troubled," and "Top Aides Confer." This last story, in the *Times* archives, mentions in the last two paragraphs periodic attacks on Cuba by exile groups, without, of course, linking these to the US-sponsored Operation Mongoose. Such might fall outside the slogan, "All the News That's Fit to Print." Hitchcock's written word visuals likewise both provide and withhold information. And basing his reading predominantly on Hitchcock's visual storytelling, Spoto, who favors *Topaz* over *Torn Curtain*, suspects that Hitchcock suspects something beyond what could be found in the newspapers. Spoto writes that with "all the little people caught in the cogs of the mad machines of the super-powers...Hitchcock's moral cynicism, his deep distrust of politics, his contempt for international big business, have never come across so clearly as in this film" (432-33).

Thus, in light of John Dewey's famous claim that "'politics is the shadow cast on society by big business,'" Chomsky notes that:

It is only natural that state policy should seek to construct a world system open to US economic penetration and political control, tolerating no rivals or threats. A crucial corollary is vigilance to block any moves toward independent development that might become a "virus infecting others," in the terminology of planners. That is a leading theme of postwar history, often disguised under thin Cold War pretexts that were also exploited by the superpower rival in its narrower domains. (*Hegemony* 15-16)

In other words, global populations have been subjected to one protection racket after another. And in *Topaz*, the head of the spy ring planted by the USSR in the French intelligence services, Devereaux's old friend Jacques Granville, as the story turns out, is a sociopath loyal neither to Devereaux, nor to France, but only to his own personal gain. This is basically Uris's theme in the novel *Topaz*: love of country versus self-aggrandizement. But this could be said of global business elites as well. It is their institutional duty to be loyal neither to their fellow national (or global) citizens nor to the very national states that support their pursuit of profits and power. This is why, of all three endings Hitchcock filmed, the one that has Granville escape (like Gavin Elster in *Vertigo*), seems to me the most honest.

Again, both *Torn Curtain* and *Topaz* offer audiences the superiority of Western "democracy" as politically naïve consumerism. In *Topaz*, the CIA "rescues" the vacationing Kusenovs in front of Den Permanente, the famous Copenhagen department store, another instance, perhaps, of product placement. Toward the end of the film, the formerly Communist Kusenov will begin to appreciate to the delights of Western consumerism. The close-up of Kusenov watching the woman adroitly attaching a petal onto a statuette in the Royal Porcelain Factory, while the Soviet agent watches him in turn, seems Hitchcock's acknowledgment that art for art's sake is embedded in the political. In both capitalism and Communism, that means unequal power relations. Most importantly, the middle-class travel fantasy, negotiating foreign places coveted by the affluent, acquires the added excitement of dangerous border crossings and other transgressions. What could be more thrilling than a game of espionage while on tour with possible thermonuclear war at stake?

The Unreliable Narrative

Of course, audiences already knew the Cuban missile crisis averted such a war. Hitchcock's real suspense, then, must lie in individual deaths and what becomes of relationships. In *Topaz*, people die verifying missiles that U2 photographs had already revealed. The film ends in Paris. A man idly casts a newspaper on a bench near the Arc de Triomphe. It is a copy of the *New York Herald Tribune*, bearing the headline, "Cuban Missile Crisis Ends: U.S. Scraps Plans to Bomb Bases." In the official narrative, President Kennedy stared down Soviet Premier Nikita Khrushchev, forcing him to withdraw the offensive nuclear weapons threatening the United States. Of course, Kennedy agreed to withdraw Jupiter missiles in Turkey aimed at Russia. But those missiles were obsolete anyway since the US could easily target Russia with Polaris missiles from nuclear submarines. Nor did crisis resolution stop President Kennedy from proceeding with covert operations to topple the Castro regime (Chomsky, *Hegemony* 75). Arthur Schlesinger later called the Cuban Crisis "the most dangerous moment in human history" (74).

It may cast a certain irony on *Topaz*, then, to consider that it was not Western agents but a lone Soviet naval officer who saved the world from criminal elites on both sides. For what is less well known is that during the tensest moment of the crisis a US Navy destroyer was dropping signaling depth charges on a Soviet submarine, trying to coax it to surface. Almost tragically, this only caused its captain and third officer to panic and agree to launch a nuclear-armed torpedo. But a third commander, Vassily Arkhipov, blocked the order, avoiding by a hair's breadth a nuclear exchange (Chomsky, *Hegemony* 74). While Khrushchev's decision, against Kremlin counsel, to put missiles in Cuba was "an act of criminal lunacy," writes Chomsky, it was nevertheless a response to the greater criminal lunacy of US policy, given the risks of likely consequences.[9] "We understand the truism very well when considering the actions of official enemies," Chomsky explains, "but find it hard to apply to ourselves" (78). The plausibility remains, according to historian Thomas Patterson, that "'the origins of the October 1962 crisis derived largely from the concerted U.S. campaign to quash the Cuban revolution' by violence and economic warfare" (qtd. in Chomsky, *Hegemony* 80).

At the domestic level, American propaganda explains poverty as originating not with an inherently unjust political economy but with an inherently vicious and undeserving poor (predominantly people of color) seeking handouts from the state even unto Socialism, itself portrayed as decadent. There is a famous sequence in *Topaz* in which Andre Devereaux watches from across the street of Harlem's Hotel Theresa (we get his "silent cinema" point of view) as his contact Phillipe Dubois (Roscoe Lee Browne) bribes Rico Parra's aid José Uribe (Don Randolph) to help him photograph a secret treaty with the Soviet Union contained in Parra's red briefcase. Spoto points out the contrast in New York's palatial St. Regis Hotel and the "Theresa Hotel crowded with maids, visitors, pressmen, prostitutes and political sycophants" (428). The hotel is in fact associated with Rico Parra's slovenliness, a change Hitchcock made to Rico's appearance in the novel. In the film he dresses in baggy, unkempt fatigues. He and his staff drink heavily while carrying on the regime's administrative work. Hitchcock provides an unsavory close-up of a half-eaten hamburger staining an important document that Rico recovers as if to highlight what slobs these revolutionaries are, slumming, acting as if they are in solidarity with people of African descent in the US.

As in *Torn Curtain*, the plot of *Topaz* transpires amid international intrigue between rival systems of the Cold War that, in one profound but invisible way, are almost identical: those systems' three-tiered class structure. The Soviet Union destroyed workers cooperatives—socialism—and renamed as "Socialism" the organization of a kind of industrial czarism, a definition that ironically suited both the Bolshevik and US propagandists alike. But is not an oligarchy of big business owners analogous to the Party? (Chomsky constantly refers to corporate "planners"). Below that executive branch in the West was the professional-managerial class, analogous to the coordinator class of a Communist command economy. Both hierarchies handed decisions down to workers excluded from decision-making participation (Albert 181-82). Both systems "bought off" their populations, one with guaranteed jobs, housing, education, health care, the other with the "freedom" of no such guarantees, but the considerable if uneven affluence siphoned, we must remember, from the poor of Third World countries, which created a higher standard of living (for whites) in the post-World War II decades, especially. Of course, the West enjoyed free speech under a unique historical situation in which speech could pose no serious threat to the capitalist system with its prevailing "necessary illusions." What was missing in both systems, of course, was universal democracy originating in the one place it counts most: the workplace.

Both *Torn Curtain* and *Topaz* take for granted the culture of the above-mentioned three-tiered employer/employee schema. Since Hitchcock and his 1960s audience can hardly be expected to think past the basic social structure common to rival camps, Cold War espionage tales can only add a certain genre flavor to the usual domestic issues of middle-class, heterosexual relationships within capitalist culture. The story demands that we find Andre Devereux locked in a marriage in which both partners have affairs. He betrays Nicole with his fellow spy, Juanita; Nicole in turn has an affair with the very top-level French traitor, code named Columbine, that Andre seeks. And this, for further irony, proves to be his best friend from World War II French Resistance days, Jacques Granville. The red Legion of Honor lapel emblems that both men wear thus vibrate with irony. The audience identifies with Andre as a member of the professional managerial class. He is, furthermore, a genuine French patriot who believes an alliance with the US is best for France, also calculated to gratify Hitchcock's audience. Although he works for government, he strikes us as the ideal corporate employee who "takes ownership," devotes himself so fully to the company, as though he is an owner, that it both depletes his marriage and fuels an illicit passion for his tragic mistress, Juanita (a social condition further recognizable to Hitchcock's audience).

Juanita in turn enlists loyal espionage from her servants, the Mendozas, to oppose a regime that has confiscated her property. But where the dialectic of history once asked, "Which would you rather be, the master or the slave?" at last the Hegelian *aufheben*—a whole new question—lifted itself up from the previous one and asked, "Who says you have to be either one?" The employer/employee schema ensued. In later capitalism, perhaps Chomsky's notion of a democratic, libertarian socialism might arise, one that can ask, "Who says one has to be either an employer or an employee?" as worker cooperatives become prevalent. While Hitchcock's films are certainly predicated on the employer/employee schema, we may be able to detect a certain tendency in his films to critique that arrangement. Hitchcock's image of the tortured Mendozas in the configuration of the *Pietá*, for example, shows that, aside from the religious reference, their suffering attests to the Cuban Revolution as simply replacing one oppressive employer with another.

Accordingly, what we take for granted in Hitchcock's universe is that in idealistically working for the US, Andre nevertheless serves a structure of dominance. And so does Jacques, albeit selfishly. He serves a rival state also organized on an industrialized class system. Hitchcock's cinematic narration knows this on misanthropist if not institutional terms. *Torn Curtain* and *Topaz* tacitly assume, in the political unconscious, a rather shared ideological system that makes gangsters of modern states while the director instinctively questions it, not from a partisan political standpoint, least of all from a radical dissident one. Rather, Hitchcock made films about human fallibility. Had he known in the 1960s and 1970s what Chomsky was saying about capitalism's doctrinal system, its Orwellian language and "the art of disappearing unwanted facts" (*Hegemony* 193), Hitchcock might have smiled wryly at Chomsky's fallibility as well. Throughout his career Hitchcock was quite comfortable around left-wing artists. Many of them were eventually blacklisted while he was not, largely because he was just too "realistic" and cynical, too temperamentally "apolitical" to identify with any of their fallible causes (McGilligan 414). Although he could appreciate their concerns he may have believed too deeply that institutions cannot be much altered because they grow out of unchangeable human nature. It is left for Hitchcock to observe human behavior as a sensitive artist and a moderate Democrat in an America of Keynesian economics.[11] Alfred Hitchcock presents, then, voyeuristic movies observing individual characters' behavior. To dissidents, however, the torture and death of the Mendozas in *Topaz* (brought on by Andre's espionage) is institutional behavior relative to an imperial America still enjoying its own New Deal. And, in a sense, Michael's cruel disregard for Sarah in the opening of *Torn Curtain*, is also institutional behavior.[12]

Both a shrewd observer and exploiter of society's imp of the perverse, yet seemingly innocent of ideology critique, Hitchcock was able to make films and cultivate a persona that emitted none of the partisan vibes that would bring his work to HUAC's censorious attention in the 1940s and 1950s. And when he failed at the box office it was not due to alienating whole swaths of his audience on political or religious grounds. Of course, to US dissidents with perhaps a naiveté of their

The Unreliable Narrative 191

own, Hitchcock takes for granted institutions of dominance as though they are simply endemic to the Human Condition. Even so, at one point in Hitchcock's *Topaz*, a wall lamp frames the American agent McKittrick (Edmon Ryan) such that it appears to give him devil's horns. Later, Kusenov remarks that in defecting to the Americans, "I have made my bargain with the devil." Neil Sinyard argues that in *Torn Curtain*, Michael "would sell his soul...for ultimate knowledge: he is Faust" (274). Precisely because Hitchcock, the consummate artist, is no self-conscious dissident in his Cold War films, his cinema becomes all the more interesting as, paradoxically, the worldly innocent eye.

Notes

1. Michael Walker finds key narrative parallels between *Torn Curtain* and *Psycho* (1960): "Each film...begins with the heroine experiencing a blockage in her relationship with the hero that creates a sense of insecurity" (96-97).

2. In the novel, Leon Uris portrays Andre's first love Nicole as just a spoiled aristocrat.

3. Such corrosive activities characterize an economic system predicated on competition rather than cooperation. See, for example, muckraking journalist Jim Hightower, "A Corporate 'Foreign Legion' Has Taken over America's Intelligence and Military Functions: Our Taxes Pay Spies to Work for Rich Shareholders—and Pay for the Corporatization of War Itself," *The Hightower Lowdown*, vol. 14, no. 4, April 2012.

4. The Tivoli Gardens and the Nimb Fountains where Michael and Sarah have lunch, and the Copenhagen's ceramics scene where the Kusenovs escape, figure prominently in Gordon Hessler's cult film, *The Girl in a Swing* (1988). Hessler served as story editor for *Alfred Hitchcock Presents* (1960-62), then became associate producer (1962-64). From 1964-65, he produced *The Alfred Hitchcock Hour* (Leitch 136).

5. This is perhaps Hitchcock's wry comment on Chief Justice Oliver Wendell Holmes's (in)famous limitation on free speech in the Supreme Court's decision in *Schenck v. United States* under the Espionage Act of 1917, a precedent Holmes and other Supreme Courts later reversed. But the earlier ruling has been used ever since in defense of censorship.

6. If I may add this observation to Michael Walker's striking parallels between *Torn Curtain* and *Psycho*.

7. Whereas Donald Spoto attributes *Topaz*'s success to its ingenious use of color, Paula Morantz Cohen sees the film's employing a complex color-coded design repre-

senting the interplay of nationalities as detracting from the more engaging focus on one couple with secret and duplicitous feelings, as in *Notorious* (Spoto 427-28; Cohen 156-57). Consistent with Cohen's remark about the intermixing of color among all sides, moreover, is the mixing of Juanita's and Rico's blood. For it appears to me that the bullet may well have passed through her body and into Rico's own left hand at just the place on her back where he clutches her body to his.

8. Juanita de Córdoba is thinly disguised as the real-life Juanita Castro, the sister of Fidel and Raúl. She became disillusioned with her brothers' revolution, saying that they had made Cuba "a prison surrounded by water."

9. Similarly, in *Torn Curtain*, Michael Armstrong's double-dealing "defection" could itself be called "an act of criminal lunacy."

10. A question I like to raise is whether envisioning an alternative political economy based on worker cooperatives that are not male-, white-, straight-dominated, and so on, might in some ways enhance our perceptions of Hitchcock's plot structures and poetics.

11. This refers to the prescriptions of economist John Maynard Keynes, who sought to stabilize capitalism through substantial redistribution of wealth and government interventions. Marxist economist Richard Wolff, however, argues that capitalism's very dynamic *must* oscillate between Keynes and Friedrich Hayek's deregulated "free markets." It thus remains exploitive and unstable. I would add that the dynamic has profound psycho-social implications that manifest in Hitchcock's films.

12. Raymond Durgnat's early readings of *Torn Curtain* and *Topaz* remain valuable as institutional critique.

Works Cited

Albert, Michael. *Parecon: Life after Capitalism*. Verso, 2003.
Allen, Richard. *Hitchcock's Romantic Irony*. Columbia UP, 2007.
Berger, John. *Ways of Seeing*. British Broadcasting Corporation and Penguin, 1972.
Bernays, Edward. *Propaganda*. Introduction by Mark Crispin Miller. Ig Publishing, 1928, 1955, 2005.
Chomsky, Noam. *Chronicles of Dissent: Interviews with David Barsamian*. Common Courage Press and AK Press, 1992.
---. *Hegemony or Survival: America's Quest for Global Dominance*. Metropolitan, 2003.

---. *Necessary Illusions: Thought Control in Democratic Societies.* South End Press, 1989.

---. *Year 501: The Conquest Continues.* South End Press, 1993.

Cohen, Paula Morantz. *Alfred Hitchcock: The Legacy of Victorianism.* U of Kentucky P, 1995.

Durgnat, Raymond. *The Strange Case of Alfred Hitchcock: Or, The Plain Man's Hitchcock.* The MIT Press, 1974.

Jacobs, Steven. "Sightseeing Fright: Alfred Hitchcock's Monuments and Museums." *The Journal of Architecture*, vol. 11, no. 5, 2006, pp. 593-601.

Leitch, Thomas. *The Encyclopedia of Alfred Hitchcock: from Alfred Hitchcock Presents to Vertigo.* Checkmark, 2002.

McGilligan, Patrick. *Alfred Hitchcock: A Life of Darkness and Light.* ReganBooks, 2003.

Modleski, Tania. *The Women Who Knew Too Much: Hitchcock and Feminist Theory.* Routledge, 1988.

New York Times. "Top Aides Confer: U.S. Forces Maneuver Off Puerto Rico—Link Is Denied." 22 Oct. 1962, pp. 1, 16.

Sinyard, Neil. "'The Loyalty of an Eel': Issues of Political, Personal, and Professional Morality in (and around) *Torn Curtain.*" *Hitchcock's Moral Gaze*, edited by R. Barton Palmer, Homer B. Pettey, and Steven M. Sanders, SUNY Press, 2017, pp. 271-85.

Spoto, Donald. *The Art of Alfred Hitchcock: Fifty Years of His Motion Pictures.* Dolphin, 1979.

Tilly, Charles. *Coercion, Capital, and European States: AD 990-1990.* Basil Blackwell, 1990.

Ture, Kwame. "Black Power Speech (1996)." *Youtube*, uploaded by Donnie Mossberg, 5 Dec. 2012. www.youtube.com/watch?v=IMYTN0-2ugI

Uris, Leon. *Topaz.* McGraw-Hill, 1967.

Walker, Michael. "A Hitchcock Compendium: Narrative Strategies in *Torn Curtain.*" *Hitchcock Annual*, 2005-2006, pp. 95-120.

"Even our friends spy on us": Espionage and Emotion in Hitchcock's *Topaz* and *The Short Night*

By Ken Mogg

[Jay Presson Allen] considered Hitchcock…much more romantic and wistful than the more grounded and perceptive Alma…
—Walter Raubicheck & Walter Srebnick (118)

Staging the encounter with the [Lacanian] Real is Hitchcock's essential cinematic project.
—Eric Savoy (228, n1)

Poe's most considerable narrative legacy to Hitchcock is the expert crafting of emotional responses in audiences. The key to that legacy is the concept of the sublime, the simultaneous experience of delight and terror…
—Dennis R. Perry (1)

Hitchcock, who in April 1945 had supervised the initial compilation and editing of footage from Bergen-Belsen and other concentration camps, knew how the world goes, and was prepared to hint at it in his films. His deepest intuitions about the world, with its dark side, were probably formed by his having lived through the First World War, and having afterwards made films that allegorized its horrors, notably the Ivor Novello vehicle, *The Lodger* (1927).[1] The perceptive Dennis Perry takes up this idea when he comments specifically on the espionage films: "Much of Hitchcock's work, like Poe's, is implicitly apocalyptic. His many spy films, for example, suggest frightening threats against Western civilization…Hence, these stories are often about the protagonists becoming…aware of the depth of corruption in unexpected places" (47-48). Espionage in the spy films, like forensics in the films featuring police procedures and courtrooms, intrigued Hitchcock, and provided him with ready-made material to convey his disabused view of the world, at a human rather than cerebral level.[2] Perry's emphasis on the sublime, and a *simultaneity* of emotions, goes to the essence of Hitchcock's working method. That method involves nothing less than the director outflanking the audience who must finally watch, "spellbound."[3] Although this method runs through the films from the 1930s onwards, its paradigm is the *Storm Cloud Cantata* scene in the first version of *The Man Who Knew Too Much* (1934), and is worth recalling.

    The scene, and the cantata, aren't just about storm clouds, but that's a good place to start. The setting is the circular Royal Albert Hall, London, and Jill (Edna Best) has bought herself a ticket in the medium-priced tier seats, knowing vaguely that the political assassins who have kidnapped her pre-pubescent daughter intend some malevolence. (By contrast, the film audience understands very precisely that an assassination of a dignitary will be attempted when a clash of cymbals occurs at a climactic moment.) Hitchcock commissioned respected Australian composer Arthur Benjamin to write the cantata. The lyrics, sung by a female soloist backed by a massed choir and full orchestra, refer to "nameless fear, / And panic [that] overtook each flying creature of the wild." This exactly fits Leonard B. Meyer's characterization of musical suspense "which seems to have direct analogies in experience in general...[For example,] the low, foreboding rumble of distant thunder on an oppressive summer afternoon... Similarly in music the state of suspense involves an awareness of the powerlessness of man in the face of the unknown" (28-29). In other words, a low-intensity sublime already exists here, by virtue of the analogy with man-in-nature—but undoubtedly Hitchcock, like T.S. Eliot, the author of "Tradition and the Individual Talent" (1921), appreciated how in good art "any semi-ethical criterion of 'sublimity' misses the mark," and what matters is "the intensity of the artistic process" (Eliot, par. 14). That's what the multi-layered Storm Cloud Cantata scene is finally about. For one thing, the dialogue had earlier referred to Sarajevo, and nothing less than war-versus-peace feels at stake. For another, Hitchcock keeps the occasion down-to-earth (while further complicating our emotional response) because we experience the cantata not in an abstract, or merely aesthetic, way but through the searching eyes and ears of Jill. Her feeling of powerlessness has its precise parallel in the film audience's inability to do anything except watch spellbound.

Further, it may be mentioned here that the Hitchcock project with the greatest potential for sublimity, an adaptation of *We, the Accused* (1935) by Ernest Raymond, never got made, to Hitchcock's permanent regret. Nonetheless, it remains a touchstone in his oeuvre. It would have been a manhunt story loosely based on the case of one Samuel Furnace (not Dr. Crippen, as often said), in which wife-killer Paul Presset goes on the run with his young mistress, fellow schoolteacher Myra Bawne, and for a few short weeks they know life "perhaps…intensified to the utmost" (Raymond, *We, the Accused* 328). Hitchcock always sympathized with Paul. As late as 1972, interviewed by Charles Thomas Samuels, he averred that "the murderer [in Raymond's story]…did nothing worse than rid himself of a bitch of a wife" (239-40).[4] Early in the manhunt, the reader is introduced to Inspector Boltro, whose dedication to bringing the couple to book is absolute. Later, at the Old Bailey, Paul encounters someone equally set against him, the prosecutor Sir Hayman Drewer, who seems a close relative of the icy judge in Robert Hichens's *The Paradine Case* (1933). A key passage is the one already quoted: "Perhaps all life, [Paul] thought, was beauty threatened by danger…" (327-28). In turn, right from the early days, Hitchcock had been ready to show the ruthlessness of authorities, such as the intelligence-boss "R" (Charles Carson) in *Secret Agent* (1936)—adapted from two of Somerset Maugham's "Ashenden" stories—who thinks nothing of dispatching the Royal Flying Corps to shoot up a train bound for Constantinople carrying both the fleeing German spy (Robert Young) and Ashenden himself (John Gielgud), as well as innocent civilians.

So the world, in Hitchcock's eyes, was not always a pretty place, although it might at the same time be beautiful, and that is one source of the sublime that surfaces in both *Topaz* (1969) and Hitchcock's last project *The Short Night* (screenplay by David Freeman[5]). By this final decade or two of his life, Hitchcock (1899-1980) had refined his youthful *Weltanschauung*, although perhaps not by much, seeing no need. Basically, he felt that this was how people were, and the world would always reflect it—and Hitchcock's films, in turn, would reflect it, or hint at it. A good part of Hitchcock's art was to leave us feeling that he had covered all bases, including even the speculative. Freeman notes:

"[Hitchcock] did seem to me a man absolutely intent on correcting the Universe…If God couldn't get it right the first time around, Hitch was going to have a go at it and see what he could do" (53). Accordingly, the films were candid without being nihilistic, being prepared to point to possibilities, if only for "next time." Even the traitor father of Alicia in *Notorious* (1946) is allowed to voice such a hope. (You almost feel that Hitchcock, on principle, would allow the Nazi cause a "fairer" hearing on some future occasion, that the line had to go in the script.[6]) The bottom line, though, was that Hitchcock was a professional crowd-pleaser, which extended to his producers. To Samuels he said tersely: "We live in an industry" (250).

Altogether, it can be inferred that a guiding principle for Hitchcock as director was to give, and at times ennoble, emotional satisfaction—meaning, emotions that weren't sentimental or "pulp." Regrettably, the scripting and shooting of *Topaz* did not go smoothly even after the departure of the book's author, Leon Uris, replaced at a late stage by Samuel Taylor (*Vertigo*, 1958), who understood Hitchcock's requirements; sometimes pages of the screenplay were being delivered from Taylor's typewriter only hours before shooting. And a central love-scene with potential for sublimity had to be severely modified when it emerged that both actors (Karin Dor, Frederick Stafford) had scars from thorax surgery. (Unfazed, Hitchcock would script an even more ambitious love-scene for *The Short Night*, to be played in circumstances that definitely invite the audience to experience the contrast of delight and terror.) Still, the Cuban setting in *Topaz* was perfect for its director's needs, and he and Taylor did not waste it. We may discount the Cuban missile crisis, whose outcome was already known to the audience (contrast the impending war implicit in the 1930s films), and instead emphasize the island as a "stage" for ongoing revolution, with its inevitable dramas, plus matters of espionage touching the island but involving global powers. Cuba in *Topaz* functions like the Albert Hall in *The Man Who Knew Too Much*. Specifically, there is a degree of the sublime inherent in the events, but a related concept is that of "romantic irony" where again simultaneity is of the essence. Such a concept was first applied to Hitchcock's films by Richard Allen, meaning "the *amoral* point of view of the romantic-ironist or aesthete" that employs a *both/and* rather than *either/or* logic (or rhetoric) (xiii-xiv), but there exists a particularly nuanced definition, that of Anne Mellor, in which the poet:

romantically engages in the creative process of life by eagerly constructing new forms, new myths. And these new fictions and self-concepts [ironically] bear with them the seeds of their own destruction. They too die to give way to new patterns, in a never-ending process that becomes an analogue for life itself.[7] (5)

We shall see this process in action when discussing in detail the Cuban scenes; here, it's sufficient to note their sweep, effectively spanning the island and incorporating a political rally in the capital Havana addressed by Fidel Castro and Che Guevara. *Topaz* pointedly includes five world capitals in its representative itinerary.

Lastly, these introductory remarks should include information about double agent George Blake (born George Behar in Rotterdam in 1922), whose case reportedly "fascinated" Hitchcock (McGilligan 731), and whose complex personality provided the basis for the villain of Ronald Kirkbride's novel *The Short Night* (1968), which Hitchcock intended to film. Although Blake quickly joined the Dutch Resistance when the Nazis invaded his country, he was forced to flee to Britain where he demonstrated brilliant linguistic skills and was recruited as an intelligence officer, joining MI6, the British foreign intelligence service, in 1944. After the war, he was posted first to Hamburg (he was put in charge of interrogating German U-boat captains), and later Seoul, where he worked as a vice consul and secretly as an MI6 agent. But the outbreak of the Korean War saw the British Legation rounded up and sent north of the border where they were interned for the duration. After their release in 1953, they returned to Britain as heroes. In 1954, Blake married MI6 secretary Gillian Allan, who fairly soon gave him two sons (there was a third child who arrived after Blake's arrest for treason). Blake's subsequent postings were to Berlin and to Beirut where the British encouraged him to pose as a double agent in order to obtain information about Soviet bloc activities; in fact, his deepest loyalties by this time were with the Communist cause, and he was busily betraying British (and Allied) agents. For example, he betrayed Russian double agent Lieutenant-Colonel Pyotr Popov, a Soviet GRU (military intelligence) officer, who had been passing information to the CIA and who was arrested one day on a Moscow bus, then sentenced to death (probably by a bullet to the back of the head[8]).

Blake's own arrest came in 1961 after he was recalled from Beirut. His trial at the Old Bailey saw him sentenced to a savage 42 years in prison; in fact, it was the severity of that sentence that persuaded a fellow inmate at Wormwood Scrubs Prison, Seán Bourke, who had IRA sympathies, to assist Blake to escape in 1966 and who travelled with him to Moscow. Bourke's account of the escape and its aftermath, *The Springing of George Blake* (1970), provided Hitchcock with the exciting opening of his adaptation of *The Short Night*, plus key insights into the complexity of Blake's character. On the one hand, Blake was capable of considerable charm—he hadn't been appointed to diplomatic posts lightly—and of keeping it up for years, if necessary. With Bourke, he kept it up throughout their prison years and mostly while they were lying low together on the outside. Only once, in Hampstead, was there a hint of what was to come. One day Blake offered to help his companion who was doing stretching exercises on the floor. Suddenly he "seemed to lose control of himself. 'Get down, get down, get down!' he hissed through clenched teeth" as he pushed Bourke's head towards his knees. Only after several seconds did he stop. "He was flushed and excited. Then he started to laugh. But it was a forced, nervous laugh and I felt sure that he must realize that he had gone too far and given something away" (Bourke 183-84). Later, Bourke saw how things were between them: "The only thing at stake for Blake was his personal vanity, his only motive an insatiable thirst for power" (242). Also, he seems to have been a latent pedophile. According to Bourke, small children made him "hopelessly soft." "He would linger near a playground to watch the children at play, and when walking through the streets his eyes were constantly darting from one young person or group to another" (Bourke 224). However, Freeman's screenplay for *The Short Night* gives the character the benefit of the doubt while making his affection for his two boys literally a saving grace. In twice hesitating to fire a gun in front of them, during the film's tense climax, he indirectly ensures his escape across the Finland-Russia border.

Actually, you feel that Hitchcock would have respected Blake, by and large. Early in his MI6 days, Blake felt snubbed when the father of the aristocratic young lady he was currently dating took him aside and made it plain that there was absolutely no question of Blake's marrying her. Given British notions of class and what was fitting, the snub—as

Blake always remembered it—was understandable. Yet it rankled (Hyde 30-31). Blake's Communist sympathies had first been planted in his teenage years by a Marxist cousin. He had also toyed with the idea of becoming a Roman Catholic priest (Hyde 59). But it seems that his North Korean experience was decisive. Asked about it, he referred to

> the relentless bombing of small Korean villages by enormous American Flying Fortresses. Women and children and old people [were the targets], because the young men were in the army…It made me ashamed of belonging to these overpowering, technically superior countries fighting against what seemed to me defenseless people.[9] (qtd. in Irvine)

Recently, Blake's observations have been echoed by Christine Hong of UC Santa Cruz: "Throughout the Cold War the United States waged really destructive hot wars in the Third World, most infamously on the Korean Peninsula…an estimated 4 million [Koreans] were killed during that asymmetrical war in which the United States unleashed bombs with absolutely no regard for human life" (Hong).[10]

§

Like Castro, Che [Guevara] was not averse to world nuclear war and argued that resistance to imperialist aggression was worth the possibility of "millions of atomic war victims."
—Michael Sexton

In the *Reflections on the Revolution in France*, Edmund Burke had in fact troped the Revolution as a false sublime…the humiliation of the beautiful in the figure of Marie Antoinette…
—Vijay Mishra (14-15)

To further demonstrate the important point that Hitchcock sought on principle to "outflank" even his own material, as well as his audiences, consider that in *Topaz*, Juanita de Córdoba (Dor) tells Castro look-alike Rico Parra (John Vernon), "You make my country a prison," only to receive his measured reply, "No, you cannot judge."[11] The lines were written by Taylor. The fact is, Hitchcock chafed from the outset to rid himself of the tendentious Uris whose gift of assembling a storyline from countless "sources" and his reliance on the material's frequent shock-content had its own vigor, but wasn't Hitchcockian. Uris biographer Ira Nadel notes: "Hemingway, not Henry James, was [Uris's] model. This naturally led to…fiction filled with macho action at the expense of emotion and complexity" (8). According to Nadel, Uris first met with Philippe de Vosjoli, a "retired" member of the French secret service—and the primary source of *Topaz*—in Acapulco in 1964. Another commentator describes Vosjoli as "a short, bald-headed man" (Epstein), and thus nothing like Stafford who plays him in the Hitchcock film (as the character Andre Devereaux). Vosjoli showed Uris the draft of an autobiography, *Le Réseau Topaz/The Topaz Network*, in which he disclosed that the Americans had allowed him access to defector Anatoliy Golitsyn of the KGB (the Soviet Intelligence and Security Service), who had indicated major leaks in NATO, possibly going as high as the cabinet of French President Charles de Gaulle. Vosjoli had also used contacts in Cuba, including Castro's sister, Juanita, to provide the CIA information about Soviet missiles being installed there (Nadel 181). He initially refused to identify his sources to his French bosses, fearing that Soviet moles would pass the information to Moscow. Later events would prove that his fears were well-founded.

I shall argue here that the film *Topaz* remains timely in its emotional appeal. Properly understood—using the guidelines I've begun to sketch—it makes a moving and powerful statement. I'll argue that the final duel scene was always a favorite of Hitchcock's, and is the "correct" ending. More than once, I have watched *Topaz* alongside Eric Rohmer's *Triple Agent* (2004) and noted a subtext they share, in which the wife is demoralized by her husband's inability to be open, to tell her everything. Rohmer's comment on that is worth quoting: "All my films are spy films in a sense. They all deal with characters spying on others or being suspicious of others" (Jeffries). This anticipates by a decade the observation of Chinese espionage novelist Ha Jin apropos his *A Map of Betrayal*: "Even our friends spy on us and we do the same to them" (qtd. in Levy).[12] Few of *Topaz*'s characters feel secure for long, and several of them will betray and/or be betrayed—this in a context of false appearances amounting to what one character calls "a fairy tale." Unfortunately, Nadel is inexact when he reports on what was said at the initial story-conference after Taylor came on board, but he sums up: "After analyzing the novel, the participants noted that there was something fascinating about *Topaz*..." (187).[13] Clearly, they intended to make this the essence of their film; I think it included the "unbelievability" of what was disclosed.

In the novel, Andre Devereaux more than once finds himself on the receiving end of incredible information—or at times disinformation.[14] It includes matters like the Russian defector's revelation of a French "dirty tricks" department whose newest sub-section consists "of a group of French scientists...who will be placed in American research and industry...to conduct industrial and scientific espionage on the United States" (Uris 222). On being told this, Andre makes a rare angry outburst: "It's fantasy." The Russian takes off his glasses. "We deal in fantasy, do we not?" (Uris 223). Another time, Andre's enemies inform the French President, "Monsieur le Président, we have uncovered a fantastic plot. It is our opinion that the entire missile crisis was a gigantic hoax dreamed up between the United States and the Soviet Union [with Devereaux as dupe]." The touchy President ponders this, concluding that it may indicate a Soviet-American collusion designed to relegate France to secondary status (Uris 355). A study of the history of warfare shows that such goings-on and/or "fake news" have always existed.[15] Uris's novel plays up one of the Russian's disclosures: the existence within the KGB of the Department of Disinformation (252).[16] Hitchcock, on the other hand, probably sensed that such material verged on cliché or led him into difficulties; his hands were already full as he sought not to offend his potential French audience with successive allegations concerning France and its gullible President, something that apparently didn't trouble Uris. Working with Taylor, Hitchcock would construct, instead, a "true" parable touching on how close the world came to apocalypse, essentially a behind-the-scenes story of life and death retaining the novel's "fascination."

Here, Maurice Jarre's score could help, several times underlining the fact that a character has been caught out. A pompous French General visiting Washington DC is quickly brought to heel: Andre simply asks him to consider who told Paris about the Russian defector, and why. Could someone in Moscow, with Paris contacts, be angling to nullify the Russian's disclosures? The General is baffled, which Jarre emphasizes with a single, derisory "plunk." This deftly filmed scene gives a foretaste of the Paris scenes later. Notably, the scene in Pierre's Restaurant emphasizes some of Andre's colleagues' inability to acknowledge possible leaks in the government and in NATO. (No one seems to have heard of the "Cambridge" moles in England.[17]) Jarre starts the film's waltz in a high register, and lets it waft behind Andre's follow-up question about whether anyone present has heard of a spy organization called "*Topaz*." Predictably, one of the men at the table expostulates, "This is a fantasy!" Yet the scene has another dimension. Two of those present are in fact spies, and one of them—Henri Jarré (Philippe Noiret)—cracks up, although this isn't immediately apparent.[18] We watch sympathetically as he limps to a side table to help himself to more food, then re-joins his colleagues and chides Andre for not knowing that the Russian defector was "planted" on the Americans. Seemingly the scene ends with Andre as baffled as the French General earlier. In fact, Hitchcock and Taylor now move into high gear. While Andre checks with the Americans, successive scenes show Jarré fearful of being found out but getting no sympathy from his fellow-spy, then being further wrong-footed when a persistent Andre sends his journalist son-in-law François Picard (Michel Subor) to interview him. The scripting here parallels the ruthless scene in Hitchcock's *Murder!* (1930) in which Sir John (Herbert Marshall) tries to trick the gentle cross-dresser Handel Fane (Esmé Percy) into admitting that he is a killer. Both times, the emotional chemistry is complex, even pointing to a tractableness of the film viewer that is eyebrow-raising—but certainly, from the storyteller's point of view, serving its purpose.

Ironically, Devereaux is criticized by wife Nicole (Dany Robin) for having sent François—"a boy"—to interview the dangerous Jarré. This suggests Andre is irresponsible, uncaring. In truth, he leaves behind him a trail of people whose lives he has jeopardized. In the novel, François writes an article from material supplied by Andre about leaks and ineptitude in the French government, and is promptly murdered by the dirty tricks department (Uris 356-57). Nonetheless, both novel and film take the line that Andre is an exemplary agent. The very blandness of the character as played by Stafford may have worried Hitchcock,[19] but is both fitting—real secret agents *are* mostly bland[20]—and serves a narrative purpose. Andre is arguably "more sinned against than sinning." I used to similarly defend the character Barry Lyndon (in Stanley Kubrick's classic 1975 film), and actor Ryan O'Neal's performance, against a critic friend who felt that they didn't do enough. While Andre is not exactly a rogue like Barry, there are plenty of Russians, Cubans and French out to get him! Another of the film's ironies is that agents often have little to show for their work, and may in fact risk their own and others' lives for questionable ends.[21] In *Topaz*, we hear the American agent Michael Nordstrom (John Forsythe) congratulate Andre for obtaining on-the-ground evidence of the Soviet missile build-up in Cuba: "What you found out confirms our information from other sources, including the U-2 photos." Film theorist Barbara Creed's recent book on human-animal ethics makes a parallel point: "The terrible irony is that we experiment on animals to confirm what we already know" (13). However, is it *only* a parallel? I've suggested that Hitchcock held a *Weltanschauung* that already implies the main idea here: how (in this case) espionage and its imperatives bring out the worst and best in people, and how both those possibilities may be innate in our make-up. We, too, are creatures, but are capable of an over-determination that makes us hard.[22] Devereaux appears an essentially decent fellow, but the espionage world, like all forms of power, can corrupt.

Also, although he may be "more sinned against than sinning," he is fallible like everyone else. (Compare the title of this essay.[23]) Nicole knows of his mistress in Cuba, and the novel indicates that he has always been promiscuous, including a rumored recent affair with a Washington hostess (38). Further, the novel has been criticized for including an "irrelevant" section (277ff.) that describes how Andre and his school friend Jacques Granville smuggled Jews away from the Germans into Vichy France and later fought for the Free French. Hitchcock and Taylor saw that this was vital information, and contrived to have Nicole explain to Nordstrom about the rifle prominently featured in the Devereauxs' Washington apartment: it had been hers when fighting alongside Jacques and Andre in the Resistance. We readily sense that Nicole is bored in Washington; in fact, Hitchcock photographs her in a manner identical—hanging off a door jamb, like a child—to a moment in *The Paradine Case* (1947) where he had shown "grass widow" Gay Keane (Ann Todd) feeling similarly neglected. The information about the friendship with Jacques (Michel Piccoli) becomes timely when an exasperated Nicole flees to him in Paris while Andre seemingly dallies in Cuba.

Jacques is well off, a close advisor to the French President, and—if he were an artist—might agreeably epitomize "anything you can get away with" (as Marshall McLuhan was just then claiming for contemporary art and artists) (McLuhan and Fiore 132-36). In fact, the opportunistic Jacques is your ambiguous Hitchcock villain who will turn out to be the chief spy "Columbine": as played superbly by Piccoli, he is someone of fastidious tastes, and is highly capable. That's how he found himself accompanying General de Gaulle[24] at his Free French garrison in Algiers, leading to subsequent promotions. His betrayal of de Gaulle is only explained in the last page or so of the novel and not at all in the film. During the war, he had been sent on liaison missions to Moscow where the Soviets successfully groomed him, much as they had the moles in England. Hitchcock may have felt that this explanation was uncinematic. He and Taylor accordingly worked hard, in limited time, to make the "true parable" I have begun to describe, with an emotional intensity that takes matters to a different level.

If you generalize *Topaz's* mise-en-scène as one of hard/soft, or force versus attempts to soften/ameliorate, you won't go far wrong. A title explains that the "display of force" at a May Day parade in Moscow prompts the Russian family's attempt to defect, which we then watch in the suspenseful Copenhagen sequence featuring both a porcelain factory and the Den Permanente department store with its celebrated arts and crafts exhibit. Further, the Copenhagen sequence has played up the film's principal leitmotiv: flowers. Orson Welles would have understood. A Welles observation that should be more widely known is to the effect that in almost all serious stories "there is more lost paradise than defeat...that's the central theme in Western culture, the lost paradise" (qtd. in Byrne 28). Welles's own films are exemplars of it, being rich in an iconography that will include, say, an exotic garden or island, or its variant (e.g., a walled estate named "Xanadu," a wintry field). Hitchcock's films are the same. His first film, or parable, had the sardonic title *The Pleasure Garden* (1925), and included an ironic sequence set in the tropics. *Rebecca* (1940) has its own stagnating Xanadu, "Manderley"; *Vertigo*, set in an exquisitely-photographed San Francisco, by implication is all Lost Paradise. The pervasive floral imagery in *Topaz* is eloquent, as when Mike Nordstrom orders chrysanthemums to placate Andre and family for having tracked them down on vacation. In turn, Andre will prevail on one of his sub-agents, Philippe Dubois (Roscoe Lee Browne), who runs a florist's shop in Harlem, to seek out and photograph documents held by Rico Parra who is heading Cuba's delegation at the UN: memorably, Hitchcock shows us Andre's discussion with Dubois in the shop's cool room—filled with exotic flowers—while denying us the sound of their voices. This is one of the film's more "Brechtian" moments, which I'll interpret below. Of a different order, full of irony, is the last line spoken by the Russian defector, Boris Kusenov (Per-Axel Arosenius[25]), now resident in America and missing his home: "I'm going for a walk in the garden."[26] Note: he is a "hard" character but one who commands our fascinated respect.

Andre himself was always going to be a Lost Paradise figure; at least, the novel announces proudly that he was born in Montrichard, "the garden of France" (273). In Cuba, clearly, he feels almost at home, as his friendship with the aristocratic and beautiful Juanita ("the widow of a hero of the Revolution"[27]) appears to be of long standing, and very possibly had its erotic side from the beginning. As noted, the extended Cuban passages provide a "stage" for significant action: in that respect, they are like the *Storm Cloud Cantata* sequences in *both* versions of *The Man Who Knew Too Much* (1934, 1956), the latter sequence specifically likened by Murray Pomerance to an arcadia that speaks of life and death, or rather, both in one ("Et in Arcadia ego," as the poet reminds us[28]). That is, the Cuba passages have their self-destructive "romantic irony"; meanwhile, as in the novel *We, the Accused*, two lovers experience life "intensified to the utmost." More controversially, Hitchcock adds "down-to-earth" counterpoint (e.g., the Mendozas' calamitous, seagulls-beset picnic)—and possibly misjudges (or can't deflect) its effect on some unsympathetic audiences.[29] Wholly admirable, though, is the inventiveness he brought to Juanita herself and the sublimity her situation apropos Cuba invokes, to be demonstrated shortly. Note that Bernardo Bertolucci's *Before the Revolution* (1964)[30] had recently appeared; possibly Hitchcock already knew the remark, "Only those who have lived before the [French] Revolution know how sweet life can be."[31] In imagery of a revolution passionately upheld, or betrayed, *Topaz* employs a key Lost Paradise metaphor.

Two theorists of the sublime were the philosophers Immanuel Kant (1724-1804) and Arthur Schopenhauer (1788-1860).[32] Another was

English politician and author Edmund Burke (1729-97), who wrote important studies of both "the sublime and the beautiful"[33] and of the French Revolution (1790).[34] According to Kant, "the sublime *moves*, the beautiful *charms*."[35] According to Burke, "Whatever is fitted…to excite the ideas of pain, and danger…is a source of the sublime; that is, productive of the strongest emotion which the mind is capable of feeling" (Stern 45). Although Burke had supported the American Revolution, the excesses of the French Revolution alarmed him, so that he now drew on his aesthetic ideas to pinpoint something beautiful turned ugly, a false sublime, destructive and terrifying. He saw how the Revolution (in Mishra's words) was turned by the Jacobins "into the sublimely Gothic terror of disorderly men and women" (15). Burke's was a classic conservative appeal to anti-mob sentiment already strong in England ("the mob" was the *mobile vulgus,* "the fickle crowd") and with an artistic lineage that would extend from William Hogarth (1697-1764) to Charles Dickens (1812-70) to Hitchcock himself—whose *The Lodger* (1926) shows the mob at full roar, however ambiguously. (Is that Hitchcock himself joining them?[36]) As if following Burke, Hitchcock and Taylor sought to make their Cuban episodes speak simultaneously of a political tension that threatened to become terrifying, and another tension (the triangle of Juanita, Andre, and Rico Parra), equally explosive, involving "the humiliation of the beautiful."

Juanita's mansion is effectively her private "palace," with sea-views, a fountain, colored skylights, elegantly tiled floors, attractive modern paintings, and a contented staff. Widowed, but still beautiful, she has at least two lovers, although Andre is evidently her favorite, and their relationship extends to her clandestine intelligence-gathering for him. Although the novel soon mentions the brutal side of the Revolution, notably "the cruel mercy of Castro's chief inquisitor, Muñoz" (111), the film holds back on explicit reference to it: the unruly Harlem scenes give a foretaste. Hitchcock favored the slow build. Eventually, he shows the shocking events of the capture and torture by Muñoz (Roberto Contreras) of Juanita's servants, the Mendozas (Lewis Charles, Anna Navarro), including a final composition of their plight that is a disquieting pietà— presumably carrying anti-Communist connotations for those who want to read it thus.[37] But Juanita's impending death, on the analogy of "the humiliation of the beautiful," yet invoking the sublime, was no doubt Hitchcock's main concern as a self-styled crowd-pleaser. The novel offered him some clues. On the evening before Andre departs, Juanita wears a "particularly stunning" hostess gown (Uris 170). Earlier, alighting from her car, she had been memorably glimpsed: "In a quick, graceful movement she spun out of the driver's seat, gathered up her packages, and shut the door with a push of her heel" (119-20). If Hitchcock needed an impetus for his key scene, these suggestive images were to hand. After Rico learns from the Mendozas of Juanita's spying, he calls to her on her upstairs landing to "come down"; momentarily, she disobeys him, sweeping aside her purple robe as several of Muñoz's men dash past her to search her rooms. Then, she descends the staircase in one of the set-pieces that Perry notes were a hallmark of both Poe and Hitchcock (5). Rico of course is torn between love of his mistress and his political feelings; the mere jealously he had felt of Andre's access to Juanita is now about to be trumped by politics, leaving him no choice. Alluding to Muñoz, he speaks of Juanita's coming humiliation—"there are things that will be done to your body"—and promptly shoots her. As everyone remembers, she collapses to the floor, and her robe spreads around her in a way that reminds some critics, appropriately enough, of a blooming flower.[38]

The robe is *royal* purple, showing the full extent of Hitchcock's irony, not to mention his applied imagination, which I have called "admirable" above.[39] This is more than nose-thumbing at "Jacobins" like Muñoz who thrive during reigns of terror. Whether or not Hitchcock and/or Taylor had the French Revolution specifically in mind, or perhaps arrived at their most graphic image simply on "generic" principles, we are not finished, for there remains another likely inspiration: namely, some of the female nudes reclining on royal-purple chaise-longues of Belgian surrealist painter Paul Delvaux (1897-1994). Most famously, Delvaux's *The Sleeping Venus* (1944) combines myth and striking perspective (and a chequered floor like that of *Topaz*) that inevitably remind you of the influence of his mentor, Giorgio de Chirico (1888-1978), long admired by Hitchcock.[40] Nudity is as implicit in our last image of Juanita as it is in another way—described by Hitchcock to François Truffaut—in *Vertigo*, when Scottie (James Stewart) persuades Judy (Kim Novak) to wear her hair in a manner she had resisted (Truffaut 185-86). To call Hitchcock "devious" will not do, as his every move is made in plain sight, and that includes the very style of *Topaz*. If the Lost Paradise motif is implicit even in a pistol-duel on a deserted sports field that Hitchcock wanted for his finale, its counter-current is the everyday, down-to-earth detail that the film seems to insist on, not to everyone's delight, it must again be added. Previously, "homely" detail had worked in Hitchcock's favor, as it had seemed to guarantee authenticity, as when in *The Lodger* the Cockney policeman Joe (Malcolm Keen) had romanced Daisy (June Tripp) in her kitchen by cutting out two pastry hearts and thrusting them towards her. But by the time he made *Topaz*, Hitchcock was invoking a *void* in humanity, potentially confusing to audiences. Hitchcock and Taylor had skirted such confusion with their brilliant *Vertigo*, but *Topaz* proved more intractable.[41]

In fact, after the highly schematic *The Birds*, Hitchcock found himself a metaphysician by default—everything now looked potentially "meta" to him, in the sense of his distancing himself from the quotidian—as if he had become alienated from an everyday world whose insufficiencies he had always happily hinted at, but benignly so (as in 1943's *Shadow of a Doubt*).[42] Call it Hitchcock's "new cynicism," thrust on him against his will, whether by the logic of his successive films, by his producers,[43] or by the content of espionage novels like John le Carré's *The Spy Who Came In From the Cold* (1963).[44] In referring above to the "Brechtian" absence of the characters' voices from the Harlem florist's scene, I sensed that Hitchcock was cautioning us how life itself can easily be turned off, even as he was preparing us for the extended sequence, equally inaudible, that ensues outside the Hotel Theresa, between the florist Dubois and Rico Parra's ill-fated employee Luis Uribe (Don Randolph).[45] That sequence deftly establishes the locale,[46] contains clever mime by the two actors, and serves to remind us that this encounter has been arranged by Andre (acting in turn for the Americans)—who now watches impassively from across the street, his enigmatic moral position roughly comparable to the title character's in Rohmer's *Triple Agent*.[47] Note, though, that the audience *also* looks on, supposedly having been conditioned to do so by Hitchcock (with the flower-shop sequence), no doubt trusting to again hold us spellbound. Yet the sequence is arguably too meta and self-conscious for its own good, inviting the annoyance of unsympathetic viewers.

These (and other) weaknesses admitted, I yet feel strongly that *Topaz* has an emotional truth; which brings me to the ending Hitchcock wanted for his film but, at age 70, was pressured to drop after preview audiences reported being puzzled. Krohn quotes what Hitchcock told the French journal *Écran* (July-August, 1972):

> The best scene in the film, the sequence in the Charlety stadium [in Paris], is not in the release version…I remember seeing a very long time ago, perhaps in *Paris-Match*, a photo of a [pistol] duel in an empty stadium. The image of those two men surrounded by banks of empty seats, all alone in the middle of the playing field, with a Dubonnet ad in the background, fascinated me. (34)

Compare this with what I was told by Richard Franklin (*Psycho II*, 1983), who had watched the making of *Topaz* and later worked with several of its key personnel, including visual effects artist Albert Whitlock. Richard told me that Hitchcock had devoted more time to preparing and shooting the duel scene than any other scene in the film.[48] In 1986, he obtained permission from Hitchcock's daughter to search her late father's garage, and there he located the long-forgotten footage, which Hitchcock had smuggled from the studio. (The scene, or the bulk of it, is now viewable as an "extra" on the Universal Studios Home Entertainment DVD.) Importantly, it is a scene at once "fantastical" and "logical," and anyone who has followed what I have been claiming here for *Topaz* as a whole would surely accept the duel as the "right" ending, rather than either of the relatively perfunctory endings that were, at different times, and in different countries, officially released. Here's a description of the finale. It takes place at dawn, keeping the "icy blues and greys" that Krohn notes dominate the film, "as if the director had decided to take literally the expression 'Cold War'" (30).[49] In long-shot, the duelists, Jacques and Andre, and their seconds, enter the arena and move to their positions. We hear a muffled drum-roll.[50] Andre's second, François, makes a last-minute protest to try and stop what he senses is a one-sided contest, but the opponents are ordered to cock their pistols and prepare to fire. Suddenly, the film cuts away to a shot of the distant grandstand where high up a man enters and raises a telescopic rifle, then shoots Jacques dead. After a moment, a stunned François manages to remind Andre that Nicole will have heard the shot and be anxious. Andre joins Nicole in a corridor under the grandstand, and the two approach each other for what may be a fresh start to their relationship.

The scene is "fantastical" for obvious reasons, starting with the idea of a modern-day duel, not to mention its shock resolution (explained as the Russians not having further use for one of their agents who has been found out). Equally, the scene is impeccably "logical" because the duel was proposed by Jacques, who clearly thinks all life is a game yet brings to it his customary calculation (he knows he's a superior pistol-shot); and Andre accepts the challenge seemingly out of his inability, as usual, to refuse a hard task although this time knowing he won't just be looking on. The scene really does "outflank" both protagonists and viewers, even while staying true to its premises, among them that the Russians consistently play harder. Thus it invokes the film's initial show of force at a Moscow military parade where Kusenov (the film's true hero?) decided to defect out of conscience. Altogether, few Hitchcock endings are as enigmatic, or as poetic, as the one Hitchcock wanted for *Topaz*.[51] Its Lost Paradise trappings are patent: the chilly, barren arena is like a surreal echo of Gabriel Valley, scene of a murder in *Spellbound* (1945). And Hitchcock's intuition was certainly right about the effect of the background ads: the ones we see here around the arena fence, featuring motor oils and brands of mineral water such as "Perrier" and "Vichy" locate us in a decidedly down-to-earth France even as they eerily remind us of the stadium's absent, cheering crowds. Which in turn raises the question asked by a popular 1950s song: "Where Have All The Flowers Gone?"[52] As we'll see, David Freeman, screenplay writer of *The Short Night*, calls such allusiveness in Hitchcock "dreamlike, almost abstract…and its power is undeniable" (Freeman 246).

But I have been insisting on *Topaz* as a "true parable," both metaphysically (staging its encounter with the Real) and materially (showing the toll taken by espionage on human lives); in fact, these aspects may signify a single truth, if human beings really are as inherently goodbad as some observers, such as the philosopher Schopenhauer, tell us. The term "Real" follows Lacan's usage, meaning that which "resists and exceeds interpretation" (qtd. in Longacre 68). It thereby resembles what Kant called the unknowable "Thing-in-itself" and which Schopenhauer

"Even our friends spy on us" 213

equated with the blind cosmic "Will"—which actually seems to me closest to Hitchcock's usage in his films, where he consistently reveals the working of an implacable force (in the case of *Topaz*, beginning with the Moscow parade).[53] Schopenhauer proposed to combat the inimical effects of Will with an "ethics of compassion."[54] Similarly, compassion is an under-appreciated, but important, element/emotion in Hitchcock (yes, there is also his cynicism at times!), most obviously in his films from *The Birds* onwards,[55] and my readers will be familiar with the well-known closing montage of *Topaz* showing the tortured Mendozas and the bodies of Juanita de Córdoba and Henri Jarré. It is a montage of human cruelty and suffering (something else Schopenhauer regularly emphasized), and it invites our compassion. The only thing not clear is whether Hitchcock intended this particular montage to follow the duel: Krohn merely says that at the previews the duel scene "was followed by appropriately elegiac end music" (31).[56] Nonetheless, one can't doubt that the montage represented for Hitchcock major content. When Andre, our decent but fallible identification-figure, is re-united with Nicole under the Charlety grandstand, the pair are being given a second chance, and perhaps it extends to us all.

§

The goal was to help the audience feel Joe's ardor developing and to watch his plans become confused with his romantic longings.
—David Freeman, describing *The Short Night* (244)

We…found just what Hitch had in mind…The deep blue [Finnish] lakes, the sky always filled with thunderheads, the stands of tall straight birch trees…
—Herbert Coleman (360)

No doubt, *The Short Night* would have been thoughtfully photographed and acted, contained several effective scenes, and made a strong statement about the importance of a loving relationship in an absurd universe. (There had been a similar largesse behind the evident self-parody of 1976's *Family Plot*.) Accordingly, if the finale involving a pursuit in a car and a wild showdown on a train approaching the

Finnish-Russian border is basically old-fashioned, still the Hitchcockian context remains crucial. Screenwriter Freeman points out that Hitchcock preferred a third act where "if you wish to appeal to a wide general audience, you must allow them a certain amount of narrative comfort" (242). Hitchcock knew the finale in *The Short Night* was hokum. "He [simply] wanted to make it the best hokum he could" (Freeman 249). It's important to remember that Hitchcock dealt *primarily* in emotions, and that these will have been generating since the film started yet without all of them being resolved, or all issues worked out. Provided the finale does a good job—here let's recall T.S. Eliot's emphasis on "the intensity of the artistic process"—hokum may offer resolution enough. In this case, the film's loving couple, Joe and Carla, survive; her two boys are rescued from their murderer father (based on George Blake), who had kidnapped them; and he himself heads for Russia (the film effectively wiping its hands of him in the face of more important matters). Freeman's assessment of all this is accurate: "Nobody ever said Alfred Hitchcock didn't know how to get at an audience's collective heartstrings" (248).

Nonetheless, Freeman admits that the screenplay was unfinished: "There are a number of scenes that either need more work or that Hitchcock was not quite satisfied with..." (230). That may be putting it mildly. Nor was Kirkbride's original novel likely to provide all solutions, although it contains the gist of the film, certainly. The basic idea is that Carla, wife of escaped double agent Gavin Brand, hides out on an island in neutral Finland[57] with her two boys to await their father's joining them; meanwhile, the embittered brother of one of the men Brand had betrayed (and whom the Russians brutally killed), Joe Bailey, tracks Carla down, intending to use her to lead him to Brand and exact his vengeance. But his feelings for Carla become amorous, and the situation radically shifts, climaxing when Brand turns up. The novel here contains a gaping hole. We're told that when Joe "set out on his mission to avenge his brother's death, suspecting that Brand might well attempt a jail break, he had not anticipated the events [that followed]" (Kirkbride 100-01). A moment's thought reveals the absurdity: a man sent to prison for a lengthy term who escapes after five years does not signal the imminence of his escape! Adroitly, the film waits to introduce Joe until after the prison break, when he is encouraged to hunt for Brand by a CIA official in New York, who had been a colleague of Joe's brother.

A feature of the novel is how it enters into Carla's psychology in a way the screenplay can't easily match. Loosely drawing on George Blake, the author spells out how Carla's husband has not been honest with her. He has always seemed two contradictory people, one almost indifferent to the world around him, the other keenly in touch with his inner self but unreachable by her. "She had never got used to this incredible dualism" (Kirkbride 123). After first making love to Joe, Carla starts to awaken to all she has been missing. One night, lying in bed with her husband, she hears herself speculate that he had taken male lovers. He is angered, but doesn't deny it (135-36). Very moving is a long passage summing up her liberation. An excerpt:

> She understood now...Because she had loved a man who did not love her she had prostituted herself in a world of make-believe, convinced that it was decent, sane and safe; that promises were kept, ideals upheld, everyday issues conducted with polite sincerity.[58] (Kirkbride 151)

It may have been this decidedly Hitchcockian passage that first attracted the director to the novel. Any form of romantic liberation could always stir his imagination: hence my reference above to the largesse of *Family Plot,* in which Blanche Tyler (Barbara Harris)—standing in for Hitchcock[59]—finally almost tempts the audience to believe in the supranormal, as she convinces boyfriend George Lumley (Bruce Dern) that she "really" is psychic! (And perhaps that the world really is benign after all![60]) And if a beautiful woman is featured, as is the case with Carla in *The Short Night*,[61] Hitchcock would try all the harder to make the lovers' happiness memorable, even idyllic, although sooner or later the scales might have to fall from their eyes concerning this flawed world. In terms of the sublime, then, we can begin to connect *Topaz* to *The Short Night* via *Family Plot*: in each case the lovers' happiness is imperiled by the dark side of human nature. Think of Juanita and Andre versus rampant death-dealers like Muñoz; or delightfully ordinary Blanche and George up against sneering Arthur Adamson (William Devane), who with the help of his crony, Joseph Maloney (Ed Lauter), incinerated his foster-parents; or Carla and Joe showing remarkable survival skills when Brand and his Russian minders turn nasty. (Hitchcock apparently considered Ed Lauter to play Brand.⁶²) In each case, a degree of romantic irony is present while the audience feels "the simultaneous experience of delight and terror."

Although Blake fled to Russia via East Berlin after his prison break, Hitchcock was happy to duplicate the novel and make Finland the film's main setting. Visually, it is a "demi-paradise," its countless picturesque lakes and islands exactly suiting Hitchcock's needs. For example, the screenplay builds several scenes around the precise geography of Carla's lake and island. Joe first sees the island from a boat steered by her boys; we're told it looks "sylvan, pastoral." He spots people working, and a further note explains that the view is "like a Brueghel painting" (Freeman 132). (Pieter Brueghel the Elder, c. 1525-69, was known as "Peasant" Brueghel because of his landscapes depicting peasants at work and play; it is the activity in such paintings that the screenplay notes explicitly.) The establishing shot is followed by closer shots of three of the people, who will prove to be the Russians: the grim Olga and Hilda, and a woodchopper, "bare-chested and wielding a large axe." Here Hitchcock is almost lulling us (except for that "large axe"); but soon afterwards, the younger boy, Roy, aged eight (his brother, Neal, is aged ten), tells Joe that the island's name is "Squirrel Island," then immediately adds, "We call it Danger Island" (143). What do the brothers know?! Perhaps equally premonitory, the dark clouds that Hitchcock had called for may have reminded him, once again, of the Storm Cloud Cantata and its foreboding imagery. In any event, Freeman notes that (the romantically-inclined) "Hitch always liked to show a lot of sky" (58).⁶³

The Russian minders are an integral part of the film, suggesting the filmmakers' understanding of how Blake managed to escape from prison in England and then make his way across Europe. More than one commentator has suggested that he couldn't have done either of those things with just the help of Seán Bourke and three of his Anglo-Irish friends: the KGB must have been involved from the start.⁶⁴ More exactly, as Phillip Knightley writes: "The only story which fits the facts is that the escape was organized by the Russians who contracted out some of the work to the IRA" (294). Also, this interpretation gets around what would otherwise be an implausibility in the film itself. Early on, Hitchcock departs from the literal account of events in Bourke's *The Springing of George Blake* by having Brand, on the run, strangle the young woman, Rosemary, with whom he has been left alone for a few minutes in a bed-sitter close to the prison: no doubt Hitchcock and Freeman wanted to characterize Brand as someone out-of-control, and took license from the episode in Hampstead ("Get down, get down!") described above. But that would certainly have left the hunted Brand without assistance to reach Russia unless he were able to turn to the Russians themselves. In both novel and film, Brand arrives on the island with a Russian minder. Note: his hardships while on the run are elided, whereas a story like *We, the Accused* is all about such things, including the loneliness and the desperation. But Hitchcock's manipulation of our emotions requires that our sympathies for Brand are kept to a near-minimum.

On the other hand, the role of Joe is built up by the film. We first meet this fit and healthy 35-year-old estate-planner and insurance man (Sean Connery was one candidate to play him[65]) on an indoor tennis court in New York in a scene that Hitchcock told Freeman he had wanted to get into a film for years. Specifically, the tennis he had in mind was of a particularly strenuous kind: there were only about a dozen courts for playing it in the United States. Freeman calls it "a game so toney and upper class that it makes squash look like bowling" (234). (You can imagine Jacques Granville in *Topaz* fancying it.) He adds: "It makes a fine, strange introduction to the character. It says he lives a life different from yours." Note the implicit reference to outflanking the audience! And in the scene itself: the almost cruel touch when at the end of the game (after Joe has just vigorously outplayed his female companion) an elderly messenger in bellman's uniform "toddles" onto the court to give Joe a message on a tray: he's wanted for lunch at the 21 Club. As the tennis scene immediately follows the murder of Rosemary, the audience is subconsciously being invited to see Joe as Brand's future nemesis. Indeed, much later, when Joe swings himself up and onto a moving train, the tennis scene reveals its full import.

The appointment at the 21 Club proves to be with the bespectacled CIA official, Paul Zelfand. To enter through the main entrance, Joe "goes down the steps, [and] under the painted statues of the jockeys" (95)—again "toney," and allowing the film a touch of color connected to a sports motif which will be taken up in London and Savonlinna, Finland. Zelfand says that he doubts Brand's escape was KGB managed, but offers no proof. He simply has a hunch that Brand is still trying to reach Moscow. He puts two photos on the table, one of Carla, one of the boys. Brand is reportedly "obsessed" with his sons, and Zelfand implies that the way to find him is to locate his family, who have also disappeared. He explains that as Brand poses no active threat to the USA, or to Britain, neither of those countries' intelligence organizations will make a move to apprehend him. Pointedly he adds: "I was at your brother's funeral. I saw your face." His implied request is, will Joe do the dirty work that others won't? Before long, Joe is flying to London, where Carla and family were last seen.

Now the screenplay loses some of its momentum. At least, there are some nice scenes plus some indifferent ones, but the overall content feels slight until Joe arrives in Finland. One effective scene, with its touch of color, has him inquiring the way to Earl's Court Road from the coach of two junior soccer teams in Hyde Park. It appears that a couple of lads belonging to the team in scarlet jerseys haven't shown up, and the coach is trying to persuade one of the opposing team in yellow jerseys to swap sides. Eventually Joe receives his directions, plus, unwittingly, a clue to finding Carla's boys. The scene elaborates a passing reference in the novel to how Roy and Neal[66] are identical twins who both like to wear red shirts (9, and passim). In the film, they are particularly attached to their scarlet jerseys. When we first meet the pair they are distinctive figures in their boat, and Joe soon spots them. The contrast with the blue lake and thundery skies is certainly part of this Hitchcock touch, which the film incorporates into a motif. Emotively, it carries a reminder that liveliness and fun are not lost, that the espionage world may not be the only option, as Carla had thought. Freeman appreciated Hitchcock's technique. As partly-quoted earlier, he describes some of Hitchcock's effects as "both more and less than a particular symbol… dreamlike…[whose] power is undeniable" (Freeman 248).

He cites a couple of such moments. One day, Joe takes Carla to a roadside restaurant in Savonlinna. On the way, he pulls her aside and kisses her behind a tree. They embrace, oblivious of everything but themselves. Then a swarm of bicyclists, happy and laughing, rides by and rings their bells at the couple.[67] Later, as the couple flirt in the restaurant's garden, Carla's minder Olga (the particularly butch one) arrives to break it up and to take Carla back to the island. Joe calls out, but just at that moment the bells of the bicyclists are heard again, drowning out whatever Carla has said (178). We sense how the mood has suddenly changed, and that Joe has a tough task ahead. Freeman is right to call the general effect "dreamlike." "Logical objections fall away," he adds, "in the face of the thing itself..." (Freeman 246). And part of the effect is plainly cumulative: those bright notes of color, and cheerful sounds, stay with us. They are part of the variegated romantic irony.

Of course, by now Hitchcock has us more or less hooked, as Joe sounded hooked from the moment he exclaimed, in New York, "Jesus Christ! What am I into?" (103). Someone had just fired a shot at Zelfand but had killed a passing chauffeur instead. The unpredictability, and danger, of the espionage world are mirrored in Joe's and Carla's stories, especially once they meet. Thus what we are seeing essentially remains the Schopenhauerian Will, whose most prominent aspect is sexuality, passion.[68] Hitchcock seems to have extended the parallel to film-form itself. In the restaurant garden, Joe asks Carla, "You know we're going to make love, don't you?" His remark is also a reminder to the audience. Typically, a Hitchcock film signals what is at stake from its earliest opportunity. In *The Trouble with Harry* (1955), Jennifer Rogers (Shirley MacLaine) knows straight away from her first encounter with artist Sam Marlowe (John Forsythe) that he'd like to paint her naked, which she acknowledges by saying that it's momentarily "inconvenient." In *The Short Night*, Joe tells Carla within seconds at their first meeting that she's beautiful: she asks him not to stare. "You make me feel... naked." Such frankness, which frees up the audience, naturally extends to discussions of power.[69] In the restaurant garden, Joe takes the opportunity to mention his late brother. The latter had been a spy, motivated not by patriotism but by "the adventure of it." Carla opens up a little about Gavin:

> Yes. Yes. I don't think Gavin did any of it for the reasons they said. Money or politics. Oh, maybe a little. But mostly for adventure and to feel powerful that all these countries depend on him. It's so stupid. (Freeman 174)

This is based on Blake. We've seen that Seán Bourke thought him driven by "an insatiable thirst for power" (242). But once he reached Russia, he felt diminished. Bourke writes:

> At the height of his power and glory he had contrived to work for two Services so that he might have a double measure of power. He had betrayed the British, and now even the Russians had no further use for him.[70] He had been deprived of his reason for living.[71] (245)

Significantly, the film provides no corresponding explanation for what initially drives Joe, apart from his robustness (life-force?) and his unprofitable intention to avenge his murdered brother. The novel at least adds the information that Joe is a Catholic (Kirkbride 84), who must modify his vow of vengeance after meeting Carla and immediately think about whether he should return home.

The film, for its part, asks us to accept that libido—and then love—are Joe's sufficient motivations for remaining; thereafter, it's fair to say, we watch him evolve into as selfless a hero as the melodrama can make him.[72] Think of him leaping to the rescue onto a moving train. In real life, "selfless" is what George Blake seemingly could not be. Another prisoner in Wormwood Scrubs Prison, intelligence expert Kenneth Hugh de Courcy, convicted of fraud charges, got to know Blake closely (Hyde 60-61), and wrote of him: "I [don't] in any way dislike Blake. But I regard him as a man devoid of mercy" (qtd. in Hyde 75). In *The Short Night*, Blake's case provides an instance of Hitchcock's obsession with "'getting it right' in a literal as well as a poetic sense" (Freeman 53). The film premises the dark side of human nature, uppermost in Brand, but eventually points the audience, via Joe and Carla's relationship, to a better path. A related idea would have informed *We, the Accused*, whose original novel refers more than once to society's "lust to punish,"[73] encouraging us to question whether Paul and Myra aren't scapegoats as well as victims. In all of these cases, a simultaneity of opposed emotions offered Hitchcock opportunity to invoke the sublime.

Wherever possible, he would do it through his characters, whom he almost certainly saw as both individuals and variants on a single "plot"[74] (or Will?[75]). We seldom lose our bearings with Hitchcock. On

"Even our friends spy on us"

their way to the roadside restaurant, Joe grips Carla's hand, and her response reveals both her inhibitions and a lot about the robust Joe: "Please stop. You're hurting me. There's so much feeling in you. You either make me laugh, or you try to hurt me. It's always so extreme. Please let go of my hand" (Freeman 169). But after Olga orders Carla to come away, and Joe soon follows her, the island proves to be as subject to extremes as Cuba in *Topaz*. Not in the same way, exactly, nor in an iconic Lost Paradise sense,[76] but employing a cross-section of subjectivities, including Gavin's (who will even have a brief scene with his boys that recalls a touching moment in 1957's *The Wrong Man*). If a single scene is reserved for the sublime, it is the one in which Joe and Carla finally make love while knowing that at any moment Gavin may arrive from abroad. Fittingly, it was the part of the script that concerned Hitchcock the most (Freeman 246), corresponding in that respect to the duel scene in *Topaz* (but in another respect to the scene in *Vertigo* where, it's implied, Scottie persuades Judy to finally sleep with him). For the sublime to be activated, typically there must be a threat, and Gavin's imminent arrival provides it. Hitchcock wanted the scene to build and build.

He may even have been remembering, at some level, the famous passage in *Lawrence of Arabia* (directed by David Lean, 1962) where a camel and rider seem to take forever to emerge out of the desert. The scene in *The Short Night* is equally protracted, equally masterful. The lovemaking does not begin at once; Carla at her window does not yet know that Joe is coming, although she senses it. Her dismissive remark to Hilda, "He's coming," seems to refer to the faint sound of Gavin's motorboat approaching from across the lake. Yet when the film cuts to the far side of the island, it is Joe who is turning off his boat's motor and propelling the boat through reeds before beaching it. Now the sound of Gavin's boat can indeed be faintly heard. Simultaneously, and almost magically, Carla appears on the moonlit beach, telling Joe, "I knew you'd be here."

The sound of the two boats arriving together is a reminder that Joe's original purpose was to kill Brand, and even at this moment it isn't certain what Joe will do: part of the scene's subjective effect is to indicate that he isn't certain either. Carla asks him straight out: "[Hilda and Olga] said that's why you're here. For [Gavin]." Joe seeks to reassure her: "For you. I've come for you." However, next moment he suggests a compromise: "If he were dead, then I'd have you for myself" (Freeman 183). She agrees, and embraces him. The scene to this point is subjective in another way, as it reminds us how we may be anticipating both a big love scene and Brand eventually getting his just desserts. But Hitchcock wasn't necessarily going to oblige us, no more or less than in *Vertigo*, say. As a professional crowd-pleaser, he would acknowledge our appetites, and give us much satisfaction, yet try to steer his melodrama to an agreeably non-predictable outcome.[77] Meanwhile, in the love scene the filmmakers focused on the feelings to be played out and, crucially, on point of view. Hitchcock decided to emphasize *Carla's* subjectivity, conceiving the sound of Gavin's boat as being inside her head. Freeman explains: "The love was real and the [approaching] husband was real; but the sound of the boat was not" (247).

This highlights a particularly daring aspect of a consistently daring scene: the presence/absence of Gavin throughout. He does finally arrive on the island, but his arrival takes forever. Carla, we've seen, first crosses the island on foot to greet Joe, then a cut shows that the pair have returned together to her cabin, yet still the sound of Gavin's boat continues, even being described in the screenplay naturalistically: "Joe stands waiting as Carla goes to the window and pulls all the drapes shut, so the approaching boat can't be seen, and the sound of the motor is muffled" (184). In general terms, this was a technique that Hitchcock had used before— there are scenes in *Vertigo* and *Marnie* where you can't be sure whether what is heard/seen is real or only in a character's head—but here it's especially purposeful, maintaining the sense of threat while imbuing it with Carla's awareness of a new joy that she dearly wants to prolong. And the longer the scene is, the more sublime it feels for audiences.

True, the sound of the boat is muffled for a time, as Carla turns to face Joe across the room, and "her husband and the rest of the world [are] shut out" (184). The love scene, notes Freeman, "was pure Hitchcock. He insisted that the lovers defer pleasure and thereby, according to [him], 'intensify it'" (247). Carla makes the first move, beginning to unbutton her blouse. Joe is momentarily transfixed, then begins to open his shirt. Cut to a wider view, showing the pair gazing at one another before Joe starts to walk towards her. Then another pause,

"Even our friends spy on us"

cued by Carla's whispered, "Wait…I want to feel you looking at me." From Freeman, we know that an early discussion of the scene between him and a grinning Hitchcock was a no-holds-barred one on the director's part, elegantly pornographic. It would be part of Freeman's job to translate the "home movie" element into acceptable screen terms (15), which the screenplay manages with successive close-ups of Joe's and Carla's faces, the last two of just their eyes (Joe's "hungry and searching," Carla's "languorous and finally ready") before, in two-shot, "they step into each other's arms" and "drop gently to the floor, entwined in an embrace" (185). The scene ends with a cut to the horizon at night, and now, in the moonlight, the sound of the boat is recognizably that of a power launch. One senses a rhyme with how, earlier, Joe's conversation with Zelfand in New York had stayed tight-framed until, at the very end, a wide-shot showed the previously empty dining-room now full (185). Thus the espionage realm and the realm of love/passion both appear liable to subjective time, which is very "human" of them.

Undoubtedly, much thought at the screenplay stage of a Hitchcock film went into trying to ensure smooth continuity, and to keeping the audience attentive and on-track. There are many instances in *The Short Night* of success at doing so: for example, the cut to the moonlight and the sound of Gavin's motorboat makes a smooth transition from love-scene to arrival of the "heavy." Equally, there are some failures, including the extended sequence in which Joe tracks a package containing the boys' scarlet jerseys from London to Savonlinna: when he waits in the Helsinki Post Office for someone to claim the package, it's about as gripping as our waiting for Herr Albert at the Friedrichstrasse Post Office in *Torn Curtain* (1966). Meaning: not very![78] In several of his late films, including *Torn Curtain* and *Topaz*, Hitchcock really did seem at times to think that his authority alone, his "imprimatur," would make a scene or passage work. Unfortunately, the very centerpiece of *The Short Night*, involving Joe's conflicted feelings after meeting Carla, is never sufficiently elaborated. Freeman mentions that he had hoped to do another Joe-Carla scene before the roadside restaurant scene:

Hitchcock agreed that it was abrupt this way. A scene between Joe's [first] arrival on the island and [the roadside restaurant scene] would make the arc of his character clearer... Hitchcock agreed, but we never settled on the specific content of the scene, nor could we find a place for it that didn't slow down the action. (244)

Astutely, Freeman says of the restaurant scene:

For this scene to work, we should know, before Joe does, that he's actually falling in love. If we don't feel real libido, what Joe's doing will turn us off him. It's a very dangerous scene—all sympathy for the hero could dissolve here. (244-45)

The situation of characters possessed of strongly conflicting emotions that must be resolved is difficult to convey on film. It risks confusing, or alienating, the audience. Of course, Hitchcock and writer Ben Hecht had triumphed over similar difficulties in *Notorious*, and reportedly Hitchcock had that film in mind now ("*The Short Night*"). Did he see Joe and Carla as Cary Grant and Ingrid Bergman? And, to some extent, Brand as Claude Rains? To compare the two films is instructive. In the present context, what I think the comparison shows is that, without an element of real espionage (Brand, we've seen, is unemployed), *The Short Night* screenplay hasn't a lot of room to maneuver, and thus can't easily add scenes that would build up the characters. (By contrast, *Notorious* has two big suspense scenes in which Grant visits the house where Bergman is spying on Rains, and another scene at a race track where Grant contacts her, his hang-ups still apparent.) For its part, Kirkbride's novel employs an omniscient viewpoint to describe the Joe-Carla relationship from the inside, in passages of considerable insight and sympathy.

I'm far from saying that Hitchcock's film/screenplay hasn't got heart, only that there are reasons why audience emotion might not have hit top gear this time. To some extent, it may be a case of the director, as in *Family Plot*, aiming at a certain parodic self-distancing befitting what Freeman calls "the late winter of his life" (250). Espionage is specifically mentioned in just one line of *The Short Night*, and that is heartfelt. In the roadside restaurant, Joe ruminates: "Spying and espionage. Everybody suffers from it. The gains are vague and abstract. And the losses are all personal" (174). The line unites Joe and Carla, and may well signify the moment when we sense that he's falling in love with her, not just brashly flirting. But also it was Hitchcock's considered view, something which Freeman acknowledges while wondering whether he would have written the line if he hadn't been doing a Hitchcock script (246). I take this to indicate he simply wasn't as immersed in the Hitchcock *Weltanschauung* as the director (he hadn't worked on *Topaz*, for example), with its disabused view of the world not readily separable from feelings of compassion. What Freeman noted was Hitchcock's relative disdain for (all forms of) politics along with his, by now, near single-minded emphasis on *passion* itself,[79] and its potential. To the screenwriter of *The Short Night*, it seemed as if Hitchcock "thought of the political content of the story as a great, cosmic MacGuffin; the idealogues were the dullards, [while] those who fought for love were vital and worth our concern" (Freeman 250). That outlook is the source of much of the emotion the film would have stirred in audiences, and calls for some final remarks.

Freeman's doubts about whether, by himself, he would have critiqued spying and espionage in quite Hitchcock's way, or at all, suggest a common-sense position. In assessing popular films we tend to look for "what oft was thought but [seldom] so well express'd," which is fair enough. To try and cope with our mixed-up world, we like to stay in touch with it, and are constantly seeking out informed sources and opinions about its many aspects, not least politics. That in itself gives a sense of participation and empowerment. Leon Uris knew there was a real hunger for politics, and catered to it. But the older Hitchcock grew, the more he favored a Schopenhauerian position as opposed to a Hegelian one: Hegel thought the state represented "the whole aim of human existence."[80] By contrast, Schopenhauer scorned the state (and Hegel!). While basically he saw existence as ineffable, he further saw it as needing to be lived[81] rather than fatuously theorized about. (His major caveat was that we should live ethically and/or detachedly.) And because, for Hitchcock, passion was akin to the will to life,[82] then politics at best could only offer a dull semblance—Representation[83]—and was unlikely to liberate anybody. Hitchcock's villains are often led astray politically, and their passions perverted, whether the Nazis (including Alicia's father) in *Notorious*, amoral Jacques Granville in *Topaz*, or the over-reaching Gavin Brand in *The Short Night*. Nonetheless, Hitchcock regularly showed a degree of pity for even his villains, and with good reason. He saw that the singular Will is amoral, and blind. Consequently, "everything's perverted in a different way."[84]

Although we do our best to cope, many of us regularly find ourselves "muddling through," following popular prejudice, everyday common sense, and the like,[85] something which Freeman as a screenwriter rather specialized in. Hitchcock would consult him on "what contemporary people thought" (Freeman 240). Equally, Hitchcock's keen eye for detail was "part of the source of the power his films generate, the reason for their grip on our emotions... Hitchcock always saw human behavior fresh, even in a tired form like melodrama" (Freeman 11). Perhaps the ideal for all of us is effectively to be aware of both Will (invisible reality) and Representation (everyday appearance); they are, after all, two sides of a single coin. That way, we may stay balanced, human. For much of his life, Hitchcock clearly managed such a feat—and shared it with us. Sadly, towards the end, he ran out of energy, and/or was overly preoccupied with his conviction that only one solution to problems, whether global or personal, really mattered: he did seem to have become "unbalanced" by his concern with the meta, and less attentive to all the details of a screenplay like *The Short Night*. That wouldn't necessarily stop his film being emotionally engaging, although its flaws might cause unease among anyone wanting hard depictions of the everyday world.

For example, I'm thinking of the screenplay's depiction of the Finnish policeman, Sergeant Linnankoski. The novel initially makes of him a figure of fun, seen spying on Carla and Joe in the town, slinking after them, his hat drawn over his eyes (Kirkbride 46), like Inspector Clouzot in a Pink Panther film. Yet by the end, he has become a substantial figure who participates in the chase to foil Brand's kidnapping of Roy and Neal. He is given a motivation, and it is moving: during the War, his wife and daughters had been killed by the Russian invaders of his home in Karelian (Kirkbride 167). However, he perishes during the chase, and you can't help thinking of Gromek (Wolfgang Kieling) in *Torn Curtain*, whom Hitchcock had wanted to establish as a family man after his death (in a scene finally deleted). Frankly, in depicting Linnankoski, the screenplay of *The Short Night* lacks that degree of penetration; the character becomes a figure of fun late in the piece, along with his house-proud Finnish wife, when both of them fail to grasp the urgency of the need to pursue

"Even our friends spy on us"

Brand—but the intended note of comedy risks annoying audiences, as some scenes in *Topaz* did. Eventually, the policeman appears at his front door, and the chase can begin; at the climax, he heroically helps rescue the boys from the moving train. Note: he isn't killed. But nor does this greatly affect us emotionally, one way or another.

Hitchcockian emotion in the films had customarily been the product of a satisfying complexity, a simultaneity of emotions; that's why I have suggested that the films attended to both Representation (everyday details) and a sense of Will (underlying those details). In effect, the 1934 and 1956 Storm Cloud Cantata scenes imply the Real. Whenever Hitchcock got it right, as so often, the result was emotionally and intellectually pleasing, because everything came together, as it seldom does in life. Recall Freeman's saying that Hitchcock was "absolutely intent on correcting the Universe." Furthermore, if the contrast between delight and fright, beauty and terror, was sufficiently present, the audience felt the sublimity of it all. The principal love-scene in *The Short Night* works that way: it is the equivalent of giving the audience what the novel says Carla had never experienced with Gavin, a heightened level of feeling and insight, not requiring her to "prostitute herself in a world of make-believe." On the other hand, too much of *The Short Night* doesn't click, and parts of it, including some characters, are insufficiently developed, which limits our emotional involvement. *Topaz* had the Cuban missile crisis and the unfolding espionage revelations to give it urgency—all of the scenes with the grim-lipped Russian defector, Kusenov, are marvelous—and Andre's perils and his affair with Juanita are more than intermittently involving. Still, it bears emphasizing that both films were made or written in difficult circumstances, so due allowance should be given them.

§

Very little observation is needed to convince us that the emotions people feel in response to artworks…are evidently different from those they feel in real life.
—John Carey (48)

No human being can exist for long without some sense of his own significance.
—Rollo May (qtd. in Carey 154)

Professor Carey is a superb, no-nonsense literary critic and book reviewer, always worth reading—but film is not his forté. Practically his sole reference to film in *What Good Are the Arts?* comes when he takes Noel Carroll to task for assuming "that there is mass art on the one hand and avant-garde art on the other, and nothing [of significance] in between" (Carey 44). He thinks Carroll's notion of mass art is often vague, especially when he claims that "it has produced 'some works of the highest achievement' without revealing what that means" (Carey 45). Carey guesses it means "works that even mass art's foes can be counted on to admire, such as the films of Charlie Chaplin, Buster Keaton and Alfred Hitchcock" (45). Note: Carey doesn't say *why* such films are admirable! (To be fair, he soon adds: "set against Carroll's strengths [his shortcomings] are mere blips" (Carey 45).) He is convinced that literature, and especially English literature, is the most expressive of the arts, for good technical reasons—it is best equipped to explore inner and outer life in all its nuances and ramifications. At the same time, he cites with enthusiasm the claims of American anthropologist Ellen Dissanayake that the concept of art should be widened beyond "our post-Kantian cult of art as solitary spiritual contemplation" "to take in 'low' activities like home decoration" (Carey 34, 152). Once "we arrive at an idea of art as something done, not consumed, and done by ordinary people, not master-spirits" (Carey 152), its function and purpose, including in emotional terms, need radical re-thinking. Granted! But is Carey downgrading the art of, say, Hitchcock by telling us this? I don't think so.

For one thing, he has admitted that the "mass" films of Chaplin, Keaton and Hitchcock are admirable in practically everyone's eyes, although he doesn't actually say why, or name titles. For another thing, he nominates—and argues brilliantly for—English literature as the pinnacle of expressive art, so he's not exactly discarding "high" art, just showing that many arguments for such art's alleged superiority are fallacious in the extreme! Note that he speaks of arriving "at *an* idea of art as something done...by ordinary people" (my emphasis), not at a claim that making (or doing) such art is the only way to go. By the same token, his enthusiasm for Dissanayake's theories includes her emphasis on how art since hunter-gatherer times has served to bring people together by "making special" (think, say, of a tool painted to emphasize its social importance). Taking his cue from Dissanayake, Carey argues that today we still have predispositions "that contemporary life cannot satisfy. Primarily,...we are lonely" (35). And of popular art he observes: "It is preoccupied with romantic-sexual love to a degree unprecedented... in any previous society, and this is a response to the loneliness of the modern condition" (Carey 36). In turn, Carey praises the Czech writer Karel Capek (1890-1938), one of whose specialties was "uncovering ancient features in popular art forms" (36-37). For example, he identified the detective story as essentially a hunt. And he analyzed the content of newspapers to show that, beyond their topicality, they were recycling age-old motifs and plot-lines to convey "not so much news as 'the eternal continuity of life'" (Carey 37).

In terms of Hitchcock, this is apt. In the 1930s, he compared himself to "the editor of the successful, popular modern newspaper," and he and Charles Bennett and Angus MacPhail would meet at his apartment in Cromwell Road armed with the remarkable *Plotto: The Master Book of All Plots* (1928) to construct their latest melodrama ("Why I Make Melodramas" 77).[86] The major point of Hitchcock's essay "Why I Make Melodramas" (1937) is to affirm that "one man's drama is another man's melodrama" (76). He suggests that this went back to the Victorian theatre where "there were only two divisions of entertainment—the melodrama and the comedy. Then snobbery asserted itself. What you saw at Drury Lane was drama. At the Lyceum it was melodrama" (76). Hitchcock's espionage films, starting with *The Man Who Knew Too Much*, were all aimed at taking the audience behind the headlines in human, down-to-earth terms. At the same time, his films, with their minimal snobbery, were clearly aimed at popular audiences—but not *only* popular audiences.[87] Anyone can appreciate the creative process in Hitchcock, whether the conception of Juanita's fate in *Topaz* as "the humiliation of the beautiful" or the motif in *The Short Night* which signals hope and optimism for the Joe-Carla relationship. (This involves the sort of thing that Freeman said defies logic, "[but] which, if I may say so, is [thereby] not a bad overall summation of Hitchcock's films" (246).) In short, Carey provides broad reasons for affirming the emotive potency of Hitchcock's work, although he may not go far enough.

His explanations for why the emotions produced by art are different from those we feel in real life are witty. Getting over a real-life bereavement is different from seeing a tragic hero die onstage: "Theatre-goers are unlikely to require counselling the next day…" (Carey 48). And "If audiences really felt 'emotional torment' [a British politician's phrase] no one would buy tickets. Emotional torment is what you feel if your child has borrowed the car, is hours late getting back, and cannot be reached on his or her mobile. It is a horrible experience and no one would willingly undergo it" (Carey 48). Maybe so, but, hopefully, you still get over it by next day! Carey concludes: "the claim that high art is distinguished by its access to 'deep' emotion looks questionable, if 'deep' is synonymous with 'genuine' or 'intense'" (Carey 49). We may assume, though, that Hitchcock's *The Man Who Knew Too Much* spans both "low" and "high" art. The Storm Cloud Cantata scene includes in its mix precisely a parent's (Jill's) torment at the fate of her child, plus much else. Frankly, not even literature can match this, lacking either the graphic imagery (of the Albert Hall concert) to be edited into a mounting rhythm, nor a soundtrack with felicitous scoring to contribute to the Hitchcockian suspense. In this matter, at least, Carey could look deeper. On the other hand, what he says about modern-day "loneliness" is surely pertinent, and he is right to invoke Rollo May, as well as Dissanayake on art's origins in "mother-infant mutuality" (154). (This seems to echo Hitchcock's explanation for why people enjoy thrillers: it reminds them of when their mothers teased them by saying "boo!" (Hitchcock, "Mr. Chastity" 55).) Hitchcock's villains at a film's end are sometimes left to experience loneliness, as if that were punishment enough; also, we've noted Seán Bourke say of the real-life George Blake that, without job or family, he was "deprived of his reason for living" (Bourke 245). Patently, what draws all those concertgoers to attend the high-brow Storm Cloud Cantata hardly differs from what brings movie audiences everywhere to the cinema: a desire, at some level, to ward off loneliness and boredom, and to again feel empowerment. Here again, high and low art overlap. Also, Hitchcock's audience isn't just held spellbound by an arch-manipulator of their emotions: it has definite needs which, when these are provided for, they indulge gratefully and feel the better for it. As the case of Carla in *The Short Night* shows, the "cold" world of espionage is life-threatening if it denies those human needs.

One of the things we've seen a Hitchcock film "make special"—a big reason why we feel the better afterwards—is a recognition that we're not hard intrinsically but, rather, compassionate and capable of empathy. Our brains have "mirror neurons,"[88] meaning that we can enter the minds of others by feeling, not just by thinking. Which is just as well. Film theorist Creed quotes ethicist Peter Singer: "Were we incapable of empathy—of putting ourselves in the position of others and seeing that their suffering is like our own—then ethical reasoning would lead nowhere."[89] Hitchcock, understanding all of this intuitively, encouraged our compassion by heightening the general emotional level and "putting the audience through it," as he said (qtd. in Rebello 174). That is what we've been looking at here.

Notes

1. See, outstandingly, Williams, passim. Novello in *The Lodger* plays what *The Bioscope* called "a horror-haunted man" whose condition audiences readily associated with war neurosis (Williams 9, 22); at the same time, his films articulated "many contemporary feelings and attitudes towards the figure of the war veteran" (Williams 9).

2. Revealingly, Hitchcock said: "I've never been interested in professional criminals. The audience can't identify with their lack of feeling" (Samuels 238).

3. "In Hitchcock's terminology, the Real is that which holds us 'spellbound'" (Savoy, 228n1).

4. Hitchcock's one-sidedness here is by design. I might compare the much-praised Iranian film, *The Cow/Gaav* (directed by Dariush Mehrjui, 1971). Although married, the main protagonist appears more devoted to his pregnant cow than to his wife—which is the whole idea. Film theorist Barbara Creed praises *Gaav* for attending to "the marginalized and the plight of the outsider" (131).

5. Included in Freeman, 69-226. Earlier, unpublished drafts were by James Costigan and Ernest Lehman.

6. All part of Hitchcock's outflanking us. A corollary: his Nazis are erred humans, not mere ideologues.

7. I thank Adrian Schober for pointing me to Mellor.

8. For this version of the likely manner of Popov's execution, see Central Intelligence Agency, "A Look Back…CIA Asset Pyotr Popov Arrested."

9. One finds a similar sentiment at the start of Hitchcock's *Topaz* where a title reads: "Somewhere in this crowd [at a Moscow May Day parade] is a high Russian official who disagrees with his government's display of force and what it threatens."

10. Compare a remark of filmmaker Chris Marker (who visited North Korea

in 1957): "Extermination passed over this land. Who could count what burned with the houses?" (Cumings). More recently again, the devastation wrought by the US during the Korean War, including the use of napalm on cities, has been described by Michael Pembroke in his book *Korea: Where the American Century Began* (2018). Cited by Schauble.

11. Both lines, notes Michael Walker, "are given similar weight" (130).

12. Compare what Hitchcock said of Jeff (James Stewart) in *Rear Window* (1954): "He's a real Peeping Tom…but aren't we all?" (Truffaut 160).

13. The biographer was working from an obviously imperfect transcript. He fails to recognize Hitchcock's affirming his well-known "logic is dull" position, and informs readers, "[this] may be Sam Taylor speaking" (187).

14. An issue of *Time* recently set out Russia's superiority in the disinformation field but—predictably, given how these matters go—noted that there were "signs that the U.S. may be playing in this field [too]" (Calabresi 29).

15. In the classic Chinese historical novel *San Kuo* (or *The Romance of the Three Kingdoms*), based on events covering the period AD 168-265, the successful conqueror T'sao T'sao (or Cao Cao) begins his campaign by sending out a fake imperial edict to various regional officials and warlords, calling on them to rise up against the warlord Dong Zhuo. See also next note.

16. Historians of twentieth-century century Russian disinformation (the word was supposedly coined by Joseph Stalin) cite Soviet manuals referring to the impressive but fake "Potemkin villages" built by Grigori Potëmkin in 1783 along a route that Catherine the Great was to travel.

17. There were five such Russian deep-cover spies, or "moles," all recruited at Cambridge University in the 1930s. They were Kim Philby, Guy Burgess, Donald Maclean, Anthony Blunt, and John Cairncross. Hitchcock said that he originally conceived *Torn Curtain* (1966) after asking himself, "What did Mrs. Maclean think of her husband's [and Burgess's] flight to Russia?"

18. Noiret gives a superb performance as the frightened spy. The character was based on the real-life traitor Georges Pâques to whom Noiret bore an "uncanny" physical resemblance (Lethier 45).

19. We may infer as much from what Hitchcock told actress Barbara Leigh-Hunt about Jon Finch in *Frenzy* (1972), that Finch had come to the film with glowing recommendations but that Hitchcock found his performance lacking "the sympathetic qualities he had hoped for and which would make the audience care about the character's fate" (Dowd).

20. Compare a reviewer's comment on the principal character in Eric Rohmer's *Triple Agent* who moves "between various spy organizations. He is portrayed as bland, but that is the very essence of his character, as he must be bland" ("*Triple Agent*").

21. Certainly *The Short Night* screenplay questions the ends of espionage, as we'll see.

22. A dramatic new rethinking of human and animal nature is that of Jeremy Rifkin and others. Rifkin's *The Empathic Civilization* argues that we are not fundamentally aggressive but empathic, and that we have been steadily evolving in recent centuries towards greater empathy with our fellows. The opposite of empathy is indifference—Rifkin refers to this as the conflict between empathy and entropy. See Rifkin, passim.

23. "Spying on each other" (to single out that leitmotiv for a moment) may be an extension of what we all do more or less unthinkingly. A review of the recent Glass Room exhibit in London noted: "We all normalize surveillance as a solution to many problems…" (Miller).

24. Called General (and later President) La Croix in the novel.

25. This admirable actor was recommended to Hitchcock by Ingmar Bergman when the two directors met in Stockholm. (Bergman also recommended Sonja Kolthoff who plays Kusenov's wife.) See Chandler 295.

26. Bill Krohn notes that in a discarded draft of the *Topaz* script Hitchcock had planned to show a defecting Kusenov and his family seeing idyllic views of Russia in the clouds around the plane "carrying them away forever from their homeland —until [Hitchcock's] CIA informant told him that the plane…would be windowless" (35).

27. As Rico Parra in the film calls her.

28. "And in Arcadia I am," usually taken to refer to Death (apropos the painting by Guercino). See Pomerance, 69-76.

29. Such audiences may recognize an allusion to *The Birds* (1963) but (understandably?) find it self-indulgent.

30. Another Lost Paradise film. Its director was the youngest of "those Italians" (as Hitchcock referred to Antonioni and Fellini in particular) whose work Hitchcock admired. The film received a glowing review by Eugene Archer in *The New York Times*, September 25, 1964.

31. Attributed to French politician Talleyrand (1754-1838).

32. Christopher Janaway notes that Schopenhauer gave his own twist to Kant's conception of the sublime as affording a pleasurable sense of elevation when destructive forces are viewed from a safe distance: in watching tragedy, Schopenhauer believed, what we rise to is a sense of the serene abandonment that comes from ceasing to will (Janaway 69). I see an analogue to the way Hitchcock outflanks us and holds us

spellbound in, say, the Storm Cloud Cantata sequence/s. At such times, we approach the Real.

33. Edmund Burke, *A Philosophical Inquiry into the Origin of our Ideas of the Sublime and the Beautiful* (1756).

34. Edmund Burke, *Reflections on the Revolution in France* (1790).

35. Immanuel Kant, *Observations on the Beautiful and the Sublime* (1764). Quoted in Stern 45.

36. David Freeman twice asked Hitchcock whether he appeared in the crowd near the end of *The Lodger*. "Once he said yes, it was he. The other time he said no, it wasn't" (58).

37. Perry reminds his readers: "As a Roman Catholic…Hitchcock would have been aware of the apocalyptic visions of Mary, particularly the Fatima secret message concerning Russia that led many Catholics in the 1950s and 1960s to understand the Cold War as a religious apocalypse" (49).

38. For example: Krohn 30.

39. Elsewhere, I have referred at length to Hitchcock's ingenious imagination (Mogg 61-77 and passim).

40. See, for example, Leff 159.

41. *Vertigo* was very much a film about "The Void" (Nietzsche's term, I believe)—culminating in the nun's poetic line, "I heard voices"—but, like Scottie, disdaining the everyday, as implicit in Midge's scenes.

42. From the superb *Marnie* (1964) through *Torn Curtain* (1966), *Topaz*, and even *Frenzy* (1972), an alienation from the everyday world showed itself in Hitchcock's films. *Family Plot* (1975), though, recovered some ground.

43. Hitchcock said his producers stopped him from making *Mary Rose* and the original *Frenzy* (little relation to the 1972 film of that title), and foisted *Topaz* on him.

44. The "alienation" (anomie) of characters in Antonioni's films may have been another factor.

45. A classic instance of Hitchcock's conditioning the audience for a shock, or the unexpected, is the river-caves scene in *Strangers on a Train* (1951), with its sound of a woman's scream, preceding the murder of Miriam on the fairground's island. (Hitchcock's technique here resembles Freud's description of "tendentious" joke mechanisms.)

46. I'm grateful to Richard Modiano in the USA who enthused to me in an email about the Hotel Theresa sequence, "full of authentic detail for anyone who has been to Harlem."

47. Bill Krohn notes that "Devereaux is continually being stationed at the entrances to suspense sequences from which he watches while other people suffer and die at his behest…" (30).

48. The shooting of the scene did not go smoothly, though. On the second day, associate producer Herbert Coleman took over when Hitchcock was summoned home to join wife Alma who had become ill (Coleman 364).

49. Only parts of the Copenhagen and Cuban sequences, and brief shots of the "safe house" in Washington DC, relieve the chill.

50. Similar to that which accompanies the pistol duel in Stanley Kubrick's *Barry Lyndon* (1975).

51. Perhaps only the ambiguous penultimate scene of *Psycho* (1960), in the police cell, matches it. (Does Norman Bates, or his Mother, have the last word?)

52. The song has always been popular since Pete Seeger composed its first three verses in 1955. Additional verses were added by Joe Hickerson in 1960, making it specifically about death. Marlene Dietrich sang a German version.

53. Innumerable Hitchcock films (e.g., *Rebecca, Spellbound, Vertigo, Psycho, The Birds*) feature from the start—often the credits-sequence—the presence of a force, or its equivalent. (In *Rebecca*, and other films, it is the ever-restless sea.)

54. Janaway contrasts Schopenhauer's "ethics of compassion" with Kant's "ethics of duty," the latter ultimately a theological notion (73-74).

55. Compassion, compatible with empathy (cf. Rifkin), is felt or displayed in all of these films at several levels, as implicit in Mark's observation at the end of *Marnie* (1964), "It's time to have…compassion for yourself." Rico Parra in *Topaz* acts from compassion, or mercy, when he is forced to shoot Juanita, knowing what her fate would be at the hands of Muñoz. That moment roughly parallels Marnie's shooting of her beloved horse Forio, injured during the hunt scene.

56. Krohn further notes that all available versions of the film now end with "the joltingly upbeat [and inappropriate] Russian military march heard over the May Day Parade during the opening credits" (34).

57. In actuality, Blake escaped to Russia via East Berlin.

58. Writing on *Marnie*, David Greven argues (from a queer perspective) that normal, heterosexist culture—from which Marnie is alienated, thus making her something of a prototype for Brand's wife in *The Short Night*—is *generally* stifling and conformist, at least as regards gender and sexual normativity. (In Greven's phrase, Marnie must show "queer resilience.") See Greven 107-48 (and especially 110-13).

59. As the film's trailer indicates, Blanche and Hitchcock share a winking relationship with the audience. See also next note.

60. Although Hitchcock was never guilty of what Socrates said about "the unexamined life," a film like the wartime *Shadow of a Doubt* (1943) speculates on whether many people (e.g., the townsfolk of Santa Rosa) aren't better off, or certainly happier, not confronting the darker side of life. Blanche's "supranormal" world effectively stands for the fantasy world of "the movies."

61. The novel repeatedly refers to Carla's ash-blonde hair and long, slender legs (11, and passim). Actors Hitchcock thought might play her included Catherine Deneuve and Liv Ullmann. See *"The Short Night"* (2017).

62. Another candidate to play Brand was Walter Matthau (2017).

63. However, Hitchcock *hated* royal-blue skies, as he told Truffaut apropos shooting *To Catch a Thief* (1955) on the Côte d'Azur (Truffaut 166).

64. See, for example, Richelson, 273n.

65. Other actors considered included Clint Eastwood and Steve McQueen. See *"The Short Night"* (2017).

66. They have different names in the novel.

67. Possibly the scene borrows from one in Ralph Thomas's 1959 remake of *The 39 Steps*. If a film borrowed from one of his, Hitchcock would often borrow right back!

68. Janaway observes, "Schopenhauer is in some respects a forerunner of twentieth-century views about the unconscious mind and the influence of sexuality on our behaviour…" (46).

69. Power and sexuality (libido) are, of course, related.

70. In actuality, Bourke was incorrect. In 2007, *The Times* (November 14) reported that Blake, on his 85th birthday, had been awarded Russia's Order of Friendship by Vladimir Putin. In Moscow, he had become a colonel in the KGB and trained Soviet spies. He also re-married and had further children. On receiving the birthday honor, he said that he had led a "very full and, in the end, a happy life."

71. Below, I'll quote psychotherapist Rollo May on the dangers of feeling powerless.

72. It's also fair to say that selflessness, the opposite of selfishness, is everywhere admired, and not only by, say, Catholics!

73. For example: "Was there no pity or imagination anywhere? This lust to punish, was it not always the sign of undergrown minds?" (Raymond 299).

74. As early as his days with the Henley Telegraph Company, Hitchcock wrote in one of his stories for the house journal: "every person has a plot…and every plot is the same" ("Fedora" 26).

75. Hitchcock's much-quoted remark at the time of *The Birds*, "Everything's perverted in a different way," again suggests his belief in an ultimate Oneness. See Hitchcock's 1963 interview, as reprinted in Gottlieb (51).

76. It is *shaded* Lost Paradise, as with the Brueghel allusion and the sublime love-making scene, but no more than that.

77. In Freeman's screenplay for *The Short Night*, Brand escapes to Russia. This seems a superior resolution to those in earlier drafts, by Lehman, in which Brand was killed or arrested. See DeRosa (2010), entry for Thursday, June 24.

78. Possibly it's less gripping. There's no Countess Kuchinska (Lila Kedrova) for comic relief.

79. In this context, note that "*compassion*" is from Latin, meaning "with suffering" (suffering *with*).

80. Schopenhauer "paraphrasing" Hegel (qtd. in Janaway 7).

81. While Schopenhauer taught that "the will to life" might/should be denied or resisted, that did not include life itself—he opposed suicide. See Janaway 90-91.

82. Hence he could be single-minded about this, and Freeman could paraphrase: "[only] those who fought for love were vital and worth our concern" (250).

83. The title of Schopenhauer's magnum opus opposed (as well as apposed) the two terms: *The World as Will and Representation*.

84. See note 75.

85. I suggested above that's a reason why "even our friends spy on us" and why we "spy on each other."

86. Gottlieb slightly mis-cites the original source, corrected here.

87. I am reminded of something once told me by Jack Sullivan (*Hitchcock's Music*, 2006) which he attributed to his teacher and mentor, the famous man-of-letters Jacques Barzun: "Hitchcock is the one filmmaker who never insults your intelligence."

88. The mirror neuron system was discovered by a team of scientists working in Italy in the 1990s. Rifkin's argument in *The Empathic Civilization* is based on that discovery, and is discussed in Creed 122-23.

89. Singer, quoted in Creed 126. Compare Schopenhauer's "ethics of compassion." Also, see Haspel on *The Birds*, where he refers to the film's happy outcome that requires "a core group of ethically aware individuals" (93).

Works Cited

Allen, Richard. *Hitchcock's Romantic Irony.* Columbia UP, 2007.

Bourke, Seán. *The Springing of George Blake.* Mayflower, 1971.

Byrne, Edward (1991). "American Dreams." *The Cresset*, vol. 54, no. 5. thecresset.org/ FilmArchive/1991/Byrne_March%201991.html. Accessed 15 June 2017.

Calabresi, Massimo. "Hacking Democracy: Inside Russia's Social Media War on America." *Time*, 29 May 2017.

Carey, John. *What Good Are the Arts?* Faber and Faber, 2006.

Central Intelligence Agency. "A Look Back…CIA Asset Pyotr Popov Arrested." www.cia.gov/news-information/featured-story-archive/2011-featured-story-archive/pyotr-popov.html. Accessed 16 Oct. 2017.

Chandler, Charlotte. *It's Only a Movie. Alfred Hitchcock: A Personal Biography.* Pocket Books, 2006.

Coleman, Herbert and Judy Lanini. *The Hollywood I Knew. A Memoir: 1916-1988.* Scarecrow Press, 2003.

Creed, Barbara. *Stray: Human-Animal Ethics in the Anthropocene.* Power Publications, 2017.

Cumings, Bruce. "A Murderous History of Korea." *London Review of Books*, 18 May 2017. www.lrb.co.uk/v39/n10/bruce-cumings/a-murderous-history-of-korea. Accessed 23 Sept. 2017.

DeRosa, Steven. "*The Short Night*: The Last Script Prepared by Alfred Hitchcock." *Writing with Hitchcock.* 2010, blog.writingwithhitchcock.com/2010/06/short-night-last-script-prepared-by.html. Accessed 9 April 2017.

Dowd, Vincent. Interview with Barbara Leigh-Hunt. "'Hitchcock just wanted to be loved' says British leading lady." 9 June 2017, www.bbc.com/news/entertainment-arts-40203693. Accessed 9 June 2017.

Eliot, T.S. "Tradition and the Individual Talent." 1921. *The Sacred Wood*, bartleby.com/200/ sw4.html. Accessed 30 May 2017.

Epstein, Edward Jay. "Philippe Thyraud de Vosjoli: The French Connection." *Diary*, 26 Apr. 1980, www.edwardjayepstein.com/diary/devosjoli.htm. Accessed 6 Nov 2017.

Freeman, David. *The Last Days of Alfred Hitchcock: A Memoir Featuring the Screenplay of "Alfred Hitchcock's* The Short Night." Overlook Press, 1984.

Greven, David. "Intimate Violence: *Marnie* and Queer Resilience." *Hitchcock Annual*, no. 18, 2013.

Haspel, Paul. "California in Extremis: The West Coast Setting and 1960's Anxiety in The Birds." *Hitchcock Annual,* no. 20, 2015.

Hitchcock, Alfred. "Fedora." *Henley Telegraph*, March 1921. *Reprinted in Hitchcock on Hitchcock: Selected Writings and Interviews*, Vol. 2, edited by Sidney Gottlieb, U of California P, 2015, pp. 26-27.

---. "Why I Make Melodramas." *Stars & Films of 1937*, Daily Express Publications, 1937. *Hitchcock on Hitchcock: Selected Writings and Interviews*, Vol. 2, edited by Sidney Gottlieb, U of California P, 2015, pp. 76-77.

---. Interview by Ian Cameron and V.F. Perkins. "Hitchcock." *Movie*, no. 6, Jan. 1963. *Reprinted in Alfred Hitchcock Interviews*, edited by Sidney Gottlieb, UP of Mississippi, 2003, pp. 44-54.

---. Interview by Oriana Fallaci. "Alfred Hitchcock: Mr. Chastity." 1963. *Reprinted in Alfred Hitchcock Interviews*, edited by Sidney Gottlieb, UP of Mississippi, 2003, pp. 55-66.

Hong, Christine. Interview by Aaron Maté. "The Overlooked Past Behind U.S.-North Korea Tensions & How South Korea Could Forge Peace." *The Real News Network*, 12 Apr. 2017. therealnews.com/t2/index.php?option=com_content&task=view&id=31&Itemid=74&jumival=18857. Accessed 6 Nov. 2017.

Hyde, H. Montgomery. *George Blake: Superspy*. Futura, 1988.

Irvine, Ian. "George Blake: I spy a British traitor." *The Independent*, 30 Sept. 2006, www.independent.co.uk/news/people/profiles/george-blake-i-spy-a-british-traitor-418245.html. Accessed 6 Nov. 2017.

Janaway, Christopher. *Schopenhauer*. Oxford UP, 1994.

Jeffries, Stuart. "Agent provocateur." *The Guardian*, 26 Oct. 2004, ww.theguardian.com/world/2004/oct/26/france.film. Accessed 7 June 2017.

Kirkbride, Ronald. *The Short Night*. Pan, 1971.

Knightley, Phillip. *The Second Oldest Profession: The Spy as Bureaucrat, Patriot, Fantasist and Whore*. Pan Books, 1987.

Krohn, Bill. "A Venomous Flower: Alfred Hitchcock's *Topaz*." *Video Watchdog*, no. 74, August 2001.

Leff, Leonard J. *Hitchcock and Selznick: The Rich and Strange Collaboration of Alfred Hitchcock and David O. Selznick in Hollywood*. Weidenfeld and Nicolson, 1998.

Lethier, Pierre. "Secret Agents." *39 Steps to the Genius of Hitchcock*, edited by James Bell, British Film Institute, 2012.

Levy, Lisa. "The Rise of the Literary Espionage Novel." *Pacific Standard*, 11 Dec. 2014, psmag.com/social-justice/rise-literary-espionage-novel-genre-fiction-writing-surveillance-95829. Accessed 6 Nov. 2017.

Longacre, Jeffrey. "The Difference Between Crows and Blackbirds: Alfred Hitchcock and the Treason of Images." *Post Script*, vol. 34, nos. 2-3, 2015.

McGilligan, Patrick. *Alfred Hitchcock: A Life in Darkness and Light*. Chichester, West Sussex, Wiley and Sons, 2003.

McLuhan, Marshall, Quentin Fiore, and Jerome Agel. *The Medium is the Message*. Penguin, 1967.

Meyer, Leonard B. *Emotion and Meaning in Music*. U of Chicago P, 1961.

Miller, Nick. "The disruptive tech store with thinking for sale." *The Age (Melbourne)*, 26 Oct. 2017.

Mishra, Vijay. *The Gothic Sublime*. State University of New York P, 1994.

Mogg, Ken. "Melancholy Elephants: Hitchcock and Ingenious Adaptation." *Hitchcock and Adaptation: On the Page and Screen*, edited by Mark Osteen, Rowman and Littlefield, 2014.

Nadel, Ira B. *Leon Uris: Life of a Best Seller*. U of Texas P, 2010.

Perry, Dennis R. *Hitchcock and Poe: The Legacy of Delight and Terror*. Scarecrow Press 2003.

Pomerance, Murray. *The Man Who Knew Too Much*. British Film Institute/Palgrave, 2016.

Raubicheck, Walter and Srebnick, Walter, editors. *Scripting Hitchcock: Psycho, The Birds, and Marnie*, U of Illinois P, 2011.

Raymond, Ernest. *We, the Accused*. Penguin, 1935.

---. *Please You, Draw Near: Autobiography 1922-1968*. Cassell, 1969.

Rebello, Stephen. *Alfred Hitchcock and the Making of Psycho*. Harper Perennial, 1991.

Richelson, Jeffrey T. *A Century of Spies: Intelligence in the Twentieth* Century. Oxford UP, 1997.

Rifkin, Jeremy. *The Empathic Civilization*. Jeremy P. Tarcher and Penguin, 2009.

Samuels, Charles Thomas. *Encountering Directors*. Putnam, 1972.

Savoy, Eric. "The Touch of the Real: Circumscribing Vertigo." *The Men Who Knew Too Much: Henry James and Alfred Hitchcock*, edited by Susan M. Griffin and Alan Nadel, Oxford UP, 2012.

Schauble, John. "Korea review: Michael Pembroke on the consequences of US failure in the '50s." *Sydney Morning Herald*, 8 Mar. 2018. www.smh.com.au/entertainment/books/korea-review-michael-pembroke-on-the-consequences-of-us-failure-in-the-50s-20180307-h0x5x2.html. Accessed 14 Apr. 2018.

Sexton, Michael. Review of *Che, My Brother* by Juan Martin Guevara and Armelle Vincent. "Comrades and brothers." *The Weekend Australian*, 6-7 May 2017.

"The Short Night." Wikipedia. en.wikipedia.org/wiki/The_Short_Night. Accessed 9 Apr. 2017.

Singer, Peter. *Writings on an Ethical Life*. Harper Collins, 2000.

Stern, Emil. "Hitchcock's *Marnie*: Dreams, Surrealism, and the Sublime." *Hitchcock Annual*, 1999-2000.

"Triple Agent." Wikipedia. en.wikipedia.org/wiki/Triple_Agent. Accessed 22 June 2017.

Truffaut, François and Helen G. Scott. *Hitchcock*. Simon and Schuster, 1967.

Uris, Leon. *Topaz*. Corgi Books, 1969.

Walker, Michael. "*Topaz* and Cold War Politics." *Hitchcock Annual*, no. 13, 2004-2005.

Williams, Michael. *Ivor Novello: Screen Idol*. British Film Institute, 2003.

Down and Out in Mysterious Morocco: Ontological Uncertainty in *The Man Who Knew Too Much* (1956)

By Niklas Salmose

"My goal," writes Robert J. Corber in *In the Name of National Security: Hitchcock, Homophobia and the Political Construction of Gender in Postwar America*, "is to show that Hitchcock's textual practices were not monolithic and homogenous, but flexible; that is to say, they responded to changes in historical circumstances" (137). What communication is not permeated by the context it is produced within? Hitchcock's films, though, seem more apt to study from a contextual analytical frame than many other textual practices, which is one of the reasons why Hitchcock is the most analyzed film director in critical history. James Berger offers us a creative explanation for this: "We recognize Hitchcock because he is always, obviously, in disguise. A disguise enables us to interpret it, and there is also pleasure in disguise itself" (146). Combining Corber's and Berger's claims, we deduce that Hitchcock's films are palimpsests of their times, but at the same time mysterious, open, implicit, and ambiguous. In short, they are open for diverse interpretative methods and theoretical prospects and hence predisposed for whatever whims a critic might find reverberate through them. At times, this also means stating the obvious. Thomas M. Leitch's famous castigation of a number of conference papers on Hitchcock and the Cold War in "It's the Cold War, Stupid: An Obvious History of the Political Hitchcock" serves as an extreme critique of a common practice of interpretation: "all movies from a given period will carry a political subtext marked by the orthodoxies of that period" (5). Leitch's main argument is not that these papers were inaccurate, but points out "their obviousness and the ways that obviousness might have limited or secured their aptness" (4). It is my ambition in this essay to not state the obvious, but to offer a plausible yet intriguing postmodern reading of what I consider an important transitional postmodern text, Hitchcock's oft-neglected *The Man Who*

Knew Too Much (1956). I will return to this focal point somewhat later; first, I want to situate this analytical and methodological perspective in some seminal, contextual or postmodern readings of the film.

Corber's analysis of how postwar America creeps into Hitchcock's films *Rear Window*, *The Man Who Knew Too Much*, *Vertigo*, and *Psycho* is contextual but not obvious. He reads the history of the Cold War and identifies how sex, gender and family constructions within that political paradigm are both destabilized and reactionary[1]; then he applies these conclusions on the selected Hitchcock films, displaying a convincing reverberation of the era's more moderate attitudes towards LGBT (excuse the anachronism) issues in Hitchcock's films. His ambition is to "show that Hitchcock's representational practices were complicit with the dominant construction of social reality under the postwar settlement" (Corber 12). In his analysis of the two versions of *The Man Who Knew Too Much*, Corber meticulously outlines how the depiction of the female heroine reflects the social definition of woman in the 1930s and the 1950s respectively. The 1934 heroine is a representation of the emerging New Woman during the Jazz Age and attempts in terms of commercialism to attract a modern, female audience (Corber 131). In the 1956 version, Jo McKenna, according to Corber, illustrates an independent woman who sacrifices her freedom for conventional, cold war sexual politics (140-45). Corber's conclusion is, in accordance with US national security, that Jo as a mother has been irresponsible and unpatriotic, working outside her home and neglecting her child (145). Hitchcock's film thus confirms the social construction of motherhood and patriarchy.

Although this is not an obvious inference, it is, in my mind, an unsatisfactory and simplified interpretation of how an audience would read Jo McKenna. David Greven contradicts Corber's conclusion in "Cruising, Hysteria, Knowledge: *The Man Who Knew Too Much* (1956)," and articulates the unstable gender construction in the film as proof of its critical agenda:

> Neither Jo nor Ben is comfortable within the normative gender roles they have been placed in and are forced to embody. The film has its reactionary side, but in the end, in its insistence on exploring the various threats to gendered normativity from

within and without, it is one of the most ideologically unstable and unclassifiable films of the 1950s—hardly subservient, itself, to the gendered and moral codes of its era. (243)

I agree with Greven that *The Man Who Knew Too Much* is an unusually unstable 1950s Hollywood film. The ambiguity of the film can be found on very many different levels beyond gender and sexuality: in what Robin Wood identifies as a peculiar genre mix between espionage and domestic melodrama, and in how James Stewart "became the epitome of the masculine power/impotence syndrome that both structures and disturbs so many of his films" (*Hitchcock's Films Revisited* 364, 365); and in the very obscure title of the film as brilliantly discussed by Tom Cohen in volume one of *Hitchcock's Cryptonymies* (165-66). I also agree with Corber that *The Man Who Knew Too Much* is very much a product of its times—the paranoia, alienation, claustrophobia of the Cold War—but in disagreement with him, I believe the film adequately opens up its context for a critical scrutiny of what simply can be understood as an emerging postmodern society. Even if the film is, overtly, about agents, spies, secrets, conspiracy, it is likewise, at another level, portraying a fragmented, unstable postwar world.

Cohen's analysis of *The Man Who Knew Too Much* is the most ambitious attempt to deconstruct this film within a postmodern framework, focusing on semantics (especially homophones), self-reflexivity, intertextuality, modern communication, simulacra, hyperbolism, repetition, the Other, and so on. In his depiction of the Royal Albert Hall as the setting for the film's attempted assassination and its MacGuffin, he acknowledges that the Hall is "filled with high-aesthetic scores and rituals" and thus come to represent the Western hyper-capitalist and colonial world (T. Cohen 167). The proposed attack on the Prime Minister of an unknown country starting with "Ao" is in fact an attack on Western history and ideology, not very far from how Joseph Conrad sets up the anarchist attack against Western time itself in *The Secret Agent*, in this case represented by Greenwich Mean Time. The clash of the cymbals in the Royal Albert Hall signals the end to grand narratives (Lyotard) or the end of history (Baudrillard), and the concert occurs on June 6, significantly the date for D-Day (T. Cohen 211). Cohen interprets the cymbals elegantly as the crash of the ideology of symbols by itself (cymbals, sheer sound) "as a critique of the Western cognitive tradition" (236). It is my attempt in this chapter to locate how *The Man Who Knew Too Much* indeed reverberates with the postmodern attitudes and emotions as they are constituted in postwar 1950s.

My analysis is on the whole inspired by Cohen's eccentric but accurate reading of the film, but tries to construct this initiated postmodern landscape more deliberately in order to establish how Hitchcock's film quite radically identifies early spasms of the postmodern society that later postmodern critics will refer to as the plurality of meaning and world. As Angelo Restivo points out in "Hitchcock and the Postmodern," "[a]sserting a relationship between Hitchcock and postmodernity might seem—especially to those scholars who hold a strongly historicist view of the development of aesthetic forms—a misguided project or yet another example of how 'postmodernism' has become a term so all-encompassing as to have lost any critical efficacy" (Restivo 555). My reading, though, is not anachronistic in the sense that I claim that Hitchcock was fully aware of a proleptic postmodern evaluation of post-war Western world; but his film echoes the tendencies and symptoms of a fragmented and a differently organized society that postmodern critics later came to identify as a rupture (or some a continuation) of modernity. In Jürgen Habermas's tradition, one could say that Hitchcock adds a critical edge (a self-reflexive tendency) and not only a commentary to the early postmodern world his film epitomizes. Hence, Hitchcock is neither passive nor reactionary, as Corber claims. Using postmodern strategies to analyze how *The Man Who Knew Too Much* negotiates the societal changes and attitudes in the post-war world yields more accurately how radical and precise this oft-neglected Hitchcock film is in depicting a changing world and the advent of postmodernity. Paula Marantz Cohen addresses the recent interest in the second version of *The Man Who Knew Too Much*, asserting that the "further away one gets from it, the more it becomes possible to connect it with social changes that occurred in American society a decade later" (116). Globalization, shifts in colonial dominance, the emergence of new media and communication and the disintegration of traditional political and religious ideologies and morals severely altered the lives of post-war generations when compared to earlier generations' experiences. All of these changes, as we will see, are noticeable in Hitchcock's film.

Down and Out

My postmodern reading is divided into two sections although there are overlaps between them, and both are concerned with postmodern, ontological uncertainty and instability. In the first, "Down and Out in Mysterious Morocco," I deal mainly with different types of postmodern staging and self-reflexivity framed in Baudrillard's concept of *hyperreality*. Part of the staged effect of *The Man Who Knew Too Much* will be traced to the film's Hollywood aesthetics, primarily the use of Technicolor and rear-projection. The second section, "A Woolf in Sheep's Clothing," focuses on how the film deconstructs different grand narratives and dominant cultural and political ideologies and institutions, such as male authority (through James Stewart's persona), masculinity, religion, police, intelligence, diplomacy, tourism and high art. This analysis is situated in what has been named by Kristin L. Matthews as the mood of McCarthyism (738), and relates to the dichotomy of familiar/unfamiliar inherent in the uncanny as well as the function of intertextuality. Although postcolonial criticism seems a relevant tool in a postmodern analysis, I will display that a routine postcolonial reading of *The Man Who Knew Too Much* fails to comprehend the complexities involved in both Western and Moroccan representations. Finally, I will look into the dispositions of the world of postmodernity, engaging in the fragmentation of both world and individual in the film. Attention will be paid to alienation, globalization, and communication and how Hitchcock's anti-narrative style enforces the notion of fragmentation.

Down and Out in Mysterious Morocco

> So we chose Marrakesh, a place I had never seen although I had long pondered the possibility of developing a chase through the Souks…It would have been much easier to have to reproduce the Souks on a Hollywood or London stage, and twenty years ago one could have. Today audiences wouldn't accept a substitute. They demand authenticity and realism.
>
> —Alfred Hitchcock (Noble 145)

Tom Cohen confirms in his analysis how *The Man Who Knew Too Much* in so many ways communicates the postmodern ontological uncertainty. One of the more interesting ambiguities, Cohen discusses, relates to the meta-aspect of filmmaking itself. He acknowledges how the remake of the 1934 version testifies to a "self-cannibalization" or "self-plagiarism" and becomes a "reflexive hiatus within Hitchcock" (T. Cohen 194, 195, 197). Furthermore, he discusses how the scene in the taxidermist's shop becomes self-mockery and a "supposed 'red herring' that lies at the heart of the project's visit to and questioning of its own underworld" (T. Cohen 194). There are other self-reflexive moments in the film. Hank (the son) relates his experience of the many sewing machines to a television commercial, and Hitchcock appears as a tourist in the Marrakesh market together with the McKennas, watching the acrobats performing. Hitchcock's own presence in his films is an auteur signature, an interior joke, but it also directs attention towards the cinematic apparatus and its director. In *The Man Who Knew Too Much* the cameo stands out from those in the other films in that he is not only passing but actively watching a stage performance, a performance which later in itself becomes a meta text: there is a man in the middle of the crowd and he is "the teller of tales," Mrs. Drayton informs Hank and us—very much like Hitchcock.

Staging and self-reflexivity are sides of the same coin; theatrical and explicitly constructed narration necessarily draws attention to the film apparatus itself. Attention to its own production and form is a postmodern continuation of changes in philosophy and art during the early nineteenth century, what Habermas identifies as the "discourse of modernity" (45), that leads to the emerging subjectivity and self-awareness in philosophy and art. This change can be related to Brian McHale's illuminating suggestion that postmodernism deals with ontological rather than epistemological issues (10). The overall idea that the Second World War created a wound, a rupture, in the progress of western civilization, argues McHale, forms the base for fragmentation and pluralism in postmodern narratives, an ontological pluralism that defies any epistemological discourse.

Tom Cohen writes that *The Man Who Knew Too Much* "by its repetition alone, is clearly marked, notched in a way that assumes an enigmatic relationship to the oeuvre, as if held in an extraordinary reflexive hiatus within Hitchcock" (197). It is fascinating how Cohen attributes Hitchcock's "powerful phase (*Vertigo, Psycho*)" to what he names a "pause" for reflection and ontological inspection as a critique of "cinematic epistemology" and includes *The Man Who Knew Too Much* (197). Already the superficially simple but very ambiguous title of the film—*The Man Who Knew Too Much*—opens up these ontological possibilities of the film. Cohen's playful analysis of the films of Hitchcock's "powerful phase" draws attention to these films' elusive status and implicitly mocks any ambition to frame them epistemologically.

In the first part of *The Man Who Knew Too Much*, which takes place in Morocco, staging and ideas of staging reappears. Staging, as I see it, is a way of emphasizing what Jean Baudrillard calls hyperreality—that reality is somehow simulated and not real. Baudrillard defines the hyperreal not as a "false representation of reality (ideology), but of concealing the fact that the real is no longer real" (25). The ontological uncertainty, sparked off by the peculiar and incomprehensible title, is continued through the first half of the film through the use of narrative suspense techniques and the creation of a "mysterious Morocco." Jo (or Joe) McKenna utters early that they are "being watched" and hints at the seemingly fake presence of characters and their intentions; everyone, including the police, seems suspicious. As an audience we ask, together with Jo, many relevant questions and receive no answers, growing more and more frustrated with Doctor Ben's arrogant, aggressive and patriarchal behavior and ignorance. Something is going on, but exactly what? Just as Jo's intuition tells her that something is not tallying, we *feel* the alienation of the characters but we do not see it. One part of this can be contributed to the use of different languages than English and the chaotic depiction of a crowded and noisy Marrakesh filled with horns, animals, and ethnic music. Even the "what will be, will be" in *Que Sera, Sera* rings out the unknown future, both in characters' lives and in the narrative aspect of a Hollywood spectacle. In this film, *nobody* knows too much!

Another aspect of staging that aligns more with Baudrillard's concept of hyperreality is more aesthetic and an effect of particular Hollywood aesthetics: the use of Technicolor and rear-projection.

In the first Moroccan scene in the film, what Cohen calls the "cinematic bus" (61), we see an illustrative example of an aesthetic, deliberate or not, that in its mise-en-scène appears heavily staged. The position of subjects, and their respective gazes, are all constructed to create a particular alienated and vulnerable effect: they all seem alone, isolated, engulfed in their own subjectivity. The "authenticity and realism" Hitchcock aimed for (see epigraph at the beginning of this section) is sternly disrupted through the clear rupture between the rear-projection of a Moroccan desert road (is it?) and the bus carefully constructed in a Paramount studio. What stands out is the studio lightning in the interior of the bus, which evidently creates an unrealistic rendering of an authentic bus ride. It also clearly sets the characters *outside* the dusty and low-contrast Morocco landscape in the rear-projection. The use of Technicolor further contributes to this estranged experience. Julia Kristeva famously remarked that color, in comparison with black-and-white, makes unified meanings "pulverized, multiplied into plural meanings. Color is the shattering of unity" (qtd. in Neale 158). Technicolor, historically, has been associated with either dream sequences, fantasy, spectacle, animation; in other words, a diegesis with no ambition to portray reality. Eirik Frisvold Hanssen confirms this in *Early Discourses on Colour and Cinema: Origins, Functions, Meanings*:

> The technological development of different colour film systems is closely linked to specific aesthetic results and therefore, even to the specific contexts and associations colour in cinema has been connected with. The idea of colour in film as enhanced reality was challenged by the fact that the colours of Technicolor looked noticeably different than the colours of the reality which was being reproduced. (111)

In the industry, the colors of Technicolor were synchronized with skin color, and the skin color of the female star in particular, which led to other colors being misrepresented. Although Technicolor in its early two-strip days were quite hyperbolic, there was a tendency in the industry to restrain the use of color in order to avoid its symbolic value of excess (Hanssen 130). Nevertheless, Technicolor never managed to go unnoticed; hence, the colors of films using Technicolor stood out against the reality they portrayed. Hanssen, with the help of William Johnson, explains this in more technical terms:

Down and Out

> Even the subtractive colour processes by Technicolor involves separation, through its foundation in the principles of "trichromatic vision": three layers of black-and-white film record the amount of red, blue and green, which is subsequently replaced by dyes in these colors in the final print, causing, as William Johnson stated, "only the most indirect relationship between object colors and print colors." (Hanssen 160)

Here we see in the very film material an ontological issue, the separation between material and representation. Another aspect connecting Technicolor to cinematic self-reflexivity is how the Hollywood color systems "signify luxury or celebrate technology" rather than subordinate to narrative content (Hanssen 115). If we consider how Doris Day is shot in the bus scene, we notice that she is accentuated through lightning (she is most isolated from the background through heavy backlighting and immediately identified through the two spotlights in her hair) as well as color. Despite the restrained ambition of the color scheme, the colors in this scene (and the film) are slightly exaggerated and saturated. Finally, the heavy use of fill light takes away realistic contrasts and shadows that would be present in a realistic light coming from outside through the bus windows and grants the scene a strong sense of superficiality.

The unreal effect of the scene is not explicit or immediate; it is a matter of convention and suspension of disbelief. But it does create an involuntary effect of de-familiarization that, taking other aspects of the film into account, gives us what best can be described as an uncanny experience. This is confirmed by Wood when he says the film presents a "family in a world whose alienness is stressed at every point" (367). The sense of ontological uncertainty is further expanded through Jo's comparison between the unfamiliar Sahara desert and the familiar Death Valley.

> HANK: Daddy, you sure I've never been to Africa before? It looks familiar.
>
> JO: You saw the same scenario last summer, driving to Las Vegas.

The confusion of place is further established through Hank's comment that Marrakesh sounds like a drink. Tom Cohen asks, quite ironically, how can you claim that a "void and hostile landscape" feels familiar?

(198). The audience certainly dissects that statement immediately, introspecting that the reality of Hollywood is representing is in fact Hollywood itself. But in the end, as Cohen argues, this is not Africa (citation from film) "but a cinematic wasteland of Marrakesh" (198).

Staging is further explored in the brilliant scene between Louis Bernard, "French, yet Arabic, Arabic yet 'born' in Paris" (T. Cohen 212), and Jo at the balcony of the McKennas' hotel room. The scene is framed by the balcony parapet and the exterior background, the real Marrakesh, is obscured by darkness with only a few, isolate details visible. The diegetic sounds are brought to an absolute minimum; only a slow mumble of North African night creatures can be heard. Instead, there is a mysterious, exotic non-diegetic soundtrack lingering in the background dressing the scene in an uncanny suit; the situation in itself is highly familiar and ordinary, but the execution gives it dramatic intensity and nervousness. The lightning, as in the bus scene, is more theatrical than cinematic, isolating the pair further from their surroundings.

LOUIS BERNARD: Were you on the American stage Mrs. McKenna?

JO: Yes, Mr. Bernard, I was on the American stage. And the London stage and the Paris stage.

LOUIS: Oh.

JO: I though perhaps you had seen me in Paris, being French?

LOUIS: Oh, you know, the theatre requires time. And for me time is often a luxury.

JO: Have you ever been to Paris Mr. Bernard?

LOUIS: I was born there.

JO: Oh. What business are you in?

LOUIS: I buy. And sell.

JO: What?

LOUIS: Whatever gives the best profit.

JO: Now when you are in Marrakesh, what are you buying and selling?

LOUIS: You know, I would much rather talk about the stage. If you tell me what shows you are in…[KNOCK AT THE DOOR]

Obviously the dialogue, centering on stage and acting, reinforces the self-reflexive quality of the scene. However, the literary dialogue contains a significant amount of subtext; they are overtly talking about Jo's and Louis's careers, but in reality they discuss reality and commodity.[2] For a secret agent, the stage is reality—that is where he operates, acts, lies, and hides, and the stage is where the attempted assassination will take place. Louis Bernard cannot separate the two, and neither can we in the stylistic way the scene is constructed. The deliberate pauses, movements, glances, and close ups, and the overall pacing of the scene ending with the interruption of the knocks on the door, are so genuinely constructed that the scene is set galaxies away from neorealist aesthetics.

A Wolf in Sheep's Clothing

Intertextual references underscore the lack of authorial control (consider Barthes' death of the author) and the fragmentation and fluidity of reality/ies. Cohen's list of intertextual instances in *The Man Who Knew Too Much* is simply remarkable and meticulous. He makes a strong case for how the remake by its own virtue becomes an exercise in intertextual reflection, something that numerous comparative studies between the two versions testify to (Corber; Hark; Rothman; Wood, "The Men Who Knew Too Much (and the Women Who Knew Much Better)"), but the reflection also extends to the preceding film, *To Catch a Thief* (T. Cohen 194-197). Another aspect of a sort of interior intertextuality are the numerous instances of potential homophonic interpretation. As common in Hitchcock studies, Lacanian psychoanalysis informs Cohen's analysis of these homophones. Nevertheless, the recurrence of them, as shown by Cohen, are quite convincing in their importance for stimulating not only misunderstandings and misinterpretations, but also highlighting the instability of reality and its ontological uncertainty. Intertextually can offer connotations both within the filmic diegesis but also outside the film. This misunderstanding is also at the heart of the narrative structure, since the misapprehension of Chapel/Chappell ("it is not a man, it is a place") becomes significant in the film. Another such example is the dialogue around Jo's name in the beginning of the film: "Jo, without the e," Dr. McKenna clarifies to Louis Bernard in the bus. As many critics have observed, the uncertain status of Jo in terms of gender and sexual constructions in the 1950s is already established in the beginning of the film. This early exercise in delusion (so much part of the Morocco sequence) semaphores to the audience from the beginning to be attentive to how the film constantly refigures itself.

Some of Cohen's more remarkable identified intertexts include Jonathan Swift's *Gulliver's Travels* (222), Shakespeare's *Macbeth* through one of Jo's socialite friend's name MacDuff (227), the initials of Albert Hall referring to the director's own initials (225), the citation of Al Jolson in the *Jazz Singer* when Louis Bernard's painted face is smeared over Dr. McKenna's hand (217, 223), and the musical allusion to Wagner's final installment of his *Der Ring des Niebelungen–Die Götterdämmerung*—as Louis Bernard is stabbed in the back (216). The allusion to Al Jolson and the minstrel show tradition of whites dressing up as blacks emphasizes the transitory construction of identity so important for a postmodern critique of grand narratives and ideology and at the same time reinforces uncertainty surrounding the subject and object's ontological status. The mask allusion of this scene is part of a grander strategy in the film, as Greven observes: "In this film obsessed with the flimsiness of appearances and the mask-like nature of identity, the ease with which one man's identity can be transferred to another vividly literalizes the work's major themes" (233-34). The reference to Wagner's opera about the end of the world resonates with the overall impression of discontinuity of Western progress. Theodor Adorno captures this postwar mood very well in his analysis of Samuel Beckett's *Endgame*: "After the Second War, everything is destroyed, even resurrected culture, without knowing it; humanity vegetates along, crawling, after events which even the survivors cannot really survive, on a pile of ruins which even renders futile self-reflection of one's own battered state... The temporal itself is damaged; saying that it no longer exists would already be too comforting. It is and it is not" (Adorno 126, 122). This sentiment is also pronounced in the opening lines of Beckett's opening lines of *Waiting for Godot* and *Endgame*:

ESTRAGON: Nothing to be done.

CLOV: Finished, it's finished, nearly finished, it must be nearly finished

Just like Jo/e focuses our attention towards semiosis, the importance from a spectator's (and the characters') perspective of textual practice and meaning is established through the signification of text. We notice it in the opening sequence's title text that reads, "A single crash of Cymbals and how it rocked the lives of an American family"; the distinct emergency exit text on the rear window of the bus, "Issue de Secours," that signals a way out, another path, different routes to meaning and reality; and, of course, in the cryptic note about the assassination in London.

Associations to minstrel shows naturally do not only signify postmodern relativity but also address colonial issues. The same can be said of the indecisiveness of what space the bus actually traverses. "Of course, it is not really Africa honey, it is French Morocco," Jo explains to Hank on the bus. "Well, it is northern Africa," Dr. McKenna responds. To Hank it is still outside Las Vegas. And to us, as discussed before, it is really nowhere except perhaps on the studio lot in Hollywood. Just as Corber's gender reading of *The Man Who Knew Too Much* lacks a reading of how the audience actually interprets the representation of gender and family in the film (as a mild critique of patriarchal structures and conventional sexual politics), it would be easy to perform a first phase postcolonial study of the filmic text that would confirm exoticism and representation of otherness in the Moroccan sequences as Edward Said established them in his seminal book *Orientalism* (1978). It is true that Morocco provides a setting in the narrative that reinforces the sense of alienness, otherness, distress in the characters and the audience. The setting masks itself behind sunglasses, foreign language and gestures, veils and ethnic music and culture. But in no way is Morocco or its inhabitants represented in an inferior way. Postcolonial criticism tends to identify the level of excess and hyperbolism involved in the exotification of non-western geographies, but in this film, the only hyperbolism going on is Dr. McKenna's obnoxious behavior towards cultural customs in a country that "he liberated"! If anything, the white man is ridiculed through the white characters' behavior. Hank, for example, calls Arabic "arab talk" in quite a depreciatory way. As a child, and an American child, his naiveté can be excused, but his father's hyperbolic and naive behavior in the dinner scene at the Moroccan restaurant can hardly be overlooked. What I argue here is that Morocco is not on display; it is Western colonial attitudes towards Morocco that are represented. Scenes of market places, buses, restaurants, shows, do not pay much attention, either through camera work, sound, or music, to Morocco's difference or otherness. Obviously it is depicted partly exotically, but not in an extraordinary way as in classic postcolonial narratives such as in Joseph Conrad's *Heart of Darkness*, E. M. Forster's *A Passage to India* or Albert Camus' *The Outsider*. Rather whiteness is hyperbolized through a superior attitude towards the country they are tourists in. "I know this is mysterious Morocco," Dr. McKenna tells his wife as a response to her suspicions in the horse wagon on the way to their hotel. For the McKenna family their experience is indeed like a mysterious fairy tale," or "as one of those Arabic Nights" as Dr. McKenna puts it. It is also Hank's desire to encounter the exotic by choosing to travel on the wagon.

Jo, as a contrast to her husband, is much less superior towards her surroundings, not least in the restaurant scene where the only excessive culture practiced is that of the ignorant, aggressive colonizing white man. Overall, Jo is much more ambivalent, and nuanced, in relation to her own experiences, and, as Greven notices, about her own marriage and motherhood (233). "Jo and Ben are presented in this film," writes Paula Marantz Cohen, "as what Max Weber called 'ideal types' of mature gender roles in conventional 1950s terms. Their typicality is highlighted by the way Hitchcock frames them as the American couple within two sociologically contrasting contexts: the Arab culture, with its exaggerated, formalized enactment of male domination and female subordination, and the British culture" (116). It is true that they represent a type of postwar white middle class family, but I would not say that the patriarchal structure of Arab culture is as dominant as Paula Marantz Cohen claims. She might refer to the opening scene in the bus, where Hank accidentally snatches the veil of an Arab woman and consequently Louis Bernard explains why the woman's husband reacted so violently. However, that aggression is negated through Dr. McKenna's behavior throughout the film, culminating in the sedation of his wife against her will. Marta Figlerowicz acknowledges this brutal behavior, although she overstates Jo's part in this: "Until the last quarter of the film, the McKennas are represented through embarrassment. Whether by virtue of their nationality or of their professions (doctor and Broadway singer),

Down and Out

the McKennas speak loudly and brashly, in a way that instantly attracts attention" (Figlerowicz 49). Furthermore, Dr. McKenna seems highly unaware of his own superior behavior and displays no introspective qualities at all. As Cohen claims, he is not even aware of the unstable definition of his home country, Indianapolis: "That is, a site in which the word *Indian* is repeated, *remarked*. This response verbally cancels the site of 'America' as home, since it would have been the land of Indians, not of 'Americans,' who were only foreigners" (T. Cohen 203). In that sense, Dr. McKenna is in a postmodern no-man's land, lost in his and his history's ignorance. Greven argues similarly:

> Stewart's Ben is often amazingly brusque, rude, discourteous and agitated. He exudes American cultural narcissism in the restaurant, where he cannot or refuses to adapt to Arab eating customs. He waves his finger dismissively and angrily at the French police captain after Bernard is killed; with aggressive calm, he tells the British secret intelligence chief that nothing can be done to Jo and him by the British authorities; the guards at the Albert Hall seem more endangered by Ben's hectoring than by the assassination plot. (236)

Returning once again to aesthetics, the particular distancing effect that rear-projection creates establishes a space that is isolated, excluded, and perhaps even privileged. This is especially obvious during the wagon trip to the hotel where the conversation about Arab nights and Mysterious Morocco appears; notice the distinct separation between the lives of Moroccans and the lives of the American family. They are aesthetically separated from each other, just as the detachment between them is fundamental at all levels. Part of the project of postmodernism is to identify and criticize the dominant grand narratives of the Western world; postcolonial analysis offers a way to disestablish Western perspectives and tropes. It is fundamental, though, that the postmodern tools used are fine-tuned to how the responses of texts actually are carried out. To me, *The Man Who Knew Too Much* undoubtedly sets Western history and the colonial project in scrutiny. Although a film superficially about losing and rescuing a child, the protagonist's attitudes and values towards his wife, child and people are nothing else but a prototype of Jack Torrance's White Man in Stanley Kubrick's *The Shining*.

I exaggerated Dr. McKenna's one-dimensional wolfish appearance on purpose in order to underline his role as a WASP aggressor.[3] *The Man Who Knew Too Much* would not be such a great film if it worked in such didactic and clear-cut ways. As I mentioned in the introduction, Hitchcock and his films are always in disguise, and so is Dr. McKenna.[4] The truth is there is another, more vulnerable side of Dr. McKenna, a characteristic much influenced by actor James Stewart's charisma and status in the 1950s. If Jo is determined to take up her singing career again, and clearly opposes the motherly role she has been assigned by her husband and the society they live in, Ben also shows subtle hints at being unsatisfied with the male role he has to play. Greven writes about how James Stewart manages to create an undecided effect in the four characters he portrayed in Hitchcock films: "James Stewart unabashedly conveys Ben's mounting hysteria. Many intriguing avenues of discussion open up in a discussion of acting in Hitchcock. To focus first on Hitchcock's use of Stewart, in each of the four films Stewart made for Hitchcock, the affable, genial star known mythically for his 'aw-shucks' drawl and looming American likability assumes an increasingly disquieting affect" (235). This ambivalence between what Amy Lawrence names "Hitchcock's icon of American manhood" (55), and Stewart as a "darker character than the common American quintessentialist" (Coffin 134), is exactly what makes James Stewart's portrayal of Dr. McKenna go beyond the typical protagonist in 1950s Hollywood. The "masculine power/impotence syndrome" that Wood identifies in Stewart's acting aptly reveals the postmodern condition of a male in distress. A doctor in a suit and tie, Ben McKenna embodies male authority in the way he negotiates through crises. He distrusts the hotel porter's confirmation that Edward Drayton has checked out, and he aggressively refuses to believe that Ambrose Chappell Junior has no idea of what is going on. The film, in alignment with postmodern criticism, takes every opportunity to castigate dominance and authority, but Stewart's vulnerable persona, besides allowing for identification with him in a dramaturgical sense, creates a multidimensional character, fragmented and lost.

When it turns out that the kidnapper is in fact a clergyman, this becomes another deconstruction of a grand narrative and authority. The hypocrisy in religion is further demonstrated through Edward Drayton's highly moral sermon. He is, as the hired killer articulates it, "a wolf in sheep's clothes" and another example of the staging and masking game that permeates the whole film. It is ironic that it is the assassin that utters these words, as he (with the exception of Jo) seems to be the only person that manages to see things for what they are, although he himself, physically, is a highly dubious man. This transcendental quality of his presence is a major factor of the uneasiness of the hotel scene in Marrakech. When he appears in the door, interrupting Jo and Louis Bernard's discourse on staging, his inexpressible status—what are his nationality, ethnicity, intentions—creates an eerie effect that adds to the overall tense atmosphere of the scene. He is familiar, yet not. Much of this can be attributed to the successful casting of Reggie Nalder as the assassin. His haunting and distinctive features were due to severe burns disfiguring his face and created a mask-like presence which caused him to be called "the face that launched a thousand trips."

In addition to mocking religion, the film also critiques institutions and authorities such as the police, intelligence agencies, diplomacy, highbrow culture and art, socialites, and tourism. As I stated in the beginning, the use of the Royal Albert Hall as the setting for the first turning point in the film coincides with what the Hall represents in terms of high art, elitism, colonial history and architecture, the idea of empire and patriarchy. The police are ridiculed in several instances, in particular in their ineffectiveness and disbelief when Jo is calling for assistance outside the Chapel.

The general distrust of reality and its players that permeates the whole film creates a strong sense of postwar paranoia. One extraordinary film sequence that captures this postmodern paranoia is when Dr. McKenna approaches the location where Ambrose Chappell lives. This scene is nightmarish and resembles the opening dream sequence in Ingmar Bergman's *Smultronstället* (1957). This mood is rendered through the desolate street, the eerie echoes of footsteps, Dr. McKenna and later another man speeding up their walk intensively, the drifting paper in the background, the jump cut to the man who follows the doctor (who turns out to be Amrose Chappell Junior), the mysterious low-key music by Bernard Hermann that creeps into the scene, the odd camera placement when Dr. McKenna looks through the gate to the Taxidermist shop, and the use of distorted perspectives when Ben is walking towards the camera. It is brightly sunny, birds are chirping and we hear the sound of children playing; still, this scene is brilliantly uncanny and captures the postmodern paranoia that operates in the oscillation between the familiar and unfamiliar.[5]

Most critics have attributed this maladjustment to the political and social ambiguity of the Cold War. Matthews has confidently discussed how Hitchcock's *Rope* (1948) mediates the haunting and irresolute mood of McCarthyism, the familiar yet unfamiliar foe of postwar America (738). She writes:

> In all of Hitchcock's postwar films the audience's reading of the film is shaped by its reading of reading in the film. While watching Hitchcock's protagonists read or misread clues, investigate questionable normalcy, and identify problematic narratives as they seek clarity and resolution, the audience is socialized into a consensus understanding of what one must do to navigate the dangers lurking in postwar America. (Matthews 754)

What makes *The Man Who Knew Too Much* stand out is its globalizing character, since the characters' negotiation of paranoia does not take place on American soil. The Cold War paranoia is spread like a potent virus through modern communicative means. The film is obsessed with planes, buses, wagons, taxis, or places of transition such as hotels, embassies, churches, police stations, and airports. And telephones. "Telephones dominate this film," writes Tom Cohen, who continues: "A communication system seems to underlie the cinematic fabric, a switchboard of blinking lights and connectors, increasingly vertiginous in a horizontal way" (205). What Matthews interprets as reading in *Rope* being a metanarrative of reading the film and the Cold-War society, the telephone book in *The Man Who Knew Too Much*, as Cohen argues, becomes a formula for understanding the preponderance of the modern world.

On the other side of communication, the film ironically poses, visually, a sense that everybody is speaking either to themselves or to nobody. One such example is when Jo is investigating the chapel together with two policemen and a detective; in a scene in front of the police car these four characters are talking but actually not looking at each other at all. This is repeated in the Royal Albert Hall when Jo talks to the usher. These mise-en-scènes draw attention to the alienation of the film's characters much in the same manner as Michelangelo Antonioni positioned his characters in his trilogy of loneliness, especially in *L'Avventura* (1960). This aesthetic strategy is further established through the predominant use of shot-reverse-shots in dialogues and scenes of social interaction.

The shot-reverse-shot technique can at times also create a strong ironic mood, as in the "red herring" scene at the taxidermist. In the dialogue between Ambrose Chappell Junior and Dr. McKenna, the cinematic image is constructed in a way that it appears as if Dr. McKenna is talking to a stuffed tiger rather than to Mr. Chappell. This entire scene stands out as an example of postmodern irony and, although being very haunting in its initial phase, turns into what Cohen calls a "near-opera buffa" (196). From a dramaturgical position, it works as a release from the tension created by the scene leading up to this confrontation. But its humorous, almost bizarre, conclusion, when Dr. McKenna is held by a bunch of elderly taxidermists (William, Edgar, David) and is threatened by old Ambrose Chappell with a sawfish, accompanied by the rushed Herrmann score, is so apart from the film's narrative content and mood that it appears as a trenchant rupture of the narrative. The way the preserved animals move in this sequence and how humans turn into beastlike animals erase Western distinctions between animal and human and destabilize the anthropocentric view of the world.[6]

The scene at the taxidermist is unique in the film in how it momentarily interrupts the flow of the drama; this, obviously, as we have discussed above, draws attention to the very construction of the film and how Hitchcock the auteur seems, in his own subtle way, to question the dominating theory of Aristotelean drama structure so fundamental in Hollywood studio filmmaking. However, there are other instances that less explicitly *pause* the narrative. Hitchcock's use of occasional aerial shots discontinues the preeminent use of mostly eye-level camera shots in the film, such as in the knife stabbing sequence in Morocco. One particularly striking example is the shot when the Draytons bring Hank from the chapel to their car. The camera is positioned in a high angle, covering the shimmering car in the foreground and the backyard of the chapel in the background. It also stands out because it is fairly long, twenty-two seconds, and hence unusual in terms of continuity editing. Furthermore, the shot, as discussed before, conveys a strong sense of staging and theatricality through its deep focus. The lightning is classic studio lightning that makes the scene feel like an interior instead of an exterior scene. Part of the setting is evidently matte paintings which undercut the suspension of disbelief. The aerial camera angle frames this shot as a miniature world,[7] a fantasy world. One of many in *The Man Who Knew Too Much*.

"I am sorry we were gone so long …"

There is something very odd about the end of *The Man Who Knew Too Much*. From the final turning point in the film, when Dr. McKenna overthrows Mr. Drayton on the staircase, less than a minute remains until the actual end of the film. This must be one of the shortest dénouements in Hollywood film history. It is nothing but comic when the McKennas rush in to greet their sleeping friends in the hotel room and Ben excuses them: "I am sorry we were gone so long…" It must be a new American prank, as one of the guests has uttered earlier in the film. In fact, it is a postmodern prank. However unsatisfactory this ending is from a standardized Hollywood perspective, a film that translates a new, postmodern, postwar society into studio cinematic semiotics could not have ended more gratifyingly. The altogether different mood of the ending compared to the suspense story in the film, ironicized through the return of Arthur Benjamin's *Storm Clouds Cantata*, perfectly diminishes the importance of the film's intrigue (and the necessity for closure in Hollywood films) and focuses on how *The Man Who Knew Too Much* charts the changed social orders of the postmodern plural and fragmented world, the ending being nothing but a narrative fragment in itself. These fragmentations appear differently than the capitalist objectifications of female bodies through the male gaze as in *Rear Window*, *Vertigo* or *Psycho*. Instead, the scrap of the old world blown to pieces lingers in all layers of the narrative. Since the very last day of the narrative takes place during the anniversary of D-Day, June 6, the Second World War is ever present in the film as a cataclysm of past traditions and a disbelief in the project of progress and rationality. The film embodies the notion that, in Karl Marx's foreboding words, "all that is solid melts into air" (Marx and Engels 37). What a contrast that is to the Universal distribution logo, which nowadays introduces the film, capturing a coherent and secured planet. This is a work, as Hitchcock himself argued in regards to the two versions of *The Man Who Knew Too Much* in the interview with François Truffaut, made by a professional and not a talented amateur.

Notes

1. For his discussion on the unstable position of gender and sexuality, see pages 9-10 in particular.

2. Jean-François Lyotard claims that contemporary culture is in essence a commodity on the market; it rests on buying and selling in the market, and the hyper-capitalist society is in a way a new and undisputed grand narrative that organizes all social and cultural practice (8). Louis Bernard's vague and evasive reply about buying and selling could be read as part of the postmodern discourse on commodification; the film, overall, though, does not in any serious way delve into issues of money or the monetary system. The characters' agency and history seem to have nothing to do with money, and neither does the assassination attempt. Money is involved in the hit man's motive, which might suggest that morals and money are intervening in a Lyotardian way, but overall I would not suggest that commodity as a postmodern feature is very present in *The Man Who Knew Too Much*.

3. Curiously, one of the more famous scenes in Kubrick's *Making 'The Shining'* is when Jack Nicholson impersonates the Big Bad Wolf while he is slashing the door to the bedroom where his wife and son hide with an axe. Kubrick's adaption of Stephen King's novel is a good example of a narrative that questions family as a Western institution and Western colonial practices. Another interesting parallel was how both Kubrick and Hitchcock treated their respective female stars, Shelley Duvall and Doris Day. Watching the documentary by Vivian Kubrick, *Making 'The Shining'*, clearly shows how Kubrick mentally abuses Duvall in order to obtain a nervous performance by her. Reggie Nalder, who played the assassin in *The Man Who Knew Too Much*, also reported in an interview with David Del Valle that Hitchcock gave Day little encouragement and that she felt unsure throughout the shoot, an effect that Hitchcock obviously was conspiring to achieve (Del Valle).

4. For a detailed analysis of how Cary Grant's character Roger Thornhill in *North by Northwest* also plays a role, see George M. Wilson "The Maddest McGuffin: Some Notes on *North by Northwest*."

5. This scene is also very reminiscent of several scenes in Hitchcock's *Vertigo* when Scottie is stalking Judy Barton, especially in the art museum.

6. Another example of a dehumanizing aspect of the characters is how Mrs. Drayton looks like a Stepford Wife in the chapel scenes.

7. Fredric Jameson, in his engaging review of William Rothman's *Hitchcock: The Murderous Gaze* (1982), addresses both the original perspective Hitchcock as an exile had on American society and how this privileged viewpoint saw its object from objective distance, much like a miniature: "Indeed, in retrospect one is astonished by the way in which the great foreigners, the great European exiles—Nabokov and Chandler fully as much as Hitchcock himself—worked by disassemblage, taking the American misery apart in carefully framed, discontinuous episodes, sometimes as reduced as individual sentences, which then stand as the frame within which their aesthetic concerns are enshrined. It is hard to imagine an American artist greeting the 'inexhaustible richness' of American daily life with the same jubilation, but it might be argued that this miniaturizing on the exile's part reveals something about daily life in the United States which the immanence of the native, under the rumbling shadow of the el-train, is unable to focus aesthetically" (20).

Works Cited

Adorno, Theodor. "Trying to Understand Endgame." 1961. *New German Critique*, vol. 26, Spring/Summer 1982, pp. 119-50.

Antonioni, Michaelangelo, director. *L'Avventura*. Cino Del Duca, 1960.

Baudrillard, Jean. *Simluations*. Translated by Paul Foss et al., Semiotext(e), 1983.

Beckett, Samuel. *Endgame*. Faber, 1976.

---. *Waiting for Godot*. Faber, 1971.

Berger, James. "The Hitchcock Symptom: Duster Flight Patterns around 'Production Values.' A Response to Griffiths." *Postmodern Culture*, vol. 20, no. 3, 2010, pp. 146-47.

Bergman, Ingmar, director. Smultronstället. Janus Films, 1957.

Coffin, Leslie L. *Hitchcock's Stars: Alfred Hitchcock and the Hollywood Studio System*. Rowman and Littlefield, 2014.

Cohen, Paula Marantz. *Alfred Hitchcock: The Legacy of Victorianism*. UP of Kentucky, 1995.

Cohen, Tom. *Hitchcock's Cryptonomies, Volume 1: Secret Agents*. U of Minnesota P, 2005.

Conrad, Joseph. *The Secret Agent: A Simple Tale*. Cambridge UP, 1990.
Corber, Robert J. *In the Name of National Security: Hitchcock, Homophobia, and the Political Construction of Gender in Postwar America*. Duke UP, 1993.
Del Valle, David. "The Face That Launched a Thousand Trips: An Interview with Reggie Nalder." *Kinoeye: New Perspectives on European Film,* vol. 3, no. 2, 2005. Figlerowicz, Marta. "Timing and Vulnerability in Three Hitchcock Films."
Film Quarterly, vol. 65, no. 3, Spring 2012, pp. 49-58.
Greven, David. "Cruising, Hysteria, Knowledge: The Man Who Knew Too Much (1956)." *European Journal of American Culture*, vol. 28, no. 3, 2009, pp. 225-44.
Habermas, Jürgen. "Modernity: An Unfinished Project." *Habermas and the Unfinished Project of Modernity: Critical Essays on the Philosophical Discourse of Modernity*, edited by Maurizio Passerin d'Entrèves and Seyla Benhabib, Polity Press, 1996, pp. 38-55.
Hanssen, Eirik Frisvold. *Early Discourses on Colour and Cinema: Origins, Functions, Meanings*. Stockholm Universitat, 2006.
Hark, Ina Rae. "Revealing Patriarchy: Why Hitchcock Remade The Man Who Knew Too Much." *Hitchcock's Rereleased Films: From Rope to Vertigo*, edited by Walter Raubicheck and Walter Srebnick, Wayne State UP, 1991, pp. 209-20.
Hitchcock, Alfred, director. *The Man Who Knew Too Much*. Universal, 1956.
Jameson, Fredric. "Reading Hitchcock." *October*, vol. 23, Winter 1982, pp. 15-42.
Kubrick, Stanley, director. The Shining. Warner Bros., 1980.
Lawrence, Amy. "American Shame: Rope, James Stewart, and the Post War Crisis in American Masculinity." *Hitchcock's America*, edited by Jonathan Freedman and Richard Millington, Oxford UP, 1999, pp. 55-76.
Leitch, Thomas. "It's the Cold War, Stupid: An Obvious History of the Political Hitchcock." *Literature/Film Quarterly*, vol. 27, no. 1, 1999, pp. 3-15.
Lyotard, Jean-François. *The Postmodern Explained*. Translated by Don Barry et al., U of Minnesota P, 1992.

Marx, Karl and Friedrich Engels. *The Communist Manifesto*. Translated by Samuel Moore, Verso, 2012.
Matthews, Kristin L. "Reading, Guidance, and Cold War Consensus in Alfred Hitchcock's Rope." *The Journal of Popular Culture*, vol. 43, no. 4, 2010, pp. 738-60.
McHale, Brian. *Postmodernist Fiction*. Methuen, 1987.
Neale, Stephen. *Cinema and Technology: Image, Sound, Colour*. Indiana UP, 1985.
Noble, Peter. "The Man Who Knew Too Much." *Hitchcock on Hitchcock: Selected Writings and Interviews*, edited by Sidney Gottlieb, vol. 2, U of California P, 2015, pp. 144-45.
Restivo, Angelo. "Hitchcock and the Postmodern." *A Companion to Alfred Hitchcock*, edited by Thomas Leitch and Leland Poague, John Wiley and Sons, 2011, pp. 555-71.
Rothman, William. *Hitchcock: The Murderous Gaze*. Harvard UP, 1982.
Said, Edward W. *Orientalism*. Routledge, 1978.
Truffaut, François. *Hitchcock/Truffaut*. Simon and Schuster, 1983.
Wilson, George M. "The Maddest McGuffin: Some Notes on *North By Northwest*." *Comparative Literature*, vol. 94, no. 5, 1979, pp. 1159-72.
Wood, Robin. *Hitchcock's Films Revisited*. Columbia UP, 1989.
---. "The Men Who Knew Too Much (and the Women Who Knew Much Better)." Raubicheck and Srebnick, pp. 194-208.

Index

Adorno, Theodor 174, 254
The Alfred Hitchcock Hour (TV series) 191n4
Alfred Hitchcock Presents (TV series) 181, 191n4
The Alfred Hitchcock Story (book) 60
Allardice, James 181
Allen, Jay Presson 195
Allen, Richard 198
allegory of the cave 46, 48
Althusser, Louis 11, 82-83, 92, 99n22. See also Ideological State
        Apparatuses
Amis, Kingsley 65
Andrews, Julie 4, 12, 107, 112, 134n3, 170
Antonioni, Michelangelo 45, 114, 233n30, 234n44, 261
Arkhipov, Vassily 187
Arosenius, Per-Axel 178, 207, 233n25
The Art of Alfred Hitchcock (book) 17, 63
L'Avventura (1960) 261

Barry Lyndon (1975 film) 204-205, 235n50
Baruch, Bernard 19
Bass, Saul 47, 76
Batista, Fulgencio 142, 183
Baudrillard, Jean 11, 50, 52, 71n3, 245, 247, 249
Bay of Pigs invasion 183-184
Beckett Samuel, 80, 87, 98n14, 254
Before the Revolution (1964) 207, 233n30, 233n31
Benjamin, Arthur 196, 262
Bennett, Charles 229
Bergala, Alan 127-128
Berger, John 178
Bergman, Ingmar 233n25, 259
Bergman, Ingrid 8, 11, 17, 42, 97n9, 153, 166n5, 224; and
        Notorious performance 22-23, 25, 28, 32, 34
Bernays, Edward 181-182
Bernstein, Sidney 21
Bertolucci, Bernardo 207, 233n30
Biographia Literaria (1906 book) 101n34
The Birds (1963) 5, 70n2, 97n6, 122, 127, 210, 213, 233n29, 235n53,
        236n75
Blackmail (1929 film) 67, 125
Blake, David 14-15, 200-201
Blake, George (George Bahar) 199-201, 216, 220, 230, 235n57,
        236n70. See also *The Short Night*

Index

Blow-Up (1966) 45, 114
Bolshevik régime 171, 188. See also Union of Soviet Socialist Republics
Borges, Jorge Luis 52, 60
Bourke, Seán 14, 200, 216, 220, 230, 236n70
Brody, Richard 21, 22
Bronfen, Elizabeth 113-114
Browne, Roscoe Lee 171, 207
Brueghel, Pieter 216, 237n76
Buchan, John 6, 16, 64
Burgess, Guy 12
Burke, Edmund 201, 208
Burton, Richard 155-56

Camus, Albert 134n4, 256
Carey, John 227-228, 229-30
capitalism 14, 77, 81, 82, 93, 118, 133, 149, 169, 170, 176-78, 186, 192, 245, 262, 263n2; propaganda associated with 173, 187-189, 190
Carmichael, Stokely (Kwame Ture) 171
Carroll, Leo G. 8, 37, 75, 86, 102n39
Carroll, Noel 228
Castro, Fidel 140, 142-43, 151, 154, 166n2, 183-85, 192n8, 199, 201
Castro, Juanita 140, 192n8, 202
Castro, Raúl 192n8
Cavell, Stanley 77, 90, 102n40
censorship. See Production Code Administration censorship
Central Intelligence Agency 74, 99n20, 102n39, 183, 185, 186, 199, 202, 217, 231n8, 233n26
Chabrol, Claude 11, 23, 46-48, 60, 70
Chandler, Charlotte 134n8, 264n7
Chaplin, Charlie 92, 228
Chomsky, Noam 14, 169, 171-73, 181, 183-90
CIA. See Central Intelligence Agency
Coercion, Capital, and European States (1990 book) 172
Cohen, Paula Marantz 246, 256-57
Cohen, Tom 245, 248-249, 251-54, 260
COINTELPRO (Counter Intelligence Program) 171. See also Federal Bureau of Investigation
The Cold War 5, 8-20, 38, 40, 60, 74-76, 79-82, 85-86, 88-89, 91-93; and 1950s 30, 77, 79-82, 85, 89-92, 96, 96n4, 97n6, 100n31, 100n32, 101n37, 102n41, 103n45, 109-11, 114, 118, 120, 122, 125-26, 133-34, 139-47, 149-50, 154, 157-58, 160-61, 164-66, 169-73, 177-79, 185-86, 188-89, 191, 201, 211, 234n37, 243, 244, 245, 260; and anti-Cuban propaganda 154

Coleman, Herbert 213, 235n48
Coleridge, Samuel Taylor 48-49, 60, 86, 101n34. See also *Biographia Literaria*
communism in the 21st century 171
Connery, Sean 6, 58, 217
Conrad, Joseph 245, 256
Conwell, Carolyn 115, 177
Corber, Robert J. 20-21, 41, 102n41, 243-44, 246, 255
Costigan, James 231n5
Creed, Barbara 205, 231, 231n4
Crowther, Bosley 22, 26
Cuba, 141-42, 165-66, 183-84, 202
Cuban Missile Crisis of 1962 13-14, 43n3, 139-41, 145, 147, 157, 160, 166, 184, 187, 198, 203, 227
Cuban Revolution 166n1
Cummings, Robert 57, 121

Dalí, Salvador 50, 56, 59
Dassonowsky, Robert 12-13
Day, Doris 15, 63, 132, 251, 263n3
de Gaulle, Charles 149, 157, 161, 202, 206
de Vosjoli, Philippe 202
Delirious New York: A Retroactive Manifesto of Manhattan 50-51
Derrida, Jacques 97n8, 132
"The Difference Between Crows and Blackbirds: Alfred Hitchcock and the Treason of Images" 97n6
Dissanayake, Ellen 228-29
Donath, Ludwig 112, 170, 175
Dor, Karin 8, 13, 154-55, 166n4, 182, 198, 201
Douchet, Jean 58-59
Dr. Strangelove; or How I Learned to Stop Worrying and Love the Bomb (1964) 86-87, 95, 96n4, 97n5, 125
Durgnat, Raymond 176, 185, 192n12

Early Discourses on Colour and Cinema: Origins, Functions, Meanings (book) 250
Eisenhower, Dwight D. (president) 142
Eliot, T.S. 78, 80, 98n12-13, 196, 214
The Empathic Civilization (book) 233n22, 237n88
Das Erdbeben in Chili (novella) 128, 135n13
Espionage Act of 1917 191n5

Family Plot (1976) 213, 215, 224, 234n42, 235n59, 236n60

Index 271

FBI. See COINTELPRO, Federal Bureau of Investigation
Federal Bureau of Investigation 171. See also COINTELPRO
Fischer, Gisela 115, 175
Fleming, Ian 6, 16, 45, 60
Foreign Correspondent (1940) 9, 121
Forsythe, John 13, 147, 205, 219
Francesca da Rimini (ballet) 131, 178
Freeman, David 7, 14-15, 197-98, 200, 212-14, 216-19, 222-27, 229, 234n36, 237n77, 237n82
French Revolution 208, 209
Frenzy (1972) 231n19, 234n42
Freud, Sigmund 101n35, 234n45
Frye, Northrop 76, 96n3

GDR. See German Democratic Republic
German Concentration Camps Factual Survey (documentary). See
    Memory of the Camps
German Democratic Republic 111, 113-18, 120, 122-24, 126-27, 129-30, 132
Gide, André 119, 134n4
Gielgud, John 7, 197
Godard, Jean-Luc 114
The Godfather Part II (1974) 142
Gottlieb, Sidney 237n86
Grant, Cary 6, 8, 10, 17-18, 22, 24-25, 27, 31, 34, 40, 42, 47, 58-59, 63, 70, 73-74, 78, 80, 83-84, 86, 89, 91- 94, 98n13, 100n26, 100n27, 101n38, 102n42, 153, 166n5, 224, 263n4
Greenberg, Jonathan 87, 96, 101n35
Greven, David 235n58, 244-45, 254, 256-58
Griffiths, Michael 100n30, 100n32, 103n46
Gropius, Walter 129
Guevara, Che 143, 154, 199, 201

Habermas, Jürgen 246, 248
Hanssen, Eirik Frisvold 250
Hayek, Friedrich 192n11
Hecht, Ben 19, 25, 224
Hegel, Georg Wilhelm Friedrich 189, 225, 237n80
Herrmann, Bernard 77, 78, 107, 261
Hitchcock, Alfred 5-23, 25-27, 29, 31-32, 38-39, 41-42, 43n2, 45-46, 48, 52-53, 59, 62-64, 67, 69-70, 73-82, 84-96, 96n2, 97n6, 97n9, 97n11, 99n18, 99n20, 99n23, 99n24, 100n25, 100n28, 101n35, 101n37, 101n38, 102n42, 103n43, 103n44, 103n45, 107-25, 127-34, 134n2, 134n8, 139-41, 143-147, 151-53, 155, 157-58, 161-62, 164-66, 169-91, 192n10,

195-31, 231n2, 231n3, 231n4, 231n6, 231n9, 232n12, 232n17, 232n19, 233n25, 233n26m 233n30, 233n32, 234n36, 234n39, 234n43, 234n45, 235n48, 235n53, 235n59, 236n60, 236n63, 236n74, 236n75, 237n87, 243-44, 246-50, 253, 256, 258, 260-62, 263n3, 263n4, 263n5, 264; alter-ego symbolism in films of 64; Biblical symbolism in films of 127-28, 134n6; books about 11, 15, 46, 51, 156, 264n7, 237n87, 243, 245; comic approaches to espionage thriller 6; and anti-Communism 9, 114, 139-140; Communist agents in films of 9, 15, 75, 163, 186; as exile 264n7; gender relations and sexuality in thrillers of 8, 9, 10-11, 62-63, 80, 170, 243, 244, 253-56, 263n1; and German Expressionism 112, 181; German film industry experience 110-111; matriarchal figures in films of 66; melo drama in films of 9, 10, 11, 17, 22, 25-29, 32, 36, 38, 40, 42, 43n2, 108, 113, 161, 220, 222, 226, 229, 245; patriarchal content in films of 67; political content in films of 9-16, 20-21, 42, 75-76, 169, 171, 188; political ideologies 144, 190; political interpretations of films by 192n10; post modern readings of films by 243-47, 257, 260-62, 263n2; psychological elements in films of 7, 13-14, 17, 55-56, 59, 82, 123, 125, 172, 192, 215; racial depictions in films of 170; rear projection in films of 118, 175, 247, 249-50, 257; and Roman Catholicism 234n37; self-reflexivity in films of 96, 233n29, 248; technique in films of 77-78, 97-98n11, 113; and Technicolor® 15, 247, 249, 250, 251; villains in films of 225; "wrong man" category in espionage thrillers of 7, 74, 100n31. See also *Torn Curtain*, intentional artifice; *Torn Curtain* and *Topaz*, political content

Hitchcock, Alma (Reville) 134n8, 195
Hitchcock and Art: Fatal Coincidences (2000 exhibition) 111
Hitchcock's Films Revisited (book) 58, 70n2
Holmes, Oliver Wendell 191n5
House Committee on Un-American Activities (HUAC) 190

I Confess (1953) 134n4
Ideological State Apparatuses 82, 84, 92, 99n22
ISA. See Ideological State Apparatuses

Jacobs, Steven 22, 42-43n1, 135n10, 174
James Bond 55, 58, 60, 65, 109, 115, 154; films 6, 7, 12, 71n3, 155-56, 166n4, 169, 180
Janaway, Christopher 233n32, 235n54, 236n68
Jarre, Maurice 203-4
John, Lyndon B. (president) 141, 144
Johnson, William 250-51

Kael, Pauline 84, 100n26
Kant, Immanuel 207-8, 233n32, 235n54

Katyn Forest massacre of 1940 130
Keats, John 98n16, 103n43
Kedrova, Lila 4, 115, 177, 237n78
Kennedy, John F. (president) 140, 147, 184, 185, 187
Kennedy, Madge 39, 87
Kennedy, Robert F. 144, 184
Keynes, John Meynard 190, 192n11
KGB 202-3, 216, 217, 236n70. See also Union of Soviet Socialist Republics
Khrushchev, Nikita 141, 166, 185, 187
Kieling, Wolfgang 125, 174, 226
King, Martin Luther Jr. 144
Kirkbride, Ronald 14, 199, 214, 224
Kleist, Heinrich von 128, 135n13
Klemperer, Victor 123-24
Koolhaus, Rem 50-51
Korean War 199, 201, 231-232n10
Krohn, Bill 41, 211, 233n26, 235n47, 235n55
Kubrick, Stanley 86, 92, 95, 96n4, 125, 133, 204, 235n50, 257, 263n3

Lacan, Jacques 55, 195, 212, 253
The Lady Vanishes (1938) 6, 8, 53, 115, 120-21, 123
Landau, Martin 58, 74, 83
Lane, Priscilla 57, 121
Lauter, Ed 215-216
le Carré, John 7, 16, 143, 169, 210
Lean, David 221
Lehman, Ernest 10-11, 15, 75, 88, 99n20, 100n27, 103n45, 115, 231n5, 237n77
Leigh-Hunt, Barbara 231n19
Leitch, Thomas 76, 80, 97n7, 100n31, 243
Lifeboat (1944) 9, 109, 121
Lloyd, Norman 9, 15, 121
The Lodger: A Story of the London Fog (1927) 112, 195, 208, 210, 231n1, 234n36
Lyotard, Jean-François 96n2, 132, 133, 245, 263n2

"MacGuffin" 10, 18-19, 20, 21, 31, 42, 43n3, 60-61, 88, 90, 113, 175, 178, 225, 245
Maclean, Donald 12, 231n17
MacPhail, Angus 229
M.A.D. See Mutual Assured Destruction
Mad Men (TV series) 81, 99n18

Magritte, René 111, 113, 132
The Man Who Knew Too Much (1934) 5-6, 15, 45, 196-97, 207, 227, 229, 248
The Man Who Knew Too Much (1956) 5-7, 9, 15-16, 46, 52-53, 63, 67, 132, 207, 227, 243-63, 263n2, 263n6; cinematography 251, 252, 261-62; and colonialism 255-56; cultural attitudes in 256-57; dialogue 252-53, 262; editing techniques 261; rear projection in 249-50, 257; religious criticism in 258-59; special effects 262; symbolism 253-54, 260. See also *North by Northwest* and Shakespearean symbolism
Marker, Chris 231-232n10
Marnie (1964) 107, 108, 110, 165, 222, 234n42, 235n55, 235n58
Marshall, Herbert 121, 204
Martin, Rebecca 10-11, 17
Marx, Karl 91, 262
Mason, James 32, 47, 83
The Matrix (1999) 11, 45, 46-47, 50, 56-57, 61
Matthews, Kristin L. 247, 260
Maugham, Somerset 6, 51, 197
May, Rollo 227, 230
McCarthy era 77, 89, 102n41, 247, 260
McElhaney, Joe 23-25
McGilligan, Patrick 41, 185
McHale, Brian 119, 248
McLuhan, Marshall 89, 206
Mellor, Ann 198-199, 231n7
Memory of the Camps (1984, 2014 documentary) 21-22, 195. See also Nazi Holocaust
Mills, Mort 122, 174
Mogg, Ken 14, 15, 60, 107, 109
Moore, Brian 12, 115, 116
Morris, Christopher D. 78, 97n8, 98n15, 122, 132
M16 199, 200
Murder! (1930) 204
Mutual Assured Destruction (M.A.D.) 12, 133

Nabokov, Vladimir 115, 264n7
Nadel, Alan 75, 103n44, 103n46
Nalder, Reggie 259, 263n3
Naremore, James 75, 82, 92, 96n2, 97n11, 99n20, 100n27, 101n35
Nazi Germany 123, 129, 135n11
Nazi Holocaust 124, 127, 171, 195. See also *Memory of the Camps*
New York Times 184, 185, 233n30

Index

Newman, Paul 4, 8, 12, 107, 115, 120, 134n8, 170, 176
Nixon, Richard M. (president) 141
Noiret, Philippe 13, 204, 232n17
North by Northwest (1959) 5-12, 15, 17-18, 23, 29, 30-42, 46, 47-70, 70-71n2, 73-96, 96n1, 97n6, 97n10, 98n14, 99n23, 100n27, 101n35, 102n41, 103n46, 110, 113, 115, 123, 126-27, 133, 175, 263n4; censorship 41, 45-46; comparisons with *Notorious* 32-35, 36; and consumer capitalism 81-82; dialogue 88, 101n35, 102n42; location filming 70n1; and 1950s political and cultural scene 77, 80; political content 75-76, 85-87, 100n33, 102n41; sexualities of characters 41, 102n42; Shakespearean symbolism 12, 55, 76-78, 90, 98n15; symbolism 60-61, 85, 96, 97n7, 99-100n25.
Notorious (1946) 6-10, 15, 17-20, 21-32, 35-37, 38, 41-42, 43n1, 46, 62, 97n9, 110, 145, 153-54, 166n5, 175, 192n7, 198, 224, 225; and atom bomb technology 19; emotion and melodrama in 26-27, 29, 40; comparisons with *North by Northwest* 32-35, 41
North Korea 230-231n10
Novak, Kim 56, 209
Novello, Ivor 195, 231n1

Operation Mongoose 184, 185
Orr, John 102n39

Pâques, Georges 232n18
Perry, Dennis R. 195, 196
The Pervert's Guide to Ideology (2012 documentary) 55-56
Peucker, Brigitte 125-126, 135n10
Piccoli, Michel 13, 177, 205
Plato 11, 46, 48, 49, 50, 55
The Pleasure Garden (1925) 206
Poe, Edgar Allan 46, 65, 66, 70, 195
post-World War II conditions 246; Nazi activity 19-20
Production Code Administration censorship 41, 89
Propaganda (1928 book) 181-182
Psycho (1960) 5, 10, 62, 97n6, 99n23, 122, 180, 191n1, 191n6, 235n51, 235n53, 244, 249, 262
Psycho II (1983) 211
"The Purloined Letter" (short story) 65, 66, 67, 68
Putin, Vladimir 236n70

"Que Será Será" (song) 63, 249

Rains, Claude 25, 154, 224
Randolph, Don 188, 210
Rear Window (1954) 5, 15, 46-47, 53, 59, 60, 62, 64, 67-69, 110, 114, 122, 133,

231n11, 232n12, 244, 262
Rebecca (1940 film) 206, 235n53
Reville, Alma. See Hitchcock, Alma
Rifkin, Jeremy 233n22, 237n88
Ritt, Martin 7, 115, 143, 155, 169
Robin, Dany 8, 170, 204
Rohmer, Eric 11, 23, 46,-48, 60, 70, 202, 210, 233n20
Rope (1948) 110, 260
Russia: and disinformation 231n14, 231n16; and "Potemkin villages" 231n16; and spies 231n16. See also Union of Soviet Socialist Republics

Sabotage (1936) 38
Saboteur (1942) 6-7, 9, 52-53, 57, 63-64, 66-67, 121
Saint, Eva Marie 10, 11, 17, 23, 32, 34, 42, 49, 70, 74, 88, 101n37, 102n39
Salmose, Niklas 15-16
Samuels, Charles Thomas 197-198
Schlesinger, Arthur 184, 187
Schopenhauer, Arthur 107, 207, 212-213, 225, 233n32, 235n54, 236n68, , 237n80, 237n81, 237n83, 237n89
The Secret Agent (1907 novel) 245
Secret Agent (1936 film) 6, 7, 110, 197
Seeger, Pete 231, 235n52
Shadow of a Doubt (1943) 112, 210, 236n60
The Shining (1980 film) 257, 263n3; Making "The Shining" (documentary) 263n3
The Short Night (unfilmed Hitchcock project) 6-7, 9, 14, 15, 195, 197, 198, 199, 200-201, 212-227, 229-230, 233n21, 235n58, 236n61, 237n77, 237n82; casting considerations 236n61, 236n62, 236n65
Sinyard, Neil 175-76, 191 "The Snow-Man" (poem) 80-81, 99n21
Soviet Union. See Union of Soviet Socialist Republics
Spellbound (1945) 127, 235n53
Spoto, Donald 10-11, 17-18, 29, 38, 40, 63, 109, 114, 131, 134n1, 174, 177, 182, 185, 188, 191n7
The Springing of George Blake (1970 book) 15, 200, 216
Sputnik 38, 77
The Spy Who Came in from the Cold (1963 novel) 145, 210
The Spy Who Came in from the Cold (1965 film) 7, 115, 143, 145, 155, 156, 169
Srebnick, Walter 13, 195
Stafford, Frederick 8, 13, 155, 182, 198, 202, 204
Stalin, Joseph 123, 124, 130, 157, 231n16

Index

Stanislavsky, Konstantin 99n24
Stevens, Wallace 55, 80, 95, 99n19, 99n21
Stewart, James 15-16, 46, 56, 63, 101n38, 117, 209, 245, 247, 257-58
Storm Cloud Cantata (orchestral) 196-97, 207, 216, 227, 230, 234n32, 262
Strangers on a Train (1951) 52-53, 112, 134n4, 234n45
Student Non-Violent Coordinating Committee (SNCC) 171
Suspicion (1941) 112, 127
Swift, Jonathan 91, 93, 254

Taylor, Samuel 13, 143-44, 146, 150-51, 153, 162, 164, 198, 201, 203-6, 208-10, 231n14, 232n13
Tchaikovsky, Pyotr Ilyich 131, 178
Technicolor 249-250
The 39 Steps (1935 film) 6, 7, 9, 38, 53, 63-64, 110, 122, 131, 175
The 39 Steps (1959 film) 236n67
The 39 Steps (novel) 6, 64-65
Tilly, Charles 14, 169, 172-73
To Catch a Thief (1955) 15, 63-64, 68, 127, 236n63
Topaz (novel) 139, 140, 155, 157, 172, 188, 203-7, 233n24
Topaz (1969 film) 5-9, 12-16, 43n3, 46, 139-166, 169, 170-71, 177-78, 180-192n7, 192n12, 197-99, 201-213, 217, 221, 223, 225, 227, 229, 231n9, 233n26, 233n29, 234n42, 234n43, 235n48-49, 235n55; alternate endings 139, 164, 186, 202, 211-212, 235n56; political content 140-152, 154, 182-183, 186, 188, 189-190, 201, 203, 208; symbolism 182, 209
Torn Curtain (1966) 4, 6,-9, 12-15, 43n3, 46, 107-120, 121-133, 134n3, 139, 169, 170-180, 185, 190, 191n1, 191n6, 223, 226, 232n17, 234n42; coded messages 179-180; intentional artifice 113, 114, 117-118, 122, 126, 175, 188, 189, 192n12; political content 114, 118, 120, 123, 124, 127, 134n8, 141, 174-178, 186, 190, 192n9; screenplay revisions 116; special effects 174, 175; symbolism 174
Toumanova, Tamara 115, 178
Triple Agent (2004) 202, 210, 233n20
The Trouble With Harry (1955) 15, 99n20, 219
Truffaut, François 18, 19, 31, 90, 209, 236n63, 263
Truman, Harry S. (president) 142
Ture, Kwame (Stokely Carmichael) 171

Ulbricht, Walter 124, 129
Union of Soviet Socialist Republics 14, 38, 113, 115, 131, 139, 141, 142, 146, 147, 148, 149, 157, 164, 170, 171, 172, 184, 187, 188, 199, 202, 205, 206, 220, 231n16, 231n17, 232n16, 236n70. See also KGB, Russia
United States of America; suppressed political history of 171, 173, 183-85, 187,

201, 231n10
United States Supreme Court 191n5
Universal Pictures 107, 109, 111, 120, 155, 262
Uris, Leon 13, 139-40, 144-46, 149, 157, 163, 172, 183-86, 191n2, 198, 202-3, 225
USSR. See Union of Soviet Socialist Republics

Vernon, John 182, 201
Vertigo (1958) 5, 10, 13, 56, 58, 62, 64, 96n1, 97n6, 99n23, 100n28, 102n41, 114, 117, 143-144, 149, 165, 186, 198, 206, 209, 210, 221-22, 234n41, 235n53, 244, 249, 262, 263n5
Vietnam War 13, 71n3, 86, 139, 140-44, 154, 157, 165, 171-72, 176-77

Wachowski brothers 11, 45, 50
Waiting for Godot (play) 79, 80, 98n14, 254
Walker, Michael 191n1, 191n6, 231n11
Waltzes from Vienna (1934) 112, 128
We, the Accused (1935 novel) 197, 207, 217, 236n70
Weekend (1967) 114
Welles, Orson 123, 206
Western capitalism. See capitalism
Whitlock, Albert 211
Wilder, Billy 111, 134n2
Wilson, George M. 90, 97n10
Wood, Robin 8, 53, 58, 70n2, 108, 124, 245, 251, 258
World War I 9, 51
World War II 19, 30, 121, 140, 157, 170-72, 188-89, 195, 248, 254, 262; post-war Nazi activities 20
The Wrong Man (1957) 53, 221

Young and Innocent (1937) 6, 52-53, 97n9

Žižek, Slavoj 11, 53, 55-56, 66-67, 82, 181

Notes on Contributors

Craig Arthur is a writer and researcher from Dunedin, New Zealand. He studied English Literature at the University of Otago. An authority on the spy genre, he has written numerous articles on James Bond. He is currently writing a spy novel set in Australia and New Zealand.

Robert Dassanowsky is Professor of German/Austrian Studies and Visual and Performing Arts, and Director of Film Studies at the University of Colorado, Colorado Springs. He also works as an independent film producer. His articles on film, literature and culture have been widely published, and his recent books include *Austrian Cinema: A History* (2005); *New Austrian Film,* ed. (2011); *Quentin Tarantino's Inglourious Basterds: A Manipulation of Metafilm*, ed. (2012); *World Film Locations: Vienna*, ed. (2012); *Screening Transcendence: Film under Austrofascism and the Hollywood Hope 1933–1938* (2018). Dassanowsky is a delegate of the European Academy of Sciences and Arts, a Fellow of the UK Royal Historical Society, and an elected member of the Austrian Academy of Film, and the European Film Academy (EFA). He serves on the board of several literary publications and film festivals.

Jeffrey Longacre is an Associate Professor of English and Assistant Director of Honors Programs at the University of Tennessee at Martin, where he regularly teaches film studies courses on adaptation, Horror films, Alfred Hitchcock, Stanley Kubrick, and Orson Welles. In addition to Hitchcock, his scholarship includes published work on William Blake, James Joyce, and Edna O'Brien.

Rebecca Martin teaches at Pace University in New York in the areas of crime writing, detective fiction, the gothic novel and female gothic, and film studies. She holds a PhD in English and a graduate certificate in film studies from the Graduate Center of the City University of New York. Her published research is in detective fiction, the eighteenth-century gothic novel, and film studies. Recent publications include two edited collections of essays with Salem Press, *Critical Insights: Crime and Detective Fiction* (2013) and *Critical Insights: Film: Bonnie and Clyde* (2016), as well as articles on the relationship between French Poetic Realism and film noir and the pedagogy of crime fiction.

Ken Mogg has published widely on Hitchcock; his *The Alfred Hitchcock Story* (1999, revised 2008) covers every film "in loving detail" (Bill Krohn). His recent writing includes a chapter on *Alfred Hitchcock Presents* for a book on children in US television (Routledge, 2018), a profile of the director for Screen Education, no. 87 (Australia, 2017), and a chapter on "Hitchcock's Literary Influences" for *A Companion to Alfred Hitchcock* (Wiley Blackwell 2011, pb 2014). His many contributions to the online journal *Senses of Cinema* (Australia) include a monograph on the literary sources and intertexts of The Birds (no. 51, July 2009) and a two-part essay on Hitchcock and Catholicism (nos. 80 and 81, September and December 2016).

Walter Raubicheck (Editor), a professor of English at Pace University, is the co-author of *Scripting Hitchcock* (2011) and co-editor of *Hitchcock's Rereleased Films* (1991) with Walter Srebnick. He has published several other essays on Hitchcock, as well as essays on American authors such as F. Scott Fitzgerald, T. S. Eliot, and Dashiell Hammett. He is currently the editor of *Lex Naturalis*, a journal of natural law published by the Pace University Press.

Niklas Salmose is Associative Professor of English Literature at Linnaeus University, Sweden. He is an active member of the Linnaeus University Center for Intermedial and Multimodal Studies (IMS). He is part of the international research project "Nostalgia in Contemporary Culture" and is currently guest editor for a special issue on contemporary nostalgia for the journal Humanities. His recent publications include work on F. Scott Fitzgerald, animal horror, translation, nostalgia and modernism, Nordic Noir and transmediations of the Anthropocene.

Randall Spinks is an Associate Professor of writing, literature and film at Nassau Community College in New York. He is co-editor, with Bettina Caluori, of *Frame and Focus: An Anthology for Investigative Reading*, 3rd ed. Most recently, he has published articles on Ernest Hemingway and Alfred Hitchcock and is currently at work on a book on the economics and aesthetics of crime and violence in both authors. He is also working on a social-historical study of the films of Martin Ritt.

Walter Srebnick is professor emeritus of English at Pace University, New York. He is currently a museum educator at the Morgan Library and the Cloisters in New York. He co-authored *Scripting Hitchcock* (2011) which was a finalist for the Edgar Award. He has also written on medieval literature and American film and culture, and he co-edited *Hitchcock's Rereleased Films: From Rope to Vertigo* (1991).

Colophon

Cover Design by Ely Mellet and Jessica Estrella
Interior Design by Bryan Potts and Alicia Hughes
The journal was typeset in Gill Sans and Cochin
and printed by Lightning Source.

PACE UNIVERSITY PRESS
Director Manuela Soares
Associate Director: Stephanie Hsu
Marketing Manager: Patricia Hinds
Graduate Assistants: Jessica Estrella and Alicia Hughes
Student Aide: Erica Magrin

www.ingramcontent.com/pod-product-compliance
Lightning Source LLC
Chambersburg PA
CBHW061436300426
44114CB00014B/1706